iPod & iTunes *Fourth Edition*

THE MISSING MANUAL

*The book that
should have been
in the box*®

Other resources from O'Reilly

Related titles
iPod & iTunes Hacks
iPod Fan Book
GarageBand 2: The Missing Manual
Digital Audio Essentials
Adobe Encore DVD: In the Studio
Photoshop Elements 4: The Missing Manual

iPhoto 6: The Missing Manual
iMovie HD6: The Missing Manual
Mac OS X: The Missing Manual, Tiger Edition
Podcasting Pocket Guide
Podcasting Hacks

oreilly.com
oreilly.com is more than a complete catalog of O'Reilly books. You'll also find links to news, events, articles, weblogs, sample chapters, and code examples.

oreillynet.com is the essential portal for developers interested in open and emerging technologies, including new platforms, programming languages, and operating systems.

Conferences
O'Reilly brings diverse innovators together to nurture the ideas that spark revolutionary industries. We specialize in documenting the latest tools and systems, translating the innovator's knowledge into useful skills for those in the trenches. Visit *conferences.oreilly.com* for our upcoming events.

Safari Bookshelf (*safari.oreilly.com*) is the premier online reference library for programmers and IT professionals. Conduct searches across more than 1,000 books. Subscribers can zero in on answers to time-critical questions in a matter of seconds. Read the books on your Bookshelf from cover to cover or simply flip to the page you need. Try it today free.

iPod & iTunes *Fourth Edition*

THE MISSING MANUAL

J.D. Biersdorfer

POGUE PRESS™

O'REILLY®

Beijing • Cambridge • Farnham • Köln • Paris • Sebastopol • Taipei • Tokyo

iPod & iTunes: The Missing Manual, Fourth Edition

by J.D. Biersdorfer

Copyright © 2006, 2005, 2004, 2003 O'Reilly Media, Inc. All rights reserved.
Printed in the United States of America.

Published by O'Reilly Media, Inc., 1005 Gravenstein Highway North, Sebastopol, CA 95472.

O'Reilly books may be purchased for educational, business, or sales promotional use. Online editions are also available for most titles (*safari.oreilly.com*). For more information, contact our corporate/institutional sales department: (800) 998-9938 or *corporate@oreilly.com*.

Printing History:

July 2003:	First Edition. (Originally published by Pogue Press, LLC., under the title *iPod: The Missing Manual*.)
February 2004:	Second Edition.
April 2005:	Third Edition.
March 2006:	Fourth Edition.

RepKover™ This book uses RepKover™, a durable and flexible lay-flat binding.

ISBN: 0-596-52675-X
[M]   [5/06]

Table of Contents

Part Two: iPod: The Software

Part Three: Beyond the Music

Part Five: Appendixes

The Missing Credits

About the Author

 **J.D. Biersdorfer** has been writing the Q&A column for the Circuits section of *The New York Times* since 1998. She has covered everything from 17th-century Indian art to the world of female hackers for the newspaper, and has reviewed dozens of books for *The New York Times Book Review*. She has penned articles for the *AIGA Journal of Graphic Design* and *Rolling Stone*, and has contributed essays about the collision of art and technology to several graphic-design books published by Allworth Press. She studied Theater & Drama at Indiana University and now splits her time between New York City and Pennsylvania. She spends her spare moments playing the banjo and watching BBC World News. Email: *jd. biersdorfer@gmail.com*.

About the Creative Team

David Pogue (editor) is the weekly tech-review columnist for *The New York Times* and the creator of the Missing Manual series. He's the author or coauthor of 37 books, including 16 in the Missing Manual series and six in the "For Dummies" line (including Magic, Opera, Classical Music, and The Flat-Screen iMac). In his other life, David is a former Broadway theater conductor, a magician, and a pianist. Email: *david@pogueman.com*. Web: *www.davidpogue.com*.

Peter Meyers (editor) works as an editor at O'Reilly Media on the Missing Manual series. He lives with his wife in New York City. Email: *peter.meyers@gmail.com*.

Michele Filshie (editor) is O'Reilly's assistant editor for Missing Manuals and editor of four Personal Trainers (another O'Reilly series). Before turning to the world of computer-related books, Michele spent many happy years at Black Sparrow Press. She lives in Sebastopol and loves to get involved in local politics. Email: *mfilshie@oreilly.com*.

Nan Barber (copy editor) has been the proud owner of an iPod since December 25, 2005.

Chris Stone (technical reviewer) is a senior systems administrator (the Mac guy) at O'Reilly Media, Inc. He's contributed to *Mac OS X: The Missing Manual*, Tiger Edition, published by Pogue Press/O'Reilly, and is coauthor of *Mac OS X Tiger in a Nutshell*, also published by O'Reilly.

Rose Cassano (cover illustration) has worked as an independent designer and illustrator for 20 years. Assignments have ranged from the nonprofit sector to corporate clientele. She lives in beautiful Southern Oregon, grateful for the miracles of modern technology that make working there a reality. Email: *cassano@highstream. net*. Web: *www.rosecassano.com*.

Acknowledgements

I would like to thank David Pogue for suggesting this book to me, and then being a terrific editor through the mad scramble of the first two editions, and Peter Meyers, Chris Stone, and the Missing Manual folks at O'Reilly for guiding me through the past couple of updates. Thanks to Apple for the iPod images and the assorted other iPod accessory companies who made their digital photography available. Much of this manuscript was written to a rotating mix of Abigail Washburn's *Song of the Traveling Daughter*, the *Battlestar Galactica: Season 1* soundtrack, and the latter works of Green Day. On a personal note, I'd also like to extend thanks to all my friends and family for putting up with all the vague iPod-related mutterings during the book's four editions, including Mary and Bobby Armstrong, Tom Biersdorfer, my parents, and my grandfather. Other occupants on the thank you list must include my supportive Internet buddies (the Wonder Women and the gang in Echo's upf_oz), and most of all, thanks to Betsy–for everything.

The Missing Manual Series

Missing Manuals are witty, superbly written guides to computer products that don't come with printed manuals (which is just about all of them). Each book features a handcrafted index; cross-references to specific page numbers (not just "see Chapter 14"); and RepKover, a detached-spine binding that lets the book lie perfectly flat without the assistance of weights or cinder blocks.

Recent and upcoming titles include:

Access for Starters: The Missing Manual by Kate Chase and Scott Palmer

AppleScript: The Missing Manual by Adam Goldstein

AppleWorks 6: The Missing Manual by Jim Elferdink and David Reynolds

CSS: The Missing Manual by David Sawyer McFarland

Creating Web Sites: The Missing Manual by Matthew MacDonald

Dreamweaver 8: The Missing Manual by David Sawyer McFarland

eBay: The Missing Manual by Nancy Conner

Building an eBay Business: The Missing Manual by Nancy Conner

Excel: The Missing Manual by Matthew MacDonald

Excel for Starters: The Missing Manual by Matthew MacDonald

FileMaker Pro 8: The Missing Manual by Geoff Coffey and Susan Prosser

Flash 8: The Missing Manual by Emily Moore

FrontPage 2003: The Missing Manual by Jessica Mantaro

GarageBand 2: The Missing Manual by David Pogue

Google: The Missing Manual, Second Edition by Sarah Milstein and Rael Dornfest

Home Networking: The Missing Manual by Scott Lowe

iLife '05: The Missing Manual by David Pogue

iMovie HD 6 & iDVD 6: The Missing Manual by David Pogue

iPhoto 6: The Missing Manual by David Pogue

iWork '05: The Missing Manual by Jim Elferdink

Mac OS X: The Missing Manual, Tiger Edition by David Pogue

Office 2004 for Macintosh: The Missing Manual by Mark H. Walker and Franklin Tessler

PCs: The Missing Manual by Andy Rathbone

Photoshop Elements 4: The Missing Manual by Barbara Brundage

QuickBooks 2006: The Missing Manual by Bonnie Biafore

Quicken for Starters: The Missing Manual by Bonnie Biafore

Switching to the Mac: The Missing Manual, Tiger Edition by David Pogue and Adam Goldstein

Windows XP for Starters: The Missing Manual by David Pogue

Windows XP Home Edition: The Missing Manual, Second Edition by David Pogue

Introduction

Remember the first time you heard about MP3 files? You could take a regular old CD, like *The Essential Johnny Cash* or an album of Strauss violin concertos played by Sarah Chang, put it in your computer's CD drive, and convert all your favorite songs into the MP3 format. And do you recall your delight when you learned that those MP3 files took up one-tenth of the space it would take to copy the CD audio files directly to your hard drive? You could leave the CD at home and rock out at your desk with your growing collection of freshly "ripped" MP3s (which sounded *almost* as good as the original CD, come to think of it).

Having a folder stuffed with tunes on your computer made working at it more enjoyable, but humans are always on the go. By 1998, the first portable MP3 players began to trickle onto store shelves, many offering 32 big, roomy megabytes (MB) of memory to store song files transferred from the computer.

Of course, most people wanted more than 30 minutes of music at a time. So, later MP3 players came with more room for music, even if they were a little bigger and a little bulkier.

Then came the iPod.

What Is an iPod?

An iPod is many things to many people, but most people think of it as a pocket-size music player that holds 100 songs, 15,000 songs, or more, depending on the model. The iPod dynasty now ranges from a screenless 512-megabyte version that can hold plenty of songs for your gym routine and never skip a beat, to a 60-gigabyte multimedia jukebox that spins out an entire TV season of *The Office*, as well as color photos along with colorful music.

Like the original Sony Walkman, which revolutionized the personal listening experience when it was introduced in 1979, Apple's announcement of the original 5-gigabyte iPod in the fall of 2001 caught the music world's ear. "With iPod, listening to music will never be the same again," intoned Steve Jobs, Apple's CEO. But even out of the Hyperbolic Chamber, the iPod was different enough to get attention. People noticed it, and more importantly, bought it. By the end of 2005, Apple had sold more than 41 million of them. The iPod was the single bestselling music player on the market, the dominant player; for the first time in modern history, Apple got to feel like Microsoft.

And no wonder. The iPod was smaller, lighter, and better looking than most of its rivals—and much, much easier to use. Five buttons and a scroll wheel could quickly take you from ABBA to ZZ Top, and every song in between.

Gleaming in a white-and-chrome case slightly larger than a deck of cards, the original iPod could hold at least 1,000 average-length pop songs (or six typical Grateful Dead live jams), and play them continuously for 10 hours on a fully charged battery. The black-and-white LCD screen offered the song information in type large enough to actually read, and a bright backlight allowed for changing playlists in the dark. And with its superfast FireWire connection, the iPod could slurp down an entire CD's worth of music from computer to player in under 15 seconds.

By the end of 2005, the iPod was zipping along on a USB 2.0 connection and showing digital photos, music videos, movies, and TV shows on its bright 2.5-inch color screen. The simple little music player grew up to be a multimedia warehouse that could *still* fit in a front shirt pocket.

Beyond the Music

But wait—there's more. Once you're done playing your tunes and watching your pictures, get ready for all the other ways the iPod can serve as your favorite gadget:

- **iPod as external drive.** You can hook up an iPod to your Mac or Windows machine, where it shows up as an extra drive (albeit a much smaller drive if you plug in your lil' old iPod Shuffle). You can use it to copy, back up, or transfer gigantic files from place to place—at a lickety-split transfer speed, thanks to its FireWire or USB 2.0 connection.

- **iPod as eBook.** The iPod makes a handy, pocket-size electronic book reader, capable of displaying and scrolling through recipes, driving directions, book chapters, and even Web pages.

- **iPod as PalmPilot.** Amazingly, the iPod serves as a superb, easy-to-understand personal organizer. It can suck in the calendar, address book, to-do list, and notes from your Mac or PC and then display them at the touch of a button.

- **iPod as GameBoy.** All right, not a GameBoy, exactly. But there are three video-style games and a memory-tugging audio quiz built into the modern iPod—perfect time-killers for medical waiting rooms, long bus rides, and lines at the Department of Motor Vehicles.

- **iPod as slide projector.** Granted, not every iPod can do pictures and music, but if you've got a full-size iPod with a color screen, all you need to do is whip out its AV cable and find a TV set to entertain your friends with a musical slide show of your latest trip to Disneyland.

You know how Macintosh computers inspire such emotional attachment from their fans? The iPod inspires similar devotion: iPod Web sites, iPod shareware add-ons, an iPod accessory industry—in short, the invasion of the iPod People.

If you're reading this book, you're probably a Podling, too—or about to become one. Welcome to the club.

What You Need to iPod

The iPod is designed to communicate with a Mac or a PC, which serves as the loading dock for tunes. Fortunately, it doesn't have especially demanding system requirements. Here's what your computer needs to use a video-enabled iPod or iPod Nano with iTunes 6:

- **A decent amount of horsepower.** For the Macintosh, Apple recommends 256 MB of RAM and at least a 500-megahertz G3 processor as a minimum, but if you want to use the video iPod and iTunes, you'll need a 500-megahertz G4 processor and a video card with at least 16 MB of memory on it.

  For the PC, you need at least a 500-megahertz Pentium-level processor and at least 256 MB of RAM. If you plan to watch and use video with your iPod and iTunes, you'll need a 1.5-gigahertz Pentium-level processor or faster and a video card with 32 MB or more of memory. (Just about everything in life is better with more memory.)

- **A recent operating system.** For the Mac, you need at least Mac OS X 10.2.8, but if you want to use any of the video features, you need to make sure your version of Mac OS X is at least 10.3.9. You'll also need Apple's QuickTime 7.0.3 multimedia software or later installed.

  On a Windows machine, you need Windows 2000 or XP to use Apple's iTunes software for Windows. Like the Macsters, Windows people also need at least QuickTime 7.0.3. for video fun.

- **A USB 2.0 connection.** Older iPods that predate the 2005 arrival of the video-playing Pod and the Nano can still use a FireWire connection for transferring songs and data, but all the new models are USB 2.0-only. USB 2.0 uses the same plug as the older, slower USB 1.1 connections, so in theory, you can move your music and movies over the slower USB pathway. In reality, you might go nuts with the long wait and overwhelming anticipation of moving 40 gigabytes of data over to your new iPod with USB 1.1.

• **A broadband connection.** Fast Internet access isn't mandatory for using the iPod, but it sure comes in handy when buying and downloading files (especially videos) from the iTunes store.

Note: These are the requirements your computer must meet to use the iPod with *iTunes*. If you have an older Mac or PC and the yearning to buy an iPod, you still might be able to use it by getting a third-party music-management program that's less fussy about operating systems than iTunes.

What You Need to iPod Shuffle

Apple's mighty mite has a few special requirements of its own, including the need for *iTunes 4.7.1* or later (earlier versions of iTunes, even iTunes 4.7, won't work with the Shuffle), so make sure you install the version that came on the iPod Shuffle CD, which should be close to the current version of the program. The Shuffle CD also includes the necessary QuickTime components needed for a happy iTunes experience.

To do the Shuffle, you also need:

• **A very recent operating system.** Apple's requirements page lists Mac OS X 10.2.8 (the highest you can go in the Jaguar world) or Mac OS X 10.3.4 or later as the minimum Mac OS you can use. Windows owners need Windows 2000 (with Service Pack 4 installed) or Windows XP (with Service Pack 2 installed).

• **A USB port.** The iPod Shuffle plugs right into the computer's USB port, and you can use either a zippy USB 2.0 connection or even one of the older (but slower) USB 1.1 ports that have been common on computers since the late 1990s.

Mac vs. Windows iPods

If they were all hanging out together one afternoon at the beach, it would be hard to tell a Windows iPod from a crowd of Mac iPods. On the outside, they look the same.

But just as Macintosh and Windows computers use totally different formats for their hard drives, so do Mac and Windows iPods. This makes perfect sense because the iPod is a kind of mini computer. (Note for nerds: Mac iPods use a filesystem called HFS Plus; PC iPods use the unappetizing-sounding FAT32. If you've ever had to back up, reformat, and reinstall your pre–Windows XP system, FAT32 may sound familiar: it's the system Windows used for years.)

So, then, how can Apple claim to sell a single iPod model that, out of the box, comes formatted for either a Mac or a PC?

It doesn't really. Most iPod models are all preformatted for the Mac, except for the Nano and the Shuffle, which are preformatted for Windows. When you run the installer software on the iPod CD, the program quietly reformats the iPod drive to

---

match your operating system (except for the Shuffle, which stays as it is, as Macs have been happily reading USB flash drives for years). Details on this process, and on the cabling differences between Mac and PC, begin in Chapter 2.

Software Differences

These days, both Mac and PC fans use the same software to manage and organize what's on the iPod: a free program called iTunes. It works almost precisely the same in its Macintosh and Windows versions. Every button in every dialog box is exactly the same; the software response to every command is identical. In this book, the illustrations have been given even-handed treatment, rotating among the various operating systems where iTunes is at home (Windows XP, Mac OS X 10.3, and Mac OS X 10.4).

However, if you're a PC fan and you don't have Windows 2000 or XP, you can't use iTunes. As described in previous editions of this book, earlier versions of the iPod came with MusicMatch Jukebox for use with Windows-formatted iPods. Apple hasn't included MusicMatch Jukebox in the iPod box since 2003. If you've snatched up an older iPod on eBay or been on the lower end of a hand-me-down—and for some reason *want* to learn how to use the antique version of MusicMatch Jukebox supported by these elderly iPods—you can download the old MusicMatch chapter, once included in previous editions of this book, from the "Missing CD" page, which is located at *www.missingmanuals.com*.

iTunes 6

This book describes iTunes version 6, which Apple released in October 2005. To claim your free copy, visit *www.apple.com/itunes*. Here's what's in it for you (see Chapter 5 for more leisurely coverage):

- A smart Search bar that helps narrow down the quest for a specific song through a giant iTunes library.

- The ability to store song lyrics as well as album-cover art, both of which are right at your fingertips on the iPod or iPod Nano.

- Source-list folders to help organize the miles of playlists populating the left side of your iTunes window.

- Video playback right in the iTunes window.

- Easy synchronization of contacts and calendars between Windows (Outlook and Outlook Express) and Mac OS X 10.4 (iCal and the Mac OS X Address Book) and the iPod.

- Photo-wrangling powers to sync up and manage picture collections stored on the iPod Photo, video iPod, and iPod Nano model.

- Easy subscription and management tools to keep all your favorite podcasts up to date, whether you play them on Pod or computer.

The iTunes Music Store, meanwhile, has a few new tricks of its own (Chapter 7):

- Music videos, television shows (by single episode or entire season), highlight reels from college football games, Pixar cartoons, and more, all for about $2 apiece.

- More than 20,000 podcasts from around the word on just about every conceivable subject (and some that are inconceivable but fun anyway).

- A Customer Reviews feature that lets you post your thoughts on music and movies for sale in the store and read the trenchant observations of other iTunes fans.

- The power to "gift" specific music to recipients, in case you want to make sure your pals absolutely get this hot album you're crazy about.

- Ever-expanding audiobook shelves, with 11,000 titles now in stock.

UP TO SPEED

Updating Your iPod for New Versions of iTunes

Apple cranks out a fresh version of iTunes at least once a year and often releases updates for the iPod's firmware (its own internal operating system), usually around the same time. If you are downloading a new version of iTunes, check for accompanying iPod software as well, as some of the new features are co-dependant. (See page 269 for instructions on updating your iPod.)

The latest version of the iPod software, sporting a typically catchy name like iPod Update 2005-11-17, is available at *www.apple.com/ipod/download*. To see your iPod's software version, go to iPod → Settings → About and look at the number next to Version. The iPod download page lists the current software numbers, if you want to compare the two.

About This Book

The tiny square pamphlet that Apple includes with each artfully designed iPod package is enough to get your iPod up and running, charged, and ready to download music.

But if you want to know more about how the iPod works, all the great things it can do, and where to find its secret features, the official pamphlet is skimpy in the extreme. And help files that you have to read on the computer screen aren't much better: You can't mark your place or underline, there aren't any pictures or jokes, and you can't read them in the bathroom without fear of electrocution.

This book is one-stop shopping for iPod reference and information. It explores iPod hardware and software—for both Macintosh and Windows—for all recent iPod models. It takes you on a joyride through the iPod subculture online and off. And it guides you through all the cool musical and nonmusical things you can do with your iPod, from looking up phone numbers to checking the weather report. You'll also find heaping helpings of the Three T's: tips, tricks, and troubleshooting.

About → These → Arrows

Throughout this book, and throughout the Missing Manual series, you'll find sentences like this one: "Open the System folder → Libraries → Fonts folder." That's shorthand for a much longer instruction that directs you to open three nested folders in sequence, like this: "On your hard drive, you'll find a folder called System. Open it. Inside the System folder window is a folder called Libraries; double-click it to open it. Inside *that* folder is yet another one called Fonts. Double-click to open it, too."

Similarly, this kind of arrow shorthand helps to simplify the business of choosing commands in menus, as shown in Figure I-1. That goes for both your computer and your iPod, whose menus feature arrows → like → these that lead you from one screen to the next.

Figure I-1:
In this book, arrow notations help simplify menu instructions. For example, "File → Add Folder to Library" is a more compact way of saying "In the iTunes File menu, choose the Add Folder to Library" option.

About MissingManuals.com

At the *www.missingmanuals.com* Web site, click the "Missing CD" link to reveal a neat, organized, chapter-by-chapter list of the shareware and freeware mentioned in this book. The Web site also offers corrections and updates to the book (to see them, click the book's title, then click Errata). In fact, you're invited and encouraged to submit such corrections and updates yourself. In an effort to keep the book as up to date and accurate as possible, each time we print more copies of this book, we'll make any confirmed corrections you've suggested. We'll also note such changes on the Web site, so that you can mark important corrections in your own copy of the book, if you like. And we'll keep the book current as Apple releases more iPods and software updates.

The Very Basics

To use this book, and indeed to use a computer, you need to know a few basics. This book assumes that you're familiar with a few terms and concepts:

- **Clicking.** This book gives you three kinds of instructions that require you to use your computer's mouse or trackpad. To *click* means to point the arrow cursor at something on the screen and then—without moving the cursor at all—to press and release the clicker button on the mouse (or laptop trackpad). To *double-click,* of course, means to click twice in rapid succession, again without moving the cursor at all. To *drag* means to move the cursor *while* pressing the button.

  When you're told to ⌘-*click* something on the Mac, or *Ctrl+click* something on a PC, you click while pressing the ⌘ or Ctrl key (both of which are near the Space bar).

- **Menus.** The *menus* are the words at the top of your screen or window: File, Edit, and so on. Click one to make a list of commands appear, as though they're written on a window shade you've just pulled down.

- **Keyboard shortcuts.** If you're typing along in a burst of creative energy, it's sometimes disruptive to have to take your hand off the keyboard, grab the mouse, and then use a menu (for example, to use the Bold command). That's why many experienced computer mavens prefer to trigger menu commands by pressing certain combinations on the keyboard. For example, in most word processors, you can press ⌘-B (Mac) or Ctrl+B (Windows) to produce a *bold-face* word. When you read an instruction like "press ⌘-B," start by pressing the ⌘ key; while it's down, type the letter B, and then release both keys.

- **Operating-system basics.** This book assumes that you know how to open a program, surf the Web, and download files. You should know how to use the Start menu (Windows) and the Dock or menu (Macintosh), as well as the Control Panel (Windows), Control Panels (Mac OS 9), or System Preferences (Mac OS X).

Tip: If you're lost on these topics, there are Missing Manual titles that cover Windows 2000, Windows XP Home, Windows XP Professional, and Mac OS X. But enough sales pressure.

If you've mastered this much information, you have all the technical background you need to enjoy *iPod & iTunes: The Missing Manual.*

Safari® Enabled

 When you see a Safari® Enabled icon on the cover of your favorite technology book that means the book is available online through the O'Reilly Network Safari Bookshelf.

Safari offers a solution that's better than e-books. It's a virtual library that lets you easily search thousands of top tech books, cut and paste code samples, download chapters, and find quick answers when you need the most accurate, current information. Try it for free at *http://safari.oreilly.com.*

Part One:
iPod: The Hardware

1

Meet the iPod

Even before you extract it from its box, the iPod makes a design statement. Its shrink-wrapped cardboard square opens like a book, revealing elegantly packaged accessories and software nestled around the iPod itself.

The first part of this book will familiarize you with the hardware portion of this parcel. This particular chapter takes a look at what's inside the box for a full-size iPod or iPod Nano. If you've got your eye on an iPod Shuffle or have just popped one out of its bright green box and want to know what to do next, skip on over to Chapter 3 for a detailed discussion of Apple's flashy little music stick.

Parts of the Pod

In addition to the nicely nestled iPod itself, the package's compartments hold all the other stuff that comes with various iPod models these days: earbud-style head-phones and their foam covers, the connection cable for your computer, and a soft-ware CD. You also get a pocket protector-style slipcover and chunk of white plastic called the iPod Dock Adapter, which works as a booster seat for your iPod to fit into many of the dock-based accessories out there.

What you get by way of instructions in the standard Apple box is a small square envelope that includes a Quick Start pamphlet and a couple of Apple-logo stick-ers. Newer iPods include some electronic documentation and short tutorials in Web page-and PDF-format (located on the iPod CD), but you have to print it out if you want to read it anywhere besides your computer screen. Good thing you have this book in your hands to fill in the gaps—and it's always ready to flip through without having to boot up your PC.

A few other bits of paper are included in the iPod's info packet. You'll probably blow right past the warranty information (basically, you're covered for one year) and the software agreement (the usual legalese that makes most people's eyes glaze over like fresh Krispy Kreme doughnuts). The software agreement includes a small section about making digital copies of music, whose sentiment is echoed right on the iPod's cellophane wrapping: *Don't steal music.*

The Screen

The LCD screen is your window into the iPod's world. You can use it to navigate the menus, see how much of a charge the battery has left, and view the name of the current playlist or song. The display on the video-enabled iPods, whose resolution is 320×240 pixels (176×132 for the Nano), also comes with a white LED backlight, so you can use your iPod in movies, concerts, and as a flashlight to find your front door lock at night.

Note: The iPods of yore, the ones with monochrome displays, have screen resolutions of 160×128 pixels for full-size models and 138×110 pixels for the iPod Mini.

TROUBLESHOOTING MOMENT

The Fingerprint Magnet

The full-size iPod's shiny chrome-and-white acrylic may be gorgeous and perfect the day you open the box. But like a white sofa in a house full of Labrador Retrievers, it's not the best combination for disguising dirt, detritus, and especially fingerprints.

Cleaning with a soft, lint-free cloth can take care of most of the mess. For dark smudges, the iKlear solution and special cleaning cloth from Klearscreen (*www.klearscreen.com*) can also shine up your iPod.

The Click Wheel

The concentric ring on the iPod's face is the clickable scroll wheel, which you use to navigate up or down lists of menu options on the screen. It lets you jump to a specific playlist, album, artist, song, or even a certain part of a song. As shown in Figure 1-1, the presence of this circular navigational tool has been a consistent feature on all iPods (except for the Shuffle) since Apple first launched the product in 2001.

When a song is playing, you can also use the wheel to adjust the iPod's volume: Spin the wheel counterclockwise to turn the volume down, or clockwise to increase the sound.

Of course, "spin" may not be quite the right word. The wheel on the 2001 iPods actually turned. But on the 2002-and-later iPods, including the iPod Mini, the turning wheel gave way to a stationary *touch wheel* and then the current *click wheel*, which you operate by dragging your finger around the ring. You've got one less moving part to go bad.

Figure 1-1:
Top row, from left: The very first iPod model from 2001, the third-generation (3G) 2003 iPod, the iPod Mini, the fourth-generation (4G) click wheel model sold by both Apple and Hewlett-Packard, the U2 Special Edition iPod, and the iPod Photo.

Bottom row, from left: The video-playing fifth-generation (5G) iPod, first introduced in the fall of 2005, and its trusty sidekick, the iPod Nano. Each of these is available in either traditional white or hipster black.

Tip: Want to personalize your Pod forever? Say it with lasers—laser engraving, that is. You can immortalize the chrome backside of your iPod with a short, two-line message of your choosing when you order an iPod at *http://store.apple.com*.

Just don't make a typo.

The Buttons

The first generations of iPods had raised, contoured control buttons—Menu, Play/Pause, and so on—hugging the outer edge of the wheel.

Beginning with the 2003 iPods, Apple made all the buttons nonmoving, touch-sensitive parts. This design offered two advantages: It kept sand and dirt from derailing the iPod's parts, and it let a red–orange glow backlight the names of the buttons when it was dark out. Many iPodders complained, though, that the new layout made it more of a thumb reach to hit the Previous and Next buttons without bringing in a second hand.

Owners of the iPods made in 2004 and beyond don't have to worry about *that*; their buttons are actual, clickable spots on the 12, 3, 6, and 9 o'clock positions *on* the scroll wheel. (Apple also ditched the red–orange glow effect.) If you're old enough to own an iPod, your thumb can probably reach them.

In any case, no matter which model you have, no matter where the control buttons have migrated, they all work the same way once you find them.

Starting from the center, here are the controls:

- **Select.** The big round button in the center of any iPod is the Select button. Like clicking a mouse on a desktop computer, you press Select to choose a highlighted menu item. When a song title is highlighted, the Select button begins playback.

- **Menu.** On early-model iPods, the Mini, and the current group of click wheel models, the Menu button is at 12 o'clock, up at the top of the circle. On third-generation iPods from 2003, Menu is the second button in the row of controls.

  Pressing the Menu button once takes you to the iPod's main screen. The latest iPods give you six options: Music, Photos, Videos, Extras, Settings, and Shuffle Songs. The iPod Nano's menu is the same, except there's no Videos category. Older iPods in various states of software updates (page 269) have variations on these menus, and the iPod Shuffle has no menu at all because it doesn't even have a *screen*.

  The Menu button is also your ticket home: If you've burrowed deep into the iPod's menu system, pressing the Menu button repeatedly takes you back one screen at a time until you're back where you started.

Note: The Menu button also controls the white backlight for the iPod's display screen. Hold it down for a few seconds to turn the backlight on or off.

- You press the **Next/Fast-forward** button once to advance to the next song in the playlist. You can also hold it down to fast-forward through the current song to get to the good parts.

- The **Previous/Rewind** button, of course, does the opposite: Press it once quickly to play the current song from the beginning; press it repeatedly to cycle back through the songs on the playlist. Hold it down to rewind through the current song, just like the Rewind button on your old tape deck.

Tip: Here's another great way to navigate the song that's now playing: Press the Select button and then use the scroll wheel to zoom to any part of the song you want; when the selection diamond reaches the spot you want, press Select again. This technique, called *scrubbing,* gives you more control and greater precision than the Previous and Next buttons.

- The **Play/Pause** button, marked by a black Play triangle and the universal Pause symbol crafted from upright parallel lines, plays or stops the selected song, album, playlist, or library. It's also the iPod's Off switch if you press it for 3 seconds. (The iPod also turns itself off automatically after 2 minutes of inactivity.)

Tip: These buttons, used in combination, also let you reset a locked-up iPod. Details in Chapter 12.

Places for Plugs

Here are the various switches and connectors you'll find on the top and bottom of your iPod:

- **Dock connector port.** Starting in 2003, Apple made the iPod's main data and power jack a flat 30-pin connector on the bottom of the device, shown in Figure 1-2. At the time, the company was including a small white charging dock inside the box with all new iPods, so this jack is often referred to as the dock connector port. You also used to get both FireWire and USB 2.0 cables in the iPod boxes of the past, but these days, new iPods can't even use FireWire to transfer data and music. As of late 2005, the entire iPod line is USB 2.0-only, which means you only get the USB cable in the box.

  You'll find much more detail on this syncing business in Chapter 2.

- **Headphone port.** On the iPod's top, you'll find the jack where you plug in the earbud-style headphones that come with your iPod. If you have an iPod Nano, though, the headphone port is on the bottom of the player (Figure 1-2).

  Fortunately, this is a standard 3.5 mm stereo plug. In other words, you're free to substitute any other Walkman-style headphones, or even to play the music on the iPod through your home sound system (see Chapter 10). Some older iPods also have a small oval notch next to the headphone port that accommodated a remote, which could be used to control the music without fumbling with the player's main controls.

- **Hold switch.** With all the control buttons on the front of the iPod, it's easy to hit one accidentally while you're putting it in or taking it out of your pocket or purse. To prevent such unintended button activity, slide the iPod's Hold switch over to reveal a bright orange bar. You've just disabled all the buttons on the front of the unit, preventing accidental bumps. (A small lock icon appears on the iPod's screen when the Hold button is on.) Slide the switch back to turn off the Hold function.

Tip: A common moment of iPod panic occurs when the device's control buttons don't seem to be working. Check the top to make sure the Hold switch isn't on. If your iPod model includes a remote control, check the Hold button on the remote as well.

Charging the Battery

Many a cloud of gadget euphoria dies instantly when the new owner realizes that the device must sit in a battery charger and juice up before any fun can happen.

Out of the box, the iPod may have enough juice to turn itself on and get you hooked on spinning the wheel. But you'll still need to charge the iPod before you use it for the first time.

Figure 1-2:
*The iPod's data and
power jack, usually called
the dock connector port,
has lived on the bottom
of the player since 2003.
Here, from top to bottom,
the iPod Nano, a video
iPod, and an iPod Photo;
note that the Nano also
has its headphone port
on the bottom of the
player. All three iPods
have the Hold switch on
top.*

Charging via USB 2.0 or FireWire Cable

You can charge your iPod over a FireWire or USB 2.0 connection, but new iPods
don't even come with FireWire cables anymore, so USB 2.0 is the only way to get a
charge unless you have an old FireWire cable from a previous Pod. If your Mac or
PC has *powered* FireWire or USB 2.0 jacks, you can charge up the iPod just by
plugging it into your computer. (For FireWire, "powered" usually means the fat-
ter 6-pin FireWire connector, not the little 4-pin connectors found on many Windows machines. For USB 2.0, you need a powered jack like those on the back of the
computer, or on a powered USB hub—not, for example, the unpowered jack at the
end of a keyboard.) The battery charges as long as the computer is on and not in
Sleep mode.

It takes about 4 hours to fully charge your iPod. Note, however, that it gets about
80 percent charged after 2 hours (Nanos only take about 90 minutes to get the 80
percent power rush). If you just can't wait to unplug it and go racing out to show
your friends, you can begin to use it after a couple of hours.

During the charging process, you may see either the Do Not Disconnect message
(if the iPod is also sucking down music from your computer), the "OK to Disconnect" message (if it's done with that), or the main menu for a few minutes before
the charging battery graphic takes over. The iPod will also warn you not to disconnect it if you've set it up to work as an external hard drive, but we'll get to that
business in Chapter 9.

Using an AC Adapter

You can also charge the battery by plugging the iPod's cable into the boxy white
AC power adapter that you can get for $30 from the Apple Store (*http://store.apple.
com*) or shops that sell iPod gear (see Figure 1-3). Apple used to include this AC
adapter with the iPod but has dispensed with all but the bare hardware minimum
to get the iPod up and playing.

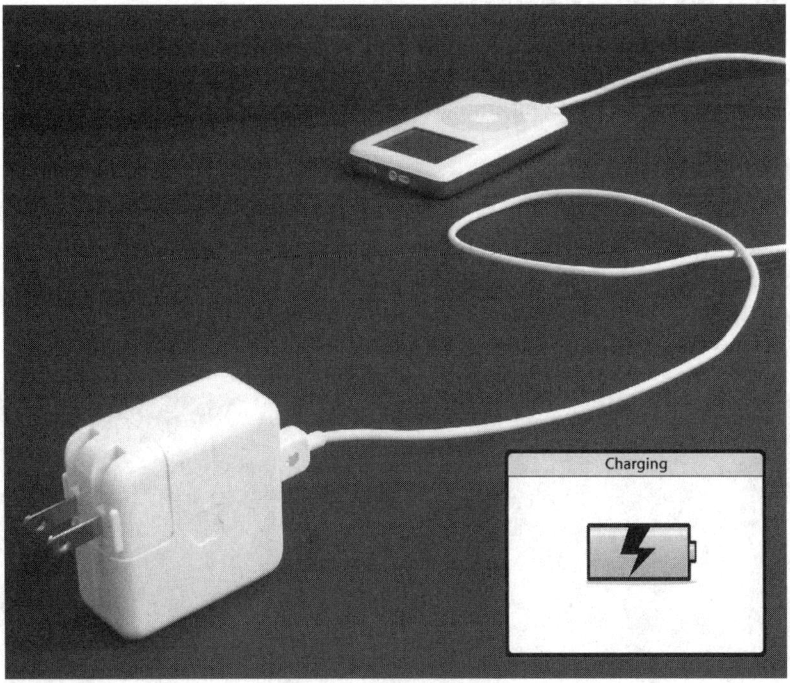

Figure 1-3:
The cable that comes with the iPod plugs into the end of the now-optional AC power adapter. Flip out the electrical prongs tucked into the adapter's end, and plug it into a regular wall socket. Run the cable between the AC adapter and iPod dock connector port (or charging dock, if you have one).

Inset: The iPod makes it graphically clear that you're charging its battery—just in case you were wondering.

You can find the AC adapter in two flavors: One that fits the USB 2.0 end of the iPod cable and one that fits the older FireWire cables. Even though you have to pay extra for it now, having an AC adapter handy has a definite advantage in that you can juice up your iPod without having to connect it to your computer.

Note: Even when fully charged, the battery in an "off" iPod drains slowly after 14 to 28 days. If, for some inconceivable reason, you haven't used your iPod in a month or more, you should recharge it, even if you left it fully charged the last time you used it.

WORKAROUND WORKSHOP

Prongs Across the World

The iPod's AC power adapter can handle electrical currents between 100 volts and 240 volts at frequencies of 50 and 60 hertz. Put another way, it works not only with the voltage in North America, but also in many parts of Europe and Asia.

Although the iPod adapter automatically converts the *voltage* of global outlets, it doesn't convert the *prongs* of the world's various outlets: round prongs, flat ones, prongs in pairs, prongs in threes, and so on.

The Apple Store sells a World Traveler Adapter Kit for the iPod: six plugs that snap onto the end of the iPod's AC adapter to adapt its prongs for electrical outlets in the United Kingdom, continental Europe, Japan, China, Korea, Australia, Hong Kong, and other parts of North America. The World Traveler Adapter Kit costs about $40 at Apple's Web site and stores.

Checking the Battery's Charge

The battery icon on the iPod's screen shows the approximate amount of gas left in the tank. When the iPod is connected to the computer, the battery icon in the top-right corner displays a charging animation, complete with tiny lightning bolt.

Battery Life

The iPod uses a rechargeable lithium ion battery. Battery life depends on which version of the iPod you have and how you use it. On the newest iPods that play video, Apple states that the 30-gigabyte model gets up to 14 hours of music playback between charges, or 3 hours of photo-and-music slideshows, or 2 hours of full-on video play.

POWER USERS' CLINIC

Maximizing Your Battery's Potential

Battery life varies. Someone inclined to settle into a long playlist and let the iPod go without interruption will enjoy more time between electricity refills than an iPodder who constantly jumps around to different songs and fiddles with controls.

Apple has several recommendations, both environmental and behavioral, for getting the most out of the battery. For example, as better power management is a perpetual goal, the company recommends always having the latest version of the iPod software installed.

While the iPod can operate without incident in temperatures between 50 and 95 degrees Fahrenheit, the iPod (like most people) works best at room temperature—around 68° F. An iPod left out in a cold car all night, for example, needs to warm up to room temperature before you play it; otherwise, it may have trouble waking up from sleep mode. It also may present the low battery icon onscreen. (If this happens to you, wait until the iPod warms up, then plug it into its power adapter and reset it by pressing the Menu and Select buttons on all click wheel iPods—or Menu and Play/Pause buttons on older iPods—until the Apple logo appears.)

Using the Hold switch (page 18) can make sure that a sleeping iPod doesn't get turned on, and therefore run its battery down, by an accidental bump or nudge while in a purse or pocket. Pausing the iPod when you're not listening to it is a

good way to save power, especially if you tend to get distracted and forget that the player is set to repeat songs and playlists over and over.

Jumping around the iPod's music library with the Previous and Next buttons can also burn down the battery sooner rather than later. Like a laptop, the full-size iPod stores its data on a tiny hard drive, and hard drives can be power hogs. To save power, the iPod lets its hard drive stop spinning as often as possible—by playing upcoming music from a built-in memory chip. Pushing the iPod's buttons to change songs forces the iPod to start its hard drive spinning again, which requires energy.

The iPod's memory cache works best with song files that are smaller than 9 MB. That's plenty for songs in the MP3 or AAC formats (Chapter 4). But if you're listening to AIFF tracks you copied straight from the CD without compression (you know who you are), the larger file sizes may overload the cache, and your battery won't last as long.

That backlight, while illuminating, is also a power drain. Use the light sparingly for better battery life.

What about the iPod's charge when you're *not* using it? Turns out that it quietly sips juice even when it's turned off. In 14 days (or much sooner), the battery will empty itself completely. In short, treat the iPod as you would a pet snake: Give it a big meal every few days.

The bigger 60-gigabyte model is rated for up to 20 hours of music-spinning, or 4 hours of slideshows, or 3 hours of movies. The wee iPod Nano gets up to 14 hours of music between charges, or 4 hours of photo slideshows scored to your favorite music tracks.

But you can expect shorter life in the real world (see the box on page 20 for more details). If your iPod is conking out too soon, contact Apple Support by phone or Web. Originally, Apple made the iPod without a replaceable battery, at least until it faced a spate of power cells with early deaths (and owner complaints). Apple now offers a $59 battery replacement program and a special AppleCare warranty just for iPods.

Note: If you don't mind voiding your iPod's warranty—or if it's already expired—and you're up for a little manual labor, you can pry the case open and replace the battery yourself (page 248).

Earphones: Apple's or Otherwise

The iPod comes with a set of white earbud-style headphones (Figure 1-4). These aren't just flimsy freebies tossed in the box, either. They're designed with the iPod's amplifier in mind.

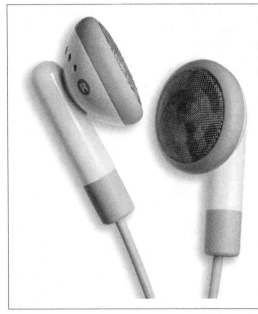

Figure 1-4:
You're supposed to wedge the iPod earbuds into your ear canals, preferably after covering each one with one of the included foam covers. As with any headphone, really loud music can damage hearing, so use the volume controls sensibly.

With a frequency response of 20 to 20,000 hertz, the iPod can cover a huge range of sounds—comparable to that of a respectable home stereo. In other words, it lets most people hear all the detailed sonic mayhem on a Pink Floyd album. To reproduce this range of frequencies, the iPod earbuds use 18 mm drivers with neodymium transducer magnets. (No, you're not expected to know what that means—but it's fun to say at cocktail parties. See the box on page 22.)

UP TO SPEED

Neodymium and Why You Care

The *driver* is the moving element in any type of speaker system, from tiny headphones to subwoofers. When an amplifier supplies power, the driver vibrates and produces sound waves.

Neodymium—which, from your cramming for that high school test in the periodic table, you may recognize as atomic number 60—is a rare-earth metal that's used in magnets, lasers, and purple glass. Its name is derived from the

Greek neos didymos, which means "new twin" (an appropriate name for a substance used in a pair of earbuds).

Apple claims that its neodymium driver is five times as powerful as the aluminum or cobalt drivers in other earbuds, capable of delivering accurate sound with minimal distortion.

Sounds good so far.

While the iPod earbuds are quite robust, they're not for everyone. Some people absolutely *hate* the sound quality. Some people don't care for the sensation of oversized chunks of foam jammed into their auditory canals. Others lack the wedge of cartilage that keeps earbud-style headphones in place, and so they can't use the iPod buds without duct tape.

Fortunately, the 3.5 mm jack on the iPod's headphone port makes it possible to use just about any type of Walkman-style headphones. If you have truly hard-to-fit ears, for example, Apple also sells a set of in-ear headphones with three different earhole cap sizes that you gently plug into your head for maximum comfort. These in-ear buddies cost $40 at *http://store.apple.com*.

Swapping out the iPod earbuds for smaller ones, or even headphones that go over the head and cover the outer ear, is perfectly fine. You can even use those big fancy noise-canceling headphones (Bose and Philips make great ones) to neutralize background noise around you and pipe more pure music directly into your head. However, if esthetics matter to you, finding white earphones that match the iPod is much less of a challenge than it used to be since Apple bucked the black and gray trends of the early 21st century.

The iPod Menus

The iPod's menus are as straightforward as its controls. You use the scroll wheel to go down the list of options you see on the screen. Then you press the Select button to pick what you want. Small arrows on the end of each menu item (like this: Settings >) indicate that another menu lurks behind it, so keep pressing Select until you get to where you want to go. (If you realize that's *not* where you want to go, press the Menu button to retrace your steps.)

Note: The menus and screens described here refer to the ones used in iPod system software 1.0 for the video-enabled iPods first released in 2005, and the mighty-mite iPod Nano.

The main screen (Figure 1-5) says iPod at the top and offers a choice of six areas to go to next: Music, Photos, Videos, Extras, Settings, and Shuffle Songs. The iPod Nano has the same set of menus except for the Videos item because it can't play video. Here's more about what's under each menu item.

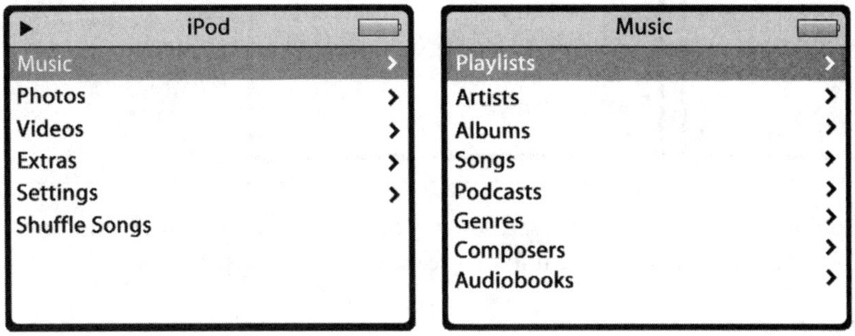

▶ iPod ▭		Music ▭
Music >		Playlists >
Photos >		Artists >
Videos >		Albums >
Extras >		Songs >
Settings >		Podcasts >
Shuffle Songs		Genres >
		Composers >
		Audiobooks >

Figure 1-5:
If you don't see this main menu (shown on the left) at the moment, press the Menu button repeatedly until you do. From here, you can drill down into any iPod function. Use the scroll wheel to slide the highlight bar down the menu, and press the round Select button to jump into the chosen menu, in this case, the Music menu.

Music

The Music menu is a big one-stop shopping center for all of the iPod's audio-related options, including tunes, audiobooks, and podcasts.

Playlists

A *playlist* is a customized list of songs that you create from the tracks in your music library. It's your own personal music mix that you can save, store, and play over and over again on your iPod or computer.

Except for On-The-Go playlists (described next), you make playlists on your Mac or PC using the iTunes software. For example, you can make a playlist called "Go For Baroque" and add all of your favorite Bach and Handel songs from your music library, in the order you want to hear them. You can also get the computer to create playlists for you with the iTunes Smart Playlists feature.

Once you save a playlist and synchronize your computer with the iPod, the file is transferred to the iPod.

All of the playlists you've created in iTunes appear in the Playlists menu (Figure 1-6). When you want to hear a particular set of songs, choose the playlist's name and press Play. When you finish listening to one playlist, pick another from the Playlists menu to keep jamming.

Playlists are not set in stone. For example, if you made a playlist called "All of Radiohead," and Radiohead puts out a new album, you can just rip the new CD on your Mac or PC, drag the files onto your existing Radiohead playlist, and update the iPod.

Figure 1-6:
Left: Scroll to the playlist you want to hear, select it, and press Play.

Right: If you highlight a playlist name and then press Select, you see a list of the songs in that playlist.

To modify or delete a playlist, use iTunes; you can't do that kind of thing on the iPod. Chapter 5 has loads more info on creating and editing playlists.

Playlists On-The-Go

Before the 2003 iPods beamed in from Apple headquarters, the only way to make a playlist for the iPod was to sit down at your computer and fire up iTunes (Chapter 5). Then you had to download the fresh, hot playlist to the iPod when it was connected.

This method didn't exactly provide instant gratification. If, while you were bopping around town, you found yourself suddenly wishing you could hear an eclectic mix of tunes from several different albums and artists, you were out of luck.

The Playlists On-The-Go feature fixes that. You scroll through your iPod's music library, choose the song you want to add, and hold down the Select button for a few seconds. The song's title blinks three times to acknowledge its addition to a special, modifiable playlist called *On-The-Go*. You're then free to scroll onward to the next song you want to add. You can press and select entire albums, artists, or even other playlists to add to your On-The-Go compilation.

To see your On-The-Go playlist, just scroll to the very bottom of the Playlists menu. Press Select to see the list of songs in it—or press Play to hear them.

For people who really love spontaneous music-mixing, it's also possible to save 'n' sync multiple On-The-Go playlists. Once you have a set list you really want to keep in the On-The-Go area of the playlists menu, scroll down to the bottom of the list and choose Save Playlist. This slides you over to another screen where your options are Cancel or Save Playlist. Press Save Playlist to have the songs immortalized as New Playlist 1 on the iPod, until you can hook up with iTunes and rename it something more memorable.

Once you save an On-The-Go playlist on the iPod, all those songs move over to New Playlist 1, and you can whip up a fresh grouping of tunes. If you opt for Save Playlist again, that new batch becomes New Playlist 2. If you have your iPod configured to automatically sync with iTunes (page 269), all the New Playlists appear in the iTunes Source list, where you can rename them. If you choose to manually update your iPod, though, you don't get to see the New Playlists in iTunes, and you have to recreate them yourself within iTunes because the program won't save them for you.

Note: The first version of the On-The-Go playlist feature held the song set in its memory *only* until the next time you connected it to the computer. Later versions of the iPod system software fixed that temporal annoyance and let you sync your spontaneous mix back into iTunes—as long as your iPod is set to automatically synchronize with iTunes on your computer.

If you tire of those tunes before you sync up again and don't want to save them, you can wipe out the temporary list by selecting the Clear Playlist option at the bottom of the On-The-Go submenu.

The Music menu holds much more than playlists, though. It has a number of categories useful for finding and playing exactly what you want to hear. Other items on the Music menu include:

- **Artists.** This menu groups every tune by the performer's name.

- **Albums.** This view groups your music by album.

- **Songs.** This is a list of every song on the iPod, listed alphabetically.

- **Podcasts.** All of your favorite prerecorded radio-style programs hang out on this menu.

- **Genres.** This menu sorts your music by type: rock, rap, country, and so on.

- **Composers.** The iPod displays all of your music, grouped by songwriter.

- **Audiobooks.** This menu lists your iPod's spoken-word content.

Figure 1-7 shows the Artists menu. To see a list of all the songs on your iPod sorted by the artist who performs them, select Artists from the Music menu, and the next screen presents you with an alphabetical list of bands and singers. Chapters 4, 5, and 6 let you know how all that song information gets attached to your digital audio files in the first place.

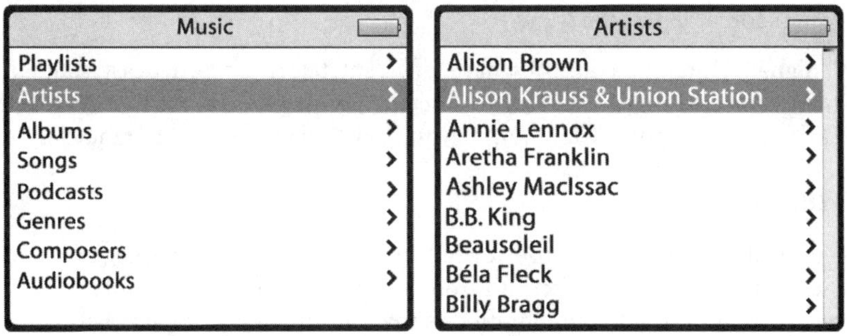

Music		Artists	
Playlists	>	Alison Brown	>
Artists	>	Alison Krauss & Union Station	>
Albums	>	Annie Lennox	>
Songs	>	Aretha Franklin	>
Podcasts	>	Ashley MacIssac	>
Genres	>	B.B. King	>
Composers	>	Beausoleil	>
Audiobooks	>	Béla Fleck	>
		Billy Bragg	>

Figure 1-7:
Click Artists to see a list of all the bands and singers in your iPod's music library. Once you select an artist, the next screen takes you to a list of all of that performer's albums. Similarly, the Albums menu shows all your iPod's songs grouped by album name.

Note: If you're a classical music buff, all bets are off when it comes to filing tidy bits of information into the Song, Composer, and Artist slots. As an article in the *New York Times* put it: "Take Saint-Saëns's First Cello Concerto, 'Violoncello in A major,' Opus 33, No. 1, with Mstislav Rostropovich as soloist and Carlo Maria Giulini conducting the London Philharmonic. Whose name should go into the 'artist' slot? And what's the 'song title'?"

Sometimes, you just have to suffer for your art.

Photos

The main difference between older iPods and the ones that appeared at the end of 2004 is the ability to display digital pictures on that bright color screen. Full-size iPods can also mimic a Kodak carousel and play slideshows on a connected television set (page 147).

The Photos menu is where you go on your iPod or iPod Nano to adjust your picture-viewing preferences. (The two TV-related settings are not available on the Nano.)

Slideshow Settings

- **Time Per Slide.** You can linger up to 20 seconds on each photo or manually forge ahead.

- **Music.** Here you can select a playlist as your slideshow soundtrack or opt for respectful silence.

- **Repeat.** As with playlists, you can have the slideshow repeat when it gets to the end.

- **Shuffle Photos.** Toggle the setting to On to randomly display each photo in the slideshow.

- **Transitions.** You can turn on the option here for a classic Hollywood wipe as you move from photo to photo.

- **TV Out.** To display your slideshow on a connected TV, select the On or Ask option. For portable slideshows on the iPod screen, choose Off or Ask. (Off does what it says, and Ask nags you to pick between your TV and your iPod's screen before it'll play the show.)

- **TV Signal.** Different countries have different television broadcast standards. When connected to a TV in North America, South America, or East Asia, select NTSC; most of Europe, China, Africa, and Australia use the PAL standard.

Photo Library

The photo library or albums you loaded on your iPod (see Chapter 6) is listed here. Select Photo Library to scroll through a pint-size visual directory of all the pictures stored in the selected album, as shown on the left in Figure 1-8. Use the scroll wheel to highlight a particular photo and press the Select button to see just that image on the screen (Figure 1-8, right). Use the Previous and Next buttons to move backward or forward through the pictures in the library.

Figure 1-8:
The Photo Library shows you teeny-tiny preview versions of all the pictures you have on your iPod. Use the scroll wheel to slide the highlight square to a certain photo (left), and press the iPod's center button to see the selected image across the entire screen (right).

Videos (5G iPods only)

That fifth-generation iPod is also a personal movie player, and with that capability, it brings a menu full of video settings and sorting options:

- **Video Playlists.** Just like music, you can make playlists of videos in iTunes.

- **Movies.** Home movies and other homemade creations can be found here.

- **Music Videos.** This submenu lists your collected music-video clips.

- **TV Shows.** A menu for iTunes store-purchased episodes and personally recorded shows.

- **Video Podcasts.** Some podcasts have pictures now; come here when they do.

- **Video Settings.** You can configure your TV playback options and also set the iPod to play video in the widescreen format or adjust it for full-screen viewing.

Playing a video works just like playing a song: browse, scroll, and select. Chapters 5, 6, and 7 tell you how to buy, sort, and organize your iPod's video collection from the iTunes side of the fence.

Extras

This menu contains all the goodies that make the iPod more than just a music player. Here's what you'll find there.

Note: The iPod models released before 2003 lack the Notes feature, Solitaire, Music Quiz, and the Parachute game.

Clock

When you choose Clock, you have the opportunity to set up live clocks in multiple cities of your choosing. This little timekeeper comes in handy if you forget your watch in any time zone! To create a clock, choose Clock → New Clock and pick your geographical location on the Region menu and then press onward to the City menu to set up the correct time. (There's more on the Clock in Chapter 8.)

Each clock you make has its own set of submenus when you press the Select button:

Alarm Clock

The iPod's alarm clock can give you a gentle nudge when you need it. To set the iPod alarm, do the following:

1. **Choose Extras → Clock → Alarm Clock → Alarm. Press the Select button.**

   The Alarm changes to On. You've just switched the alarm on (Figure 1-9, left).

2. **Scroll to Time, press Select, and spin the scroll wheel.**

   As you turn the wheel, you change the time that the iPod displays in the highlighted box (Figure 1-9, right). Press the Select button as you pick the hour, minutes, and choice of meridian for your wake-up call.

3. **Press Select again to set the time.**

   It's time to decide whether you want "Beep" (a warbling R2-D2–like noise that comes out of the iPod's built-in speaker) or music. If you choose to be alerted by music, it will play through your headphones, assuming they haven't fallen out of your ear sockets during sleep.

4. **Scroll to Sound and press Select. Choose Beep (at the top of the list), or highlight the playlist you want to hear at the appointed time. Press Select.**

   The Alarm Clock is set. You see a tiny bell icon on the main clock screen.

5. **When the alarm goes off, the iPod beeps for a few seconds—or plays the playlist you selected—until you press the iPod's Pause button.**

   If you wake up early and want to prevent the alarm from sounding, go to Extras → Clock → Alarm Clock → Alarm and press the Select button to toggle it off.

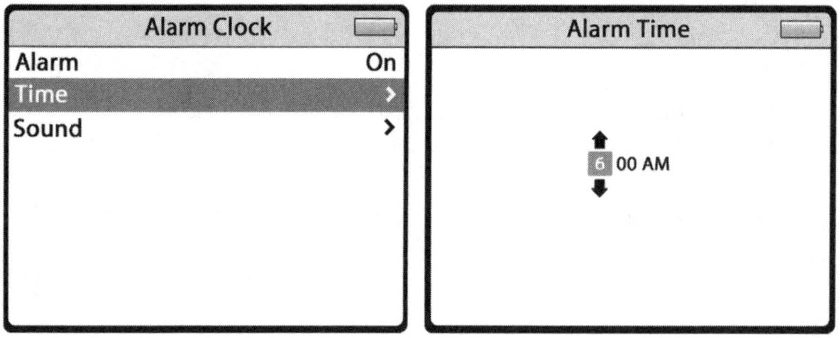

Alarm Clock	
Alarm	On
Time	>
Sound	>

Alarm Time
▲
6 00 AM
▼

Figure 1-9:
Left: Any old alarm clock lets you specify what time you want it to go off. But how many let you specify what song you want to play?

Right: Turn the dial to set the time.

Tip: You don't have to burrow all the way to the Clock option just to use your 2003-or-later iPod as a pocket watch. You can ask iPod to display the current time in its title bar whenever music is playing. To do so, choose iPod → Settings → Date & Time → Time in Title. Press the Select button to toggle the "Time in Title" display on or off.

Change City

Selecting this menu item takes you back to the Region menu so you can relocate this clock to a new town with a whirl of the wheel.

Daylight Saving Time

Here, make your current clock "Fall back" or "Spring forward" an hour by pressing the Select button to turn Daylight Savings Time off or on.

Delete This Clock

When time is *not* on your side anymore, you can get rid of the clock at hand with this menu command.

Sleep Timer

The sleep timer is like the opposite of the alarm clock: It's designed to help you fall *asleep* instead of waking you. The idea is that you can schedule the iPod to shut itself off after a specified period of music playing so that you can drift off to sleep as music plays, without worrying that you'll run down your battery.

To set the iPod's Sleep Timer, choose Extras → Clock → Sleep Timer. Scroll down to the amount of time the iPod should play before shutting down: 15, 20, 60, 90, or 120 minutes. (You can also choose to turn off the Sleep Timer here.)

Now, start the iPod playing (press Play) and snuggle down into your easy chair or pillow. The screen displays a little clock and begins a digital countdown to sleepy-land.

Your iPod will stop playing automatically after the appointed interval—but if all goes well, you won't be awake to notice.

More Extras

The remaining items on the Extras menu go far beyond music—once you know how to use them. More details about getting the most out of your iPod are revealed in Part 3 of this book, but here's what you have to look forward to:

- **Games.** You can play the historic Brick game on the iPod. On 2003-and-later models, you also get Parachute, Solitaire, and a Music Quiz (Chapter 8).
- **Contacts.** Phone numbers and addresses reside here (see the online appendix, "iPod As Organizer," available on the "Missing CD" page at *www.missingmanuals.com*).
- **Calendar.** This menu holds your personal daily schedule (see the online appendix, "iPod As Organizer," available on the "Missing CD" page at *www.missingmanuals.com*).
- **Notes.** The 2003 iPods were the first to come with a built-in text reader program that you can use to read short documents and notes (Chapter 8).

- **Stopwatch.** The iPod can serve as your timer for keeping track of your overall workout or multiple laps around the track (Chapter 8).

- **Screen Lock.** With all your stuff that's nobody's business—address book, schedule, personal photos, etc.—you may want to lock up your iPod from nosy people who'd love to scroll into your life (Chapter 8.)

Settings

The Settings menu has more than a dozen options for tailoring how your iPod sounds and looks.

Note: The following list refers to the state of the iPod menu software as of January 2006. Depending on your iPod model and the version of the iPod software you're using, you may see slight variations on the options offered.

About

The About screen displays the name of your iPod; the number of songs, videos, and photos on it; the hard drive capacity of your model; and how much disk space is free. As shown in Figure 1-10, you can also find the version of the iPod system software that your unit is currently running, as well as your iPod's serial number. (The serial number is also engraved on the iPod's back panel.)

Main Menu

The iPod has a handy personalization feature: the ability to arrange your iPod's Main Menu screen so that only the items you like show up when you spin the wheel. For example, you could insert the Calendar option onto the iPod's opening screen so that you don't have to drill down through the Extras menu to get at it.

To customize your iPod's Main Menu, start by choosing Settings → Main Menu from the main iPod menu (Figure 1-10, right). You see a list of items that you can choose to add to or eliminate from your iPod's main screen: Playlists, Artists, Clock, Contacts, Screen Lock, and so on.

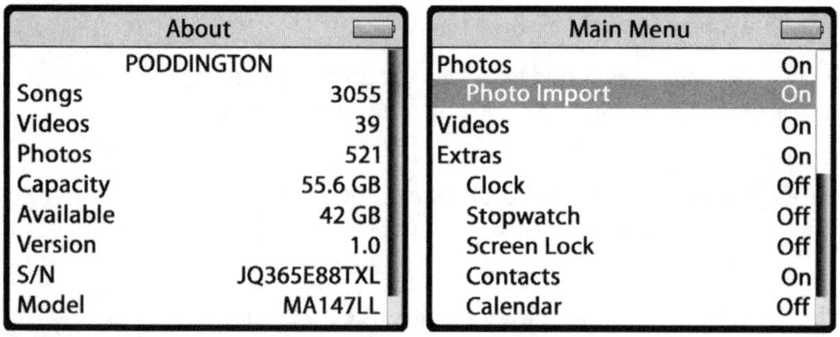

About		Main Menu	
PODDINGTON		Photos	On
Songs	3055	Photo Import	On
Videos	39	Videos	On
Photos	521	Extras	On
Capacity	55.6 GB	Clock	Off
Available	42 GB	Stopwatch	Off
Version	1.0	Screen Lock	Off
S/N	JQ365E88TXL	Contacts	On
Model	MA147LL	Calendar	Off

Figure 1-10:
Left: Among other trivia bits, the About screen shows how much space on the iPod is available for you to fill with songs and files.

Right: The Main Menu settings, just under About, can customize your iPod's main screen.

As you scroll down the list, press the Select button to turn each one on or off. You might, for example, consider adding these commands:

- **Clock,** for quick checks of the time.

- **Games,** for quick killing of time.

- **Contacts,** to look up phone numbers and call people to pass the time.

To see the fruits of your labor, press Menu twice to return to the main screen. Sure enough, in addition to the usual commands described in this chapter, you'll see the formerly buried commands right out front, ready to go.

There are also some hidden menu items for iPod accessories here. For example, you can bring the Photo Import option—used with third-party media readers or the iPod Camera Connector (page 328) to dump pictures from a digital camera onto the iPod's hard drive—up to the main menu. Likewise, here you can also activate the Voice Memos item used with attachable microphones.

Tip: To restore the original factory settings, select Reset Main Menu at the bottom of the list and Reset on the next screen.

Shuffle

When the Shuffle option is *off,* the iPod plays straight down each playlist as you originally designed it (Chapter 5). If you turn on Shuffle Songs, the iPod ambles through all the songs on your chosen playlist or album in *random* order. Press Select again to get Shuffle Albums, which makes the iPod mix up the order of the albums it plays (but not the songs within each album).

To set your Shuffle preferences, choose Settings → Shuffle from the Main menu. Then press the Select button to cycle through your three options—Off, Songs, or Albums—until you hit the one you want.

Repeat

The Repeat function works like the similarly named button on a CD player: It makes the music you're listening to loop over and over again.

To set your Repeat preferences, choose Settings → Repeat from the Main menu. Now, by pressing the Select button repeatedly, you can cycle through these three options:

- **Repeat One.** You'll hear the current song repeated over and over again, like a hippie teenager with a new Beatles 45.

- **Repeat All.** This function repeats *the current list* over and over again, whether that's an album, a playlist, or your entire song library.

- **Off.** The iPod will play the selected playlist or album once and then stop.

Tip: Be careful with the repeat functions. If you set the iPod down (or if it gets bumped when the Hold switch wasn't activated), it will cheerfully play away, over and over, endlessly, until the battery is dead.

Backlight Timer

The iPod screen's backlight is pretty, but it can be a real drain on the iPod's battery. Fortunately, you can specify how long the backlight stays on each time you press a button or turn the dial, from 1 Second to Always On. If you *never* want the iPod to light up—for example, when it's in its case and you use the remote control to operate it—you can also turn off the backlight completely.

To set your Backlight Timer preferences, choose Settings → Backlight Timer. Scroll to the amount of time you want the Backlight to stay on when you touch any iPod button—2 Seconds, 5 Seconds, or whatever—and then press Select.

For example, if you use the iPod in low-light conditions, or you have a hard time reading the screen, a ray of backlight for 5 or 10 seconds should be enough time to scroll up to a new playlist or album when you touch the controls.

Choose Always On to keep the light shining until you manually turn it off by holding down the Menu button.

Note: If you're spinning tunes as an iPod DJ in a dark club or other squinty situation, the Always On setting is handy. But, unless you have a really short set list, run the player from an AC adapter because the backlight is hungry for battery power.

Audiobooks

Serious audio book aficionados will appreciate this new setting that arrived with the latest iPods. The Audiobooks setting now lets you speed up or slow down the narrator's voice as he or she reads to you. If you later decide that the Faster setting makes your spoken novel sound like it's being read by an auctioneer, switch the setting back to Normal.

EQ

When it comes to the range of sounds, not all music is created equal. A howling heavy metal rock band produces a wider array of noises than a solo female singer armed with only an acoustic guitar.

Equalization is the art of adjusting the frequency response of an audio signal. An equalizer emphasizes or boosts some of its frequencies while lowering others. In the range of audible sound, *bass* frequencies are the low rumbly noises; *treble* is at the opposite end with the high, even shrill sound; and *midrange* is, of course, in the middle, and it's the most audible to human ears.

To save you the trouble of getting an audio engineering degree, the iPod includes a set of equalizer presets, named after the type of music (and the typical musical instruments) they're designed to enhance. Dance music, for example, usually has higher bass frequencies to emphasize the booming rhythm.

By contrast, if you're listening to your playlist of Haydn string quartets, try setting the iPod's equalizer to the Classical preset. This setting softens some of the more screechy higher frequencies while providing firm, sturdy midrange and bass frequencies that make for a mellow cello.

There are more than 20 equalizer presets on the iPod—for acoustic, classical, dance, hip hop, jazz, pop, rock, and other types of music—plus, settings that can add or reduce bass and treble sounds. They might drain the battery a little faster, and you might not be able to hear much difference, but many people prefer equalized music for the overall sound quality.

To set your iPod's Equalizer to a preset designed for a specific type of music or situation, choose iPod → Settings → EQ. Scroll down the list of presets until you find one that matches your music style, and then press the Select button. The name of the preset is now listed next to EQ on the Settings menu.

Tip: See Chapter 5 for more on equalization and how you can apply it from your computer.

Compilations

Many songs are not just by one band or singer, but are part of compilations, like greatest-hits-of-the-decade collections, movie soundtracks, and all-star tribute albums. Turning this setting to On lets you add a Compilations submenu to the main Music menu so those hard-to-sort group efforts show up as one album.

Sound Check

This ingenious setting cuts down on those jarring moments between, *say,* George Winston's New Age noodling and the latest angry Metallica thrash, by adjusting the overall volume settings.

The key to making this feature work is to remember that you have to turn it on *in two places:* once in iTunes on your Mac or PC, and once on the iPod.

Start in iTunes. Choose Preferences → Playback (⌘-comma on the Mac; Ctrl+comma in Windows), and turn on the Sound Check box. Then, on the iPod, choose Settings → Sound Check, and press the Select button to change the setting from Off to On.

The next time you sync up your iPod with the computer, the Sound Check adjustments you made in iTunes get passed along to the player.

If you don't like the Sound Check effect, turn it off *in both places.*

Clicker

Usually, each time you click an iPod button or turn its dial, you hear a little clicking sound from the iPod's built-in speaker. If you prefer to scroll in silence, simply turn the Clicker sound off here. Current iPods let you opt to have the Clicker noise play only through the headphones, only through the iPod's speaker, or both.

Some people might think the Clicker noise sounds like ants tap dancing, but others like the audio cue—especially on click wheel iPods that don't otherwise give much in the way of feedback while you're scrolling.

Date & Time

If you've just flown in from the coast and need to adjust your iPod's clock, you can change the player's date, time, and time zone settings here. These settings are especially important if the iPod needs to be punctual, like when you intend to use the Alarm Clock.

Note: If you're syncing your iPod to a Mac running Mac OS X 10.2 or later, don't bother setting your date and time on the iPod. The computer does it for you.

To manually set the clock from the Date & Time settings area:

1. **From the main menu, choose Settings → Date & Time.**

   You're going to set the time zone first. Setting the time zone is sort of a moot point if you never go far enough to change time zones. But if you travel a lot and want to change the iPod's clock with a minimum of fuss, this setting saves you from resetting the time when you land in New York after flying in from Los Angeles.

2. **Scroll to and select Set Time Zone. Pick your time zone (or a city in your time zone) from the list. Press the Select button when you're done.**

   You may notice that the iPod's list doesn't match the list of time zones found in a world atlas. Although the standard U.S. time zones are represented (with a Daylight Savings Time option for each), foreign time zones are represented by a list of major cities in each. The list isn't in alphabetical order, but starts at the International Date Line and moves eastward from Eniwetok to Auckland.

3. **Back on the Date & Time settings screen, scroll to and select Set Date & Time.**

   Use the scroll wheel to adjust the highlighted hour, minute, day, month, and year. You can also choose to have the iPod display the time in the standard 12-hour clock with a.m. and p.m. designations, or the 24-hour clock used by the military and on *M*A*S*H* reruns. Use the Next and Previous buttons on the iPod to skip over fields you don't need to change.

4. **Press the Select button for each part of today's date as you scroll to it, until everything is set.**

   Press the Menu button a couple of times to return to the main menu.

Tip: If you want the current time displayed at the top of the iPod's Main menu, press the Select button when you're in the Date & Time menu and turn "Time in Title" to On.

Contacts

This setting lets you change the sorting order of the first and last names of people in your iPod's built-in address book (see the online appendix, "iPod As Organizer," available on the "Missing CD" page at *www.missingmanuals.com*).

Language

The iPod is the United Nations of digital audio players, in that it can display its menus in most major European and Asian languages.

To set the language for the iPod's menus, choose Settings → Languages from the main iPod menu. Scroll down the list of languages and press the Select button when you find your native tongue (or the one you want to use if you're practicing vocabulary for Swedish class).

The iPod's menus now appear in the new language. To change back, return to the Language settings and scroll to a new language.

Tip: See page 250 if you accidentally change your display language to Korean and can't figure out how to change it back again.

Legal

The Legal menu contains a long scroll of copyright notices for Apple and its software partners. It's not very interesting reading unless perhaps you're studying intellectual-property law.

Reset All Settings

This command takes all your iPod's customized sound and display settings back to their original factory settings. This feature doesn't erase your music or contacts—just customized tweakings of things like the Shuffle function and Backlight Timer.

To return your iPod to its untweaked state, choose Settings → Reset All Settings. Then scroll to Reset and press the Select button. (There's a Cancel option if you decide to bail out.)

Note: Reset All Settings affects the software only. It's not the same thing as resetting the iPod itself (the hardware). Resetting the iPod involves pushing buttons to reboot the player when the iPod freezes or won't wake up from sleep mode. See page 242 to learn the procedure.

Shuffle Songs

The mystical, magical qualities of the iPod's Shuffle Songs setting (*"How does my little PeaPod always know when to play my Weird Al Yankovic and Monty Python songs to cheer me up?"*) have become one of the player's most popular features, so Apple moved Shuffle out to the main menu. Just scroll and select if you want to shuffle.

Now Playing

Highlight this command and press Select to call up the main Now Playing screen, shown in Figure 1-11. Obviously, you only see this item on the iPod's menu when you have something *playing*.

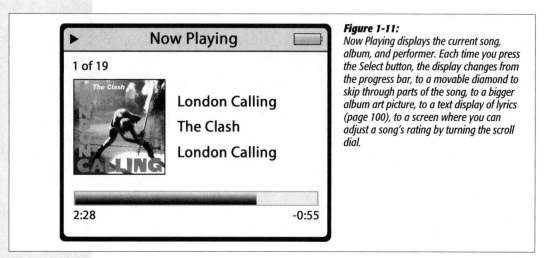

Figure 1-11:
Now Playing displays the current song, album, and performer. Each time you press the Select button, the display changes from the progress bar, to a movable diamond to skip through parts of the song, to a bigger album art picture, to a text display of lyrics (page 100), to a screen where you can adjust a song's rating by turning the scroll dial.

The iPod Sync Connection

Sleek and smart as the iPod may be, it can't do much by itself until it meets up with a computer. Once connected to a Mac or PC, however, the iPod is ready to accept whatever you want to give it—your whole music library, of course, but also everything from the complete recorded works of Tom Petty to your phone book, from news and calendar information to files too big to fit on a burned CD.

This chapter is dedicated to that concept of iPod as Satellite to Your Computer (and it concerns all iPods except the Shuffle, which has the next chapter all to itself). It explains USB 2.0 and FireWire, and how to use these connections to get songs and files off the mother ship and onto the ultraportable, ready-to-go iPod.

The iPod Software CD

The CD that comes with the iPod contains all the software you need to get up and iPodding in no time (see Figure 2-1). When you pull the disc out of the iPod's box, you see a sticker that commands you to:

"Install software before connecting iPod."

Unless you have multiple iPods and keep iTunes and all of your iPod software scrupulously up to date, you should listen to the sticker. (After you install the software, it's a good idea to check for any updates that may have occurred since that CD was made. On the Mac, choose → Software Update; in Windows, open iTunes and then choose Help → Check for iTunes Updates.)

Insert the CD and run the installer programs. Yes, there's only one CD in the box. The iPod CD installer program is smart enough to figure out what kind of computer you're using and show you only the Mac or Windows installer on the disc.

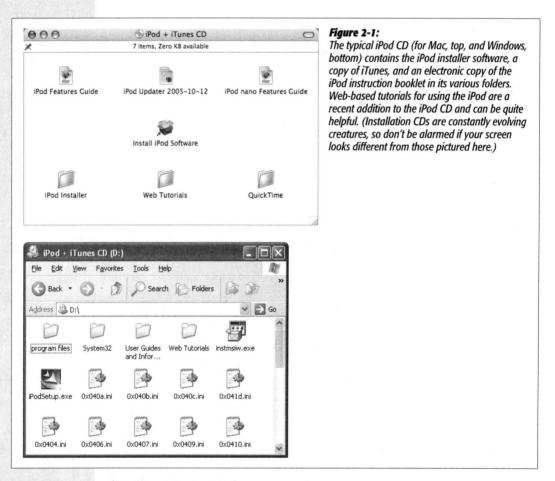

Figure 2-1:
The typical iPod CD (for Mac, top, and Windows, bottom) contains the iPod installer software, a copy of iTunes, and an electronic copy of the iPod instruction booklet in its various folders. Web-based tutorials for using the iPod are a recent addition to the iPod CD and can be quite helpful. (Installation CDs are constantly evolving creatures, so don't be alarmed if your screen looks different from those pictured here.)

The Macintosh CD

To install the software, insert the iPod CD into your Mac. If you've never used iTunes before, or you have a version you haven't updated in at least a couple of months, install the iTunes jukebox software from the CD or download the latest version from Apple's Web site (*www.apple.com/itunes/download/*).

The iPod has an operating system of its own, too (see page 22), but you don't need to install it; it's already on your iPod. However, double-clicking the installer in the iPod Installer folder puts a copy of the iPod installer program on your Mac so that you'll have it handy if you ever need to reinstall the iPod's system software.

Along the way, you'll be asked for your iPod's serial number and your registration number. When the software installer finishes, put the CD in a safe place. You'll need it if you ever need to reinstall your programs after a hard drive crash.

The first time you connect the iPod to the Mac, iTunes starts right up to greet it.

The Windows CD

If you have a PC, the software installer starts automatically when you insert the CD. The latest versions of the iPod CD for Windows ask you to connect your iPod to the PC so the installer can see if you need to format the player. (If you or someone you love has turned off the CD auto-start feature on your PC, open My Computer, and then open the icon for the CD-ROM drive. Locate and double-click the iPodSetup.exe program on the disc; you can see this icon in Figure 2-1 near the bottom. Finally, click the Install button to kick-start the installation process.)

The installer gives you all the necessary iPod drivers (utility programs that let your PC communicate with plug-in devices), plus a handsome piece of jukebox software to organize your music and download it to the iPod: iTunes for Windows. This free software is arguably the best jukebox software available for Windows. It gives you access to Apple's online 99¢-a-song music store (Chapter 7) and does a beautiful job of organizing, searching, and playing your tunes (Chapter 5).

Note: Back in Ye Olde Days of the iPod (2002), Macintosh and Windows iPods were preformatted at the factory and sold separately as Macintosh iPods or Windows iPods. Not anymore.

When you run the setup program on a Windows PC these days, behind the scenes, it actually reformats your iPod's hard drive for Windows. See Figure 2-2 for details. Be sure to install the iPod software *before* you connect the iPod to the computer.

Using USB 2.0

Way back in 2001, when the first Macintosh-only iPods first spun their scroll wheels, the only way you could connect an iPod to the computer was with a FireWire cable. This was not a bad thing, as FireWire could move 400 megabits of data per second, whipping the plastic off those pokey old USB 1.1 connections, which limped along at 12 megabits per second. With FireWire, you could transfer a CD's worth of songs to your iPod in 10 or 15 seconds and be out the door in no time.

Fast-forward to the end of 2005. FireWire is now a thing of the past on iPods, as Apple has opted to go with another technology, USB 2.0, for connecting iPods to computers. This means all iPod Shuffles, iPod Nanos, and video-enabled iPods now use USB 2.0 and *only* USB 2.0 to transfer songs and other files to the iPod.

Note: A FireWire cable with the flat, 30-pin dock connector plug from an older iPod or iPod Mini will still fit one of the newer iPods, but you can only use a FireWire connection to *charge* the Nano or iPod battery. You can't transfer data over a FireWire connection with a video iPod or iPod Nano.

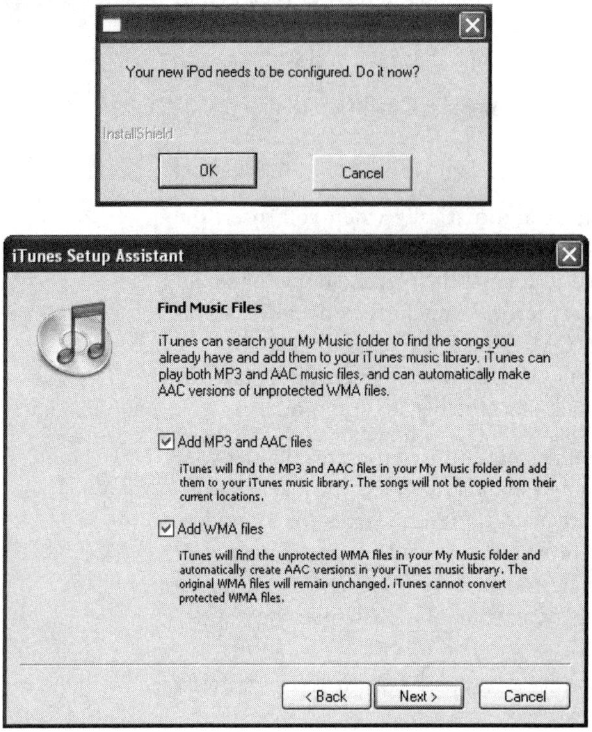

Figure 2-2:
It's not quite as dramatic a moment as watching a butterfly emerge, but the transformation of a brand-new iPod into a Windows iPod is beautiful in its own right.

Top: The installer asks whether you want to "configure" the iPod—that is, reformat it with the Windows FAT32 disk-formatting scheme.

Bottom: Once the program installs iTunes for Windows on the PC, it offers to sniff around for existing music files, including any songs in the Windows Media Audio format. Although the iPod can't play WMA files, iTunes will convert them to the AAC format for use on the iPod—if you choose to let it.

USB 2.0 can transfer data at zippy speeds of up to 480 megabits per second, which means that all those songs, photos, home movies, film trailers from the Web, and episodes of *The Office* purchased from the iTunes Music Store (Chapter 7) whistle down the wire at high speed to your connected iPod.

Note: Those are mega*bits,* not megabytes. Data transfer speeds are traditionally measured in *megabits* or *kilobits per second*; disk and file sizes are measured in *megabytes* (MB).

There are eight bits in a byte. To put USB and FireWire into more familiar terms, then, USB 1.1. can transfer files at up to 1.5 MB per second. FireWire can move 50 MB of data per second, and USB 2.0 can shuttle 60 MB per second.

Connecting Your iPod with USB 2.0

Older iPod models, including the iPod Mini, the iPod Photo, and the fourth-generation click wheel iPods (from 2004), included both USB 2.0 and FireWire cables in the box, giving you a choice of connections based on what worked best with your computer. This was helpful, as many Macs didn't have USB 2.0 ports and many PCs didn't have FireWire ports.

USB 2.0 has become widely popular in the past few years, though, and most new computers today include at least one or two USB 2.0 ports. Apple includes only a

USB 2.0 cable in the box with its iPods now, which lets you charge the iPod and sync up your music and video files.

Note: Although the company used to include a boxy white AC power adapter with new iPods, you now have to purchase it separately for about $30 from Apple's Web site or stores that sell iPod gear. The advantage to having the AC adapter means that you don't have to leash the iPod to the computer to recharge it—you just plug your iPod into the cable, the cable into the AC adapter, and the AC adapter into a wall outlet to power up.

Some Macintosh devotees were outraged when Apple dropped support for its own FireWire technology from the iPod. Ditching the FireWire hardware from the iPod's innards allowed the company to make smaller and thinner music players, but those without USB 2.0 are left with a few fairly lame options.

You can sync your iPod via regular USB, even if your machine has only regular USB (not 2.0). That's because USB 2.0 and USB 1.1 are compatible and use the same connector plug. Remember, though, that USB 1.1 is very slow compared with 2.0. You may want to plan a day's worth of activities while leaving the computer and iPod to their data-transfer duet. (A performance of Wagner's entire *Ring Cycle* or the Boston Marathon should do it.)

Another option for making a new iPod work with a slightly older computer is to add a USB 2.0 card to the machine. These expansion cards are available for about $30 for a model that fits in a spare PCI slot inside the computer; you can also find pop-in models, for about $50, that snap into the CardBus slot on a laptop. Figure 2-3 shows examples of both.

Connecting Your iPod by FireWire

If you purchased your iPod before late 2005, you probably got a USB 2.0 and a FireWire cable in the box. (Figure 2-4 shows the two types of cables.) If your iPod came with a FireWire cable and your computer has a FireWire port (also called an IEEE 1394 or, if you have a Sony computer, an i.LINK port), then you can use this cable to sync songs and charge the battery.

If you've purchased an older iPod on eBay or have been the recipient of a technological hand-me-down, connecting by FireWire goes like this: On a Mac, just plug in the FireWire cable to the FireWire port. Due to the fact that there are a couple of different types of FireWire ports on a PC, Windows owners may have more variables to deal with:

- **FireWire connector, 6-pin.** If the white FireWire cable that came with your full-size iPod fits a socket on your PC's FireWire card, great! Connect the fat end to the iPod, and you're ready to rock. (As a bonus, your iPod may even get its power charge from the same cable, depending on which brand of FireWire card you have.)

Figure 2-3:
Just because your computer didn't come with USB 2.0 doesn't mean you have to put up with agonizingly long waits to copy music, photos, and videos over to your iPod. With inexpensive expansion hardware—like this USB 2.0 card from Sonnet Technologies (top) for a desktop computer's internal PCI slot, or D-Link's USB 2.0 Cardbus card for laptops (bottom)—you can give your older computer a taste of the newer USB technology for less than $50.

- **FireWire connector, 4-pin.** The FireWire cable that comes with the full-size iPod has a fattish 6-pin connector at one end. It doesn't fit the smaller 4-pin connectors common on Windows FireWire cards.

Apple used to include a small white 4-pin adapter in the iPod box for some models. It fit over the *end* of the included 6-pin cable. With the surging popularity of USB 2.0, however, newer iPods just come with a single USB cable and no adapter. If you still prefer FireWire, though, you can get a 6-to-4 pin cable adapter at most computer stores. If you do get an adapter, just snap it onto one end of the cable and plug it into the PC's port. Then plug the other end into the iPod (or its dock, if you have one).

Your Very First Sync

For most people, the goal with any new electronics purchase is to get the new toy working right away so the fun can begin. For new iPod owners, getting to The Fun can be a very short wait. After unpacking the iPod and all its accessories, charging it up as described in Chapter 1, and installing the software, you're ready to dive in.

The First Sync with iTunes

You may already have Apple's free iTunes program and plenty of songs stored in its music library. If so, the first synchronization between iPod and computer can be astoundingly simple. As soon as you connect the new iPod to the Mac or PC,

Figure 2-4:
The FireWire cable (left) has a thicker plug than the USB 2.0 cable (right) that comes in the box with newer iPods and Minis. Another way to tell the cables apart: Look at the gray symbols on each connector—FireWire has a Y-shaped icon; USB 2.0's icon looks like Neptune's trident.

iTunes will ask whether you'd like it to copy all the music it finds on your computer. If you say yes, the program takes care of business and begins copying your entire music library to the player. Once iTunes has finished its search-and-copy mission, it displays a screen full of your songs, all neatly compiled in its Library, as Figure 2-5 proudly displays.

Figure 2-5:
The Source list (left side) displays an icon for the iPod whenever it's connected and a handy Eject button next to it, as well as your music library, playlists, songs from the Music Store, videos, podcasts, and Internet radio stations. The bottom of the window shows the number of songs and other files in the Library, and the consecutive days iTunes can play music without repeating songs.

> **Note:** You can set iTunes to also synchronize your videos, photos, podcasts, contacts, and calendars. Since you're probably just getting started here and want to get some tunes out of iTunes and onto your iPod, non-music syncing is covered a little later in the book. Check out Chapter 6 for info on moving your other digital entertainment (videos, photos, podcasts) to the iPod, and see the online appendix, "iPod As Organizer," available on the "Missing CD" page at *www.missingmanuals.com*, for the more clerical types of files (contacts and calendars).

If you decline iTunes's automatic music transfer offer, the program sets your iPod to manual update. This means you have to drag songs and videos from iTunes to the iPod; see page 47 for more on that and why it can be a *good* thing.

If you don't have an older copy of iTunes or any MP3 files on your hard drive already, you'll have to snag some songs from your music CDs (Chapter 5) or buy some songs from the iTunes Music Store (Chapter 7). Once you have a library of music built up that you'd like to transfer to the iPod, just plug it in, let iTunes open, and watch the two machines talk music together.

Longtime Windows warriors who have a large collection of songs in Microsoft's Windows Media Audio (WMA) format, take heart: Your songs are not trapped in an iPod-unfriendly format forever. iTunes offers to convert your WMA files to Podworthy AAC files and personally escort them onto your new player. See page 77 for more on audio formats and which ones are good for the iPod.

Varying the Auto-Transfer Theme

The beauty of the iTunes/iPod system is that whatever music you add to your Mac or PC gets added to the iPod automatically, effortlessly, and quickly. You've always got your entire music collection with you. Just plugging in the iPod inspires iTunes to open up and begin syncing.

It's conceivable, however, that you won't always want complete and automatic syncing to take place whenever you connect the Pod. Maybe you use the iPod primarily as an external hard drive (Chapter 9), so you don't especially care to have iTunes jumping up like a West Highland terrier every time you plug in the iPod. Maybe you want to synchronize only *some* of your music, not all of it.

Fortunately, you're in complete control of the situation.

Stop Auto-Opening iTunes

If you like, you can command your jukebox software to open only when *you* want it to, rather than every time the iPod is plugged in. Just open iTunes, plug in the iPod, and, in the Source list, click its icon.

Then, click the iPod-shaped icon in the bottom-right part of the iTunes window (circled in Figure 2-6, left). The iPod Preferences box appears. Click the Music tab in the box to turn off the "Open iTunes when this iPod is attached" checkbox. (Older versions of iTunes keep all these preferences in one box, so yours may look a little different if you haven't updated lately.)

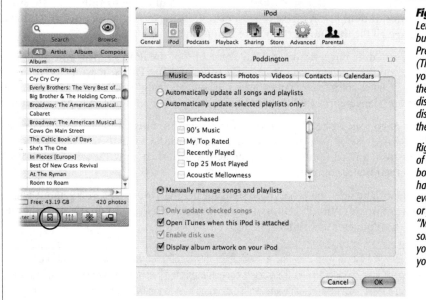

Figure 2-6:
Left: Click the circled button to call up the iPod Preferences dialog box. (The second button takes you to equalizer settings; the third controls screen displays. The last button dismounts the iPod from the computer.)

Right: On the Music tab of the iPod Preferences box you can choose to have the iPod update everything automatically, or just certain playlists. "Manually manage songs and playlists" lets you move just the songs you want to the iPod.

Transfer Only Some Songs

The auto-sync option pretty much removes any thought process required to move music to the iPod. But if you'd rather take control of the process, or you just want to transfer *some* songs or playlists, you can change the synchronization settings. If you just got done turning off iTunes from opening every time you plug in your iPod, you already know how to get to the iPod Preferences box. If you skipped that section, here's how.

1. With the main iTunes window open, click the name of your iPod in the Source list on the left side of the window.

2. Look at the bottom of the iPod window for the four small buttons along the right side (see Figure 2-6, left).

3. Click the first button on the left, which has a small graphic of an iPod on it, to open the iPod Preferences dialog box.

In iTunes 6, the iPod Preferences box is divided into multiple parts, depending on what kind of iPod you have and what operating system your computer's running. Click the Music tab in the dialog box, and then decide how you want to control the syncing process. Your choices are described in the following sections.

Complete automatic synchronization

The option to "Automatically update all songs and playlists" works as advertised. Your computer's music collection and your iPod's are kept identical, no matter what songs you add or remove from the computer.

If you have a PalmPilot or PocketPC, you may be thinking to yourself: "Ah, sweet synchronization! I won't have to worry about losing any data because everything is updated all the time no matter where I input them!"

There is a difference, however: Unlike a palmtop, the iPod's synchronization with the computer is a one-way street. If a song isn't in iTunes, it won't be on your iPod. Delete a song from iTunes, and it disappears from the iPod the next time you sync up. Many people find this out the hard way and are none too happy about it.

This, of course, is the iPod's system for preventing music piracy. If song copying were a two-way street, people could wander around with their iPods, collecting songs from any computers they came across, and then copy the whole mass back up to their home computers.

On the bright side, the autosync system means that you never worry about which songs are where. With the autosync option, what is in the computer's music library is on the iPod, and that's that.

Tip: Got a 4-gigabyte iPod Mini and a 13-gigabyte music collection already in iTunes? If you're set to autosync, iTunes will offer to personally select enough music to fill up the peewee Pod when you plug it in. If you'd rather take matters into your own hands, jump over to the "Manually manage songs and playlists" section on the next page.

Sync up only selected playlists

Choosing to sync up only certain playlists can save you some time because you avoid copying the entire music library. This tactic is helpful when, say, you have a workout playlist that you fuss with and freshen up each week. You can choose to update only that playlist instead of waiting around for the whole iPod to sync. (This feature is also handy if you're in a multi-iPod household. Each iPodder can maintain a separate playlist and set her iPod Preferences to sync up just that set of songs. Page 122 tells you how to craft powerful playlists that are all your own.)

Once you turn on "Automatically update selected playlists only," you're shown a list of the playlists you've created (see Chapter 5). Turn on the ones you want synchronized.

Tip: The iTunes library is a vast and wonderful repository, but sometimes it can be a little *too* vast. Big libraries can make iTunes a little sluggish, and some folks would prefer to have multiple libraries, to better organize their collections, rather than having to wade through one big library.

If you've got the Big Library Blues, check out Libra (*http://homepage.mac.com/sroy/libra/*), a $10 bit o' shareware for Windows and Macintosh. With Libra, you can create, rename, and delete multiple iTunes libraries. You can also swap them in and out of the program depending on what you're in the mood for, whether it be your 9,000-song jazz collection or your complete catalog of Mozart recordings. Another great reason to use Libra is if you live in a home with only one computer, shared by multiple people.

Manually manage songs and playlists

There may be times when you don't want any automatic synchronization at all. Do any of these situations sound familiar?

- You've deleted some audio files from your hard drive that you still want to keep on your iPod, but if you leave automatic syncing turned on, iTunes will erase any songs from the iPod that it doesn't have itself.

- You live in a multiple iPod household, where several different iPods drop by the iTunes library to get some songs for the road from the master collection.

- You've got yourself a Nano as well as a 60-gigabyte iPod, and you only want your high-energy workout tracks on the smaller player.

- You have your music collection scattered between the home computer and the work machine (don't worry, we won't tell your boss), and you want to be able to update the iPod from both places.

The solution to all these scenarios is to turn on the manual control option. In iTunes for Mac or PC, choosing "Manually manage songs and playlists" in the iPod Preferences box means that no music will be autocopied to the iPod. You'll have to do all the work yourself.

Note: When you turn on this option, iTunes says, "Disabling automatic update requires manually unmounting the iPod before each disconnect." It's telling you that, from now on, when you're finished working with the iPod, you'll have to click the Eject button next to its name in the Source list or the button in the lower-right corner of the iTunes window. This action safely releases the iPod from the computer's grip.

Once you've clicked the "Manually manage songs and playlists" option in the Preferences box, you'll now have to drag songs onto the iPod from the iTunes library hand over mouse, as shown in Figure 2-7. After you close the iPod Preferences box, click the small triangle next to your iPod in the Source list. It reveals all the songs and playlists on the iPod, which work just like any other iTunes playlists (see Chapter 5).

To delete songs off the iPod, click its icon in your iTunes Source list. Then, in the main song list window, click the songs you don't want anymore, and press Delete. The songs will vanish, both from the iPod's list in iTunes and from the iPod itself.

Tip: The "Only update checked songs" option in the iPod Preferences box (see Figure 2-6) can be useful in this situation. It ensures that iTunes will update the iPod only with songs whose title checkmarks you've turned on. If you have songs that aren't part of your iTunes music library, make sure they're unchecked— and therefore unerased—during an automatic synchronization.

Figure 2-7:
You can add songs to the iPod playlists by dragging them out of your main iTunes Library list, delete them by clicking their names and then pressing the Delete key, click the New Playlist button (the + icon) to create a fresh playlist, drag playlists onto playlists to merge them, and so on.

TROUBLESHOOTING MOMENT

"Do Not Disconnect"

The universal symbol for NO!, pictured as a circle with a slash through it (Ø), is a common sight when the iPod is connected to the Macintosh or PC. It appears whenever the two drives are busy exchanging music and data (and probably a little hard-disk humor on the side). If you're using the iPod as an external hard disk, or you've turned off the iPod's automatic synchronization feature, you'll see a lot of this Dr. Ø.

Breaking the connection while all this is going on can result in lost files and possibly a scrambled song. So, if you need to unplug the iPod and get going for work, be sure to *unmount* it properly (remove its icon from the screen) first.

Macintosh. You can disconnect the iPod by clicking the Eject button in the iTunes window (or, in the iTunes Source

list, next to the iPod icon); by dragging the desktop icon of the iPod into the Mac's Trash; or by Control-clicking the iPod icon on your screen and choosing Eject from the shortcut menu. Clicking the iPod icon and pressing ⌘-E will also set it free.

Windows. With the iPod selected in the iTunes Source list, click the Eject button in the lower-right corner of the window to unmount the iPod safely. In the iTunes Source list, there's also a conveniently located Eject button next to the iPod icon.

When you've ejected the iPod correctly, its screen flashes a large happy checkmark (older iPods) or pulls up the standard main menu, ready for action (2003-and-later models).

Note: Music libraries have a tendency to outgrow a computer's hard drive. Figuring out how to get the iPod to keep syncing after you've moved that 14-gigabyte iTunes music collection to a roomy new external hard drive (or a whole new computer) has become a frequently asked question. Never fear—it *can* be done, and with a minimum of teeth-gnashing. See page 257 for more information.

---

iPod-to-Computer Copying

The iPod was designed to be the destination of a one-way trip for your tunes: Music slides down the cable *to* the iPod, but songs on the player never make the trip back to the Mac or PC.

This design was perfectly intentional on the part of its creators. As noted earlier, Apple's position appears on a sticker on every iPod: "Don't steal music." If the iPod let you copy music both ways, people might be tempted to turn the device into a pocket music-sharing service, capable of copying free copyrighted songs from computer to computer.

The truth is, though, that not everyone who wants to upload songs from the iPod to a computer is stealing music. You may have perfectly legitimate reasons for wanting to be able to do so.

For example, say your computer's hard drive self-destructs, vaporizing the 2,945 MP3 files that you've made from your paid-for CD collection. You legally own those copies. Shouldn't you have the right to retrieve them from your own iPod?

Most people would answer "yes." Some might even thump their fists on the table for emphasis. And then they would clear their throats and ask, "Well, how can I do it—should I ever need to copy files off my iPod?"

Note: Once again, the following methods are printed here not to encourage you to steal music, but instead to help you back up and manage the songs that you already own.

The Hidden World of the iPod

Turning the iPod into an external hard drive (Chapter 9) lets you copy everyday computer files back and forth from your Mac or PC. But when it comes to your *music* files, you won't even be able to *find* them. The iPod and its music management programs use a special database for storing and organizing the music files—and it's invisible.

The name of the super-secret invisible iPod music folder is called iPod_Control. You can find it yourself with a little poking around on Windows and Mac OS X. If you don't fancy yourself an intrepid explorer of your computer's software secrets, there are several software utilities for both the Mac and PC that can also make it visible.

If you're using a new iPod and a relatively recent edition of iTunes, though, there's one more caveat to be concerned with: Most of the actual song titles look like license-plate numbers, like AOWC.m4a or PGDP.mp3. (Previous versions of the iPod's software simply displayed the song title as it was stored in your iTunes Music folder, like Come Fly With Me.m4a.) As shown in Figure 2-12, Windows itself can display artist and album information for each song, but that's still not much help when you're looking for a specific song.

Even if these file names look like gibberish, iTunes can make sense of them and display the song titles and artist information properly when you copy the iPod's Music folder back to your new or newly repaired computer. If you want to cherry-pick certain songs off the iPod by title, well, there's plenty of free and inexpensive software to do the job. Here are a few of the easiest and most reliable ways to catch the music.

Copying Files to the Macintosh

A quick search on "iPod" on the VersionTracker.com Web site (*www.versiontracker. com*), or on any of the hardcore iPod fan sites like iLounge (*www.ilounge.com*) or iPoding (*www.ipoding.com*), will bring up plenty of Mac-friendly iPod programs.

Tip: On the other hand, you may find it quicker to download these programs directly from the "Missing CD" page at *www.missingmanuals.com*.

Senuti

The name of this clever program doesn't make much sense until you see the tagline: everything in reverse. Not only does the program spell iTunes backward, it does a 180-degree turn on the whole music transfer process and allows you to upload tracks from your iPod instead of just downloading them. Senuti, shown in Figure 2-8, offers built-in search tools for scanning the iPod for specific songs, and it displays your iPod's playlists so that you can see what you've been listening to. If you like it, the programmer has set up a PayPal account for donations from the grateful.

Figure 2-8:
Senuti offers a peek inside your iPod's hidden music cupboard and provides a great big Copy button in the top-right corner to restore copies of your lost tracks back to your Mac's hard drive.

iPod.iTunes

With eight different modes that let you synchronize the iPod and iTunes in both directions (iPod to iTunes and iTunes to iPod), the latest version of iPod.iTunes from CrispSofties lets you keep the music, videos, and playlists on multiple iPods on multiple Macs up to date. You can also use the program to do a full restore of your media collection from your iPod back to your Mac after a hard-drive failure. The software, which costs about $35 if you decide to keep it after the free trial period ends, works with Mac OS X 10.2 and later.

iPod Viewer

For beginners, the nicely designed iPod Viewer program (see Figure 2-9) makes the whole copying-to-the-Mac procedure very simple. iPod Viewer 3.0 is designed for Mac OS X 10.2 (Jaguar) and later; iPod Viewer 1.5.2 is designed for Mac OS X 10.1.

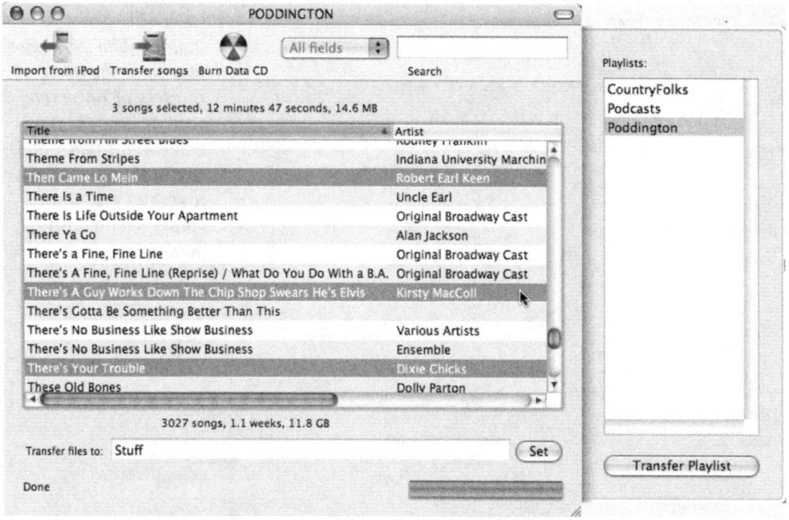

Figure 2-9:
The free iPod Viewer program lets you select some or all of the songs and playlists you want to copy to the Mac. You also get the option of picking what folder to put imported songs into. Just click the Transfer Songs button to start copying. You can also make a backup of the imported files by clicking the Burn Data CD button.

Once you install iPod Viewer, open the program with your iPod attached to the Mac. You'll be asked to select your iPod from a list, and you can also specify where you'd like to copy the songs to on your Mac. The iPodViewer software lets you copy all the songs on the iPod or just those on specific playlists. You can also burn a data CD at the same time to make sure you have a disc-based backup.

TinkerTool

You know how in those Invisible Man movies, people could see him only if he had a hat or a coat or a mask on, or he spilled something on his invisible self? It was all about revealing his hidden aspects.

You can do the same thing with your invisible iPod files with the aid of some help-ful freeware by way of Germany. TinkerTool is a system utility for Mac OS X that can make hidden files visible.

Once you've installed TinkerTool on your Mac, you'll see an icon for it in System Preferences ( → System Preferences). Click TinkerTool; in the box that pops up, turn on "Show hidden and system files," and then click the Relaunch Finder but-ton. Figure 2-10 shows the way.

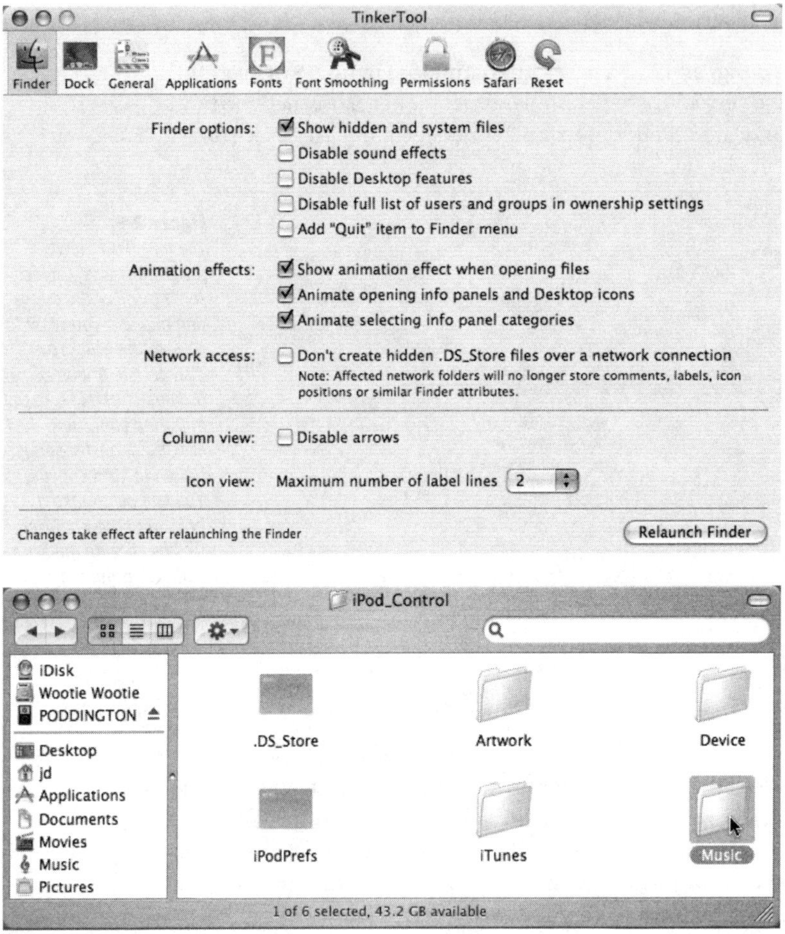

Figure 2-10:
Top: In the TinkerTool Finder preferences box, in the "Finder options," turn on the box "Show hidden and system files" to see a lot more on your iPod after you relaunch the Finder.

Bottom: With the hidden files out in the open, courtesy of TinkerTool, you can grab the iPod's entire Music folder and copy it to your hard drive to restore your iTunes library after a nasty hard-drive failure.

When the Finder restarts, you see all the formerly secret invisible system files right there on your screen, as though someone had spilled paint on the Invisible Man.

You see a lot of .DS_Stores all over the place, but step over them and connect your iPod to the Mac. (Make sure you've turned on its external disk feature, as described in Chapter 9.)

Double-click the iPod's icon to see all the files that live on it, including the iPod_ Control folder that holds all of your music files (Figure 2-10, bottom). You can click through the folders from iPod_Control → Music → F00 (all the iPod's music folders are named F-something). Because the song titles are likely squished into code that only the iPod can understand (unless you're using early versions of iTunes 4 or an older iPod), TinkerTool is best used for a full restore of your music collection, which you can do by copying the Music folder into iTunes, where the program can interpret the peculiar file names and translate them back into English.

Tip: The Spotlight file-finder program that comes with Mac OS X 10.4 normally won't scan the iPod's Music folder when searching for files, but thanks to a free program called Spodlight (available on the "Missing CD" page at *www.missingmanuals.com*), the iPod gets included in the search.

You can even search for specific keywords in the song's name and have the program turn up matching files on the iPod. Even though the song names may be garbled by the iPod's database, if you double-click one to listen to it, it gets copied right back into iTunes under its proper name.

PodWorks

Combining a nice interface with plenty of iTunes-like organizational abilities, Pod-Works lets you sort, search, and hear previews of the songs you want to copy back over to your Mac. The program can also copy playlists and On-The-Go playlists. PodWorks costs a mere $8, but you can sample a limited trial version to get a feel for it.

iPodRip

Whether it be an operating system upgrade that inadvertently trashes your hard drive and takes your tunes with it or some other hardware calamity, iPodRip can restore both your music and your sanity. The software can excavate your playlists and other supported audio files from the iPod's hard drive and copy them safely back to your Mac OS X system (10.2 and later).

The program, shown in Figure 2-11, has a free trial version, but it costs only $15 to buy—a small price to pay if you're facing the prospect of reripping 500 CDs to restore your music collection.

Copying Files to Windows

Getting songs from the iPod is also possible in Windows. You may not even need to download extra freeware or shareware.

Note: When a free or shareware program is mentioned on these pages, you can download it from the "Missing CD" page at *www.missingmanuals.com*.

Figure 2-11:
iPodRip offers a rather comforting—and familiar—interface. In the program's preferences, you can choose to import your songs and playlists into iTunes, onto your desktop, or to the disk or folder icon of your choice. It, too, is available from the "Missing CD" page at www.missingmanuals.com.

Making Windows work for you

Connect the iPod to the PC, and then proceed like this:

1. **Open My Computer.**

   You can do this from an icon on your desktop or the Start menu.

2. **On the list of drives connected to the computer, double-click the iPod.**

   Its icon appears in the list as long as you've turned on the external disk option (described on page 204).

3. **Choose Tools → Folder Options.**

   The Folder Options dialog box pops up (see Figure 2-12).

4. **Click the View tab; turn on "Show hidden files and folders." Click Apply.**

   As though by magic, the iPod_Control folder reveals itself.

5. **Open the iPod_Control folder, and then open the folder within labeled Music.**

   You see a series of folders with names that only a computer could love, like F07, F08, and so on. If your old hard drive died and took all of your song files with it, copy the entire Music folder over to the PC's new hard drive.

6. **Drag the folder over to the hard drive icon to copy all the music back to the PC.**

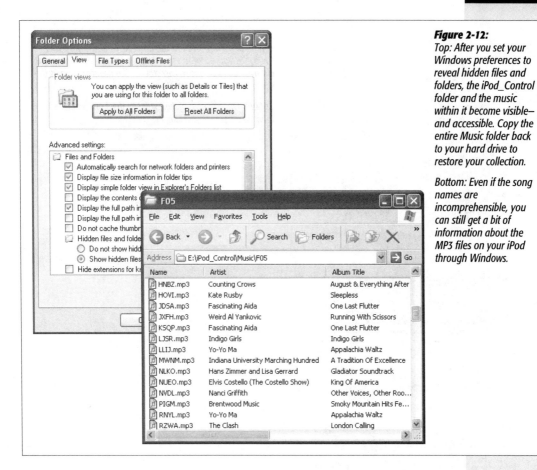

Figure 2-12:
Top: After you set your Windows preferences to reveal hidden files and folders, the iPod_Control folder and the music within it become visible— and accessible. Copy the entire Music folder back to your hard drive to restore your collection.

Bottom: Even if the song names are incomprehensible, you can still get a bit of information about the MP3 files on your iPod through Windows.

EphPod

Until Apple released Windows-compatible versions of the iPod, the EphPod program was one of the few options PC fans had for using the original Mac-only iPods. Even with the arrival of Windows-blessed iPods, the free EphPod continues to be a superior and beloved Windows utility for managing the iPod.

Once you launch EphPod and acquaint it with the iPod connected to your PC, it can show you the songs stored on your iPod. To copy them to your PC, see Figure 2-13.

XPlay

XPlay was one of the first commercial programs to let Windows fans use the original Mac-based iPods. The program's sales suffered once Apple released the

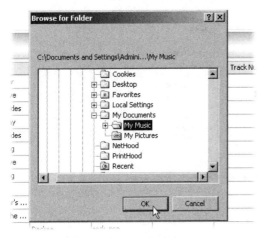

Windows-compatible iPods in 2002, but it still offers plenty of management features that can ease the process of using the iPod with Mac or Windows, like drag-and-drop updates for music and Outlook contacts.

You can download the full program for $30 at *www.mediafour.com*. A free trial version is available, too. See Figure 2-14 for instructions.

PodPlus

This $15 chunk of shareware from the folks at iPodSoft.com does many things, including downloading news headlines and horoscopes to your iPod. It also lets you copy your playlists and songs back to your PC in case of an emergency.

Figure 2-14:
In this exciting XPlay action shot, an album by the Old Crow Medicine Show is about to be copied off the iPod. XPlay is a highly versatile program for iPod management in its own right, and it can also recognize Macintosh-formatted iPods connected to a PC.

PodUtil

PodUtil is one of those rare freeware creatures that comes in versions for Mac OS 9, OS X, and Windows 2000 and XP. No matter which version you use, once PodUtil scans your iPod's hard drive, it presents you with a list of songs that you can then copy to your computer.

Note: iPodRip, described on page 53, also comes in a version for Windows 2000 and XP. However, you need to have iTunes 4.5 or later installed to use it.

Anapod Explorer

If you've ever wished you could browse through the files on your Windows iPod as easily as you browse through the files on your PC, take a look at Anapod Explorer from Red Chair Software (*www.redchairsoftware.com*). This $30 program can serve as a substitute for iTunes, as well as get under the iPod's hood and push your music and data files around, even copying them back to the PC.

As shown in Figure 2-15, Anapod Explorer lets you access your iPod's contents from any Web browser and play its music via any MP3 program of your choice. The program can also transfer photos and videos from the iPod. For people who get giddy at the thought of databases, the program has an embedded database engine (Anapod-SQL), so you can search the iPod using almost any criteria you can imagine and (*gasp!*) even generate reports in HTML or XML. A limited trial version is available to try before you buy.

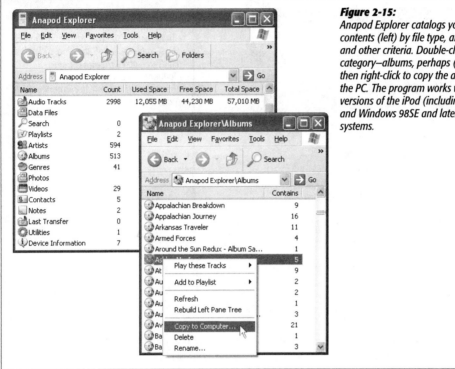

Figure 2-15:
Anapod Explorer catalogs your iPods contents (left) by file type, artist, album, and other criteria. Double-click on a category—albums, perhaps (right)—and then right-click to copy the album back to the PC. The program works with all versions of the iPod (including the Shuffle), and Windows 98SE and later operating systems.

The iPod Shuffle

It may not have all the colorful bells and whistles of its big siblings, but the screen-free iPod Shuffle is just right for many people. The Shuffle, Apple's lightest and least expensive member of the modern iPod family, is a no-nonsense portable jukebox that puts the focus squarely on the sound.

You can store up to one gigabyte of your favorite songs, podcasts, audiobooks, or data files on an iPod Shuffle, and with its minimum of fragile, scratchable parts, you don't have to worry about cracking its screen or busting its hard drive if you accidentally drop it. The iPod Shuffle has a lot to offer, and this chapter shows you how to tap into its full potential.

Meet the iPod Shuffle

Just by looking at Figure 3-1, it's pretty obvious that the iPod Shuffle is much different from the bigger iPods and iPod Nanos described previously. For starters, it's barely over three inches tall, there's no display screen, and the click wheel looks like it shrank in the dryer. And you don't even need a cable to do the Shuffle—this tiny music machine plugs directly into your computer's USB port.

A regular iPod has a miniature hard drive to store 30 to 60 gigabytes of music and data, but like the iPod Nano, the iPod Shuffle uses a small chip of flash memory to store its contents. This is the same type of memory used in the ubiquitous USB flash drive (snapped on the end of a keychain or tucked in a shirt pocket) that has replaced floppy disks as a way to carry around files from computer to computer.

Unlike hard drives, which are moving, spinning things that can skip if bumped and break if dropped, flash memory can take a lickin' and keep on rockin' because

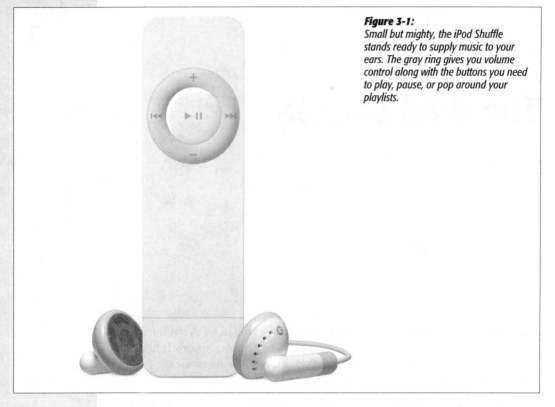

Figure 3-1:
Small but mighty, the iPod Shuffle stands ready to supply music to your ears. The gray ring gives you volume control along with the buttons you need to play, pause, or pop around your playlists.

there are no moving parts in there. Flash memory does have its limits, though, as it's still pricier and currently capable of much smaller capacities than miniature hard drives.

Yet the iPod Shuffle has room enough on the inside to hold about 125 to 240 songs, depending on which one of the two models you buy—the 512-megabyte baby or the roomier version that affords you a full gigabyte for your tunes. And because there are no moving parts and no LCD screen to worry about smashing, you can use the iPod Shuffle for more high-impact audio adventures, like your aerobics workout at the gym, your morning run over rough terrain, or to loan your kids for an hour.

Even though it can't haul your entire collection around, the iPod Shuffle can still get you through a day of music. You can conveniently load up the Shuffle with songs from your existing (or future) iTunes library with the click of a button.

And don't let its name fool you, either—you don't have to shuffle your songs if you don't want to. You can manually load up an existing playlist and listen to it in the order you designed it (see page 64). You can even use your iPod Shuffle as a USB flash drive to move big files between computers (see page 71).

Setting Up the iPod Shuffle

Inside the Shuffle's bright green box, you'll find a pair of Apple's trademark white iPod headphones, a neck strap for turning your new music player into sonic jewelry, and, of course, the iPod Shuffle itself. You also get an instruction booklet, two sets of foam earbud cushions, a wallet card describing the Shuffle's controls, and a CD of software to install on your Macintosh or Windows computer.

Now might be a good time to go over the iPod Shuffle's system requirements again, especially if you flipped directly to this chapter in a rush to start Shuffling.

Macintosh mavens need:

- Mac OS X 10.2.8 or Mac OS X 10.3.4 (or later).
- A Mac with a built-in USB port (and not a third-party USB card).
- The software included on the iPod Shuffle CD.

If you have an older Mac that doesn't have high-powered USB ports (which includes most USB 1.1 connections), you need Mac OS X 10.3.6 or later. If you're a few decimals behind on your system updates, go to the menu and choose Software Update to download the latest revision of the Mac OS.

Windows folks need:

- Windows 2000 (with Service Pack 4 or later) or Windows XP (with Service Pack 2 or later).
- A PC with either a built-in USB port or third-party USB card installed.
- The software included on the iPod Shuffle CD.

Installing the Software

A sticker on the iPod Shuffle tells you to install the software first. The CD supplies you with a recent version of iTunes and iPod Update software, which includes the iPod Shuffle's operating system, should you ever need to reinstall it (page 274).

If you already have an iPod and have been using iTunes with it—and scrupulously update both the player and the program within seconds after Apple releases new versions—it is possible to just plug the Shuffle into the computer and have iTunes welcome it aboard.

If you have never used an iPod or iTunes with your computer, you'll definitely need to install the software on the iPod CD that ships with the Shuffle.

If you have a brand new computer with iTunes 6 (or later) already installed, you should be good to go. Check your version number on the Mac at iTunes → About iTunes, or at Help → About iTunes on a Windows system.

There's only one CD in the box, and it contains all the Windows and Macintosh software needed to use the iPod Shuffle. So, just pop in the disc and follow the onscreen instructions to install the software packages on your PC or Mac.

Unless you've changed the way Windows handles compact discs, the iPod CD should spin right up, ask what language you want to use for the installation, and then walk you through the steps of installing iTunes and the iPod files on your PC. On a Mac, once the CD appears on the desktop, double-click to open it and then double-click on the Install iPod Software icon to get the ball rolling.

Apple changes the iPod installer CD frequently as it introduces new versions of iTunes and the iPod system software, but the discs are worth exploring, even after you put the programs on your computer. You can usually find electronic copies of the iPod manuals (helpful for when you lose your quick-start guide) and Web-based tutorials right there on the disc waiting for you.

Making the USB Connection

Once the software has been installed and the computer restarted, plug in your iPod Shuffle by pulling off the white plastic cap on the bottom and inserting the flat, silver USB connector into an available USB port on the computer. Your new pal iTunes should open after a few seconds, with your new iPod Shuffle listed in the iTunes Source list, ready for you to add the music.

The Shuffle can connect to either a USB 1.1 or a USB 2.0 port on your computer, as shown in Figure 3-2. Although both types of USB connections work for copying songs between computer and Shuffle, USB 2.0 is much quicker. USB 1.1 pokes along at about 12 megabits per second, while USB 2.0 burns up the wire at 480 megabits per second.

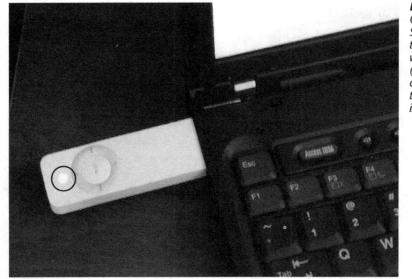

Figure 3-2:
On many computers, the Shuffle plugs right into the USB port and gets to work. The status light (circled) above the control ring glows softly to let you know the iPod is charging.

The Shuffle's serial number (which iTunes asks you to type in and register with Apple the first time you use the player) is printed in extremely small gray type on the back of the iPod. If you don't have a microscope handy to read it, the serial number can also be found in larger type on the white barcode sticker affixed to the bottom of the green box your Shuffle came in.

You'll notice the music-transferring speed difference if you use the Autofill function in iTunes (page 66) to automatically load up your Shuffle to the max, as USB 1.1 can really make you wait when loading up a full gigabyte of songs.

The first time you connect your iPod Shuffle, iTunes asks you to name it and register it with Apple before it gets down to the business of playing music. iTunes also offers to fill up your iPod with as many songs as it can, but you might want to wait until you get comfortable with the Shuffle before deciding what you want on it. As with a regular iPod, one of the first things you should do is gas up your battery with power before you roam too far with it (see the next section for details on charging).

If you have a computer where the USB ports are on the back or too close together to wedge in the iPod Shuffle next to your printer or scanner's connection, you can get a USB extension cable in most computer stores or pick up a $30 iPod Shuffle dock from Apple at *http://store.apple.com*.

Due to their design, some Mac models like the iMac G3 or the big white eMac are going to need some sort of extension cable anyway because the Shuffle is too wide to cram into those closely spaced ports.

Charging Up the Battery

Like most other portable devices, the iPod Shuffle runs off of a battery when it's not plugged into a power source somewhere. Many flash memory players use disposable AAA batteries that you have to keep adding, like quarters into a payphone, to keep going. But the Shuffle has its own rechargeable battery that you can fill up with power just by plugging it into your computer.

To connect the iPod Shuffle to your Mac or PC, just yank off the white plastic cap on the Shuffle's bottom to expose the silver USB connector and plug it into the nearest available powered USB port. Make sure the Shuffle is firmly plugged into the USB port because if it's not fully connected, neither iTunes nor the computer may acknowledge it.

Once you connect the iPod Shuffle to the computer, the battery starts charging. Once your Shuffle is connected, a ghostly amber light from within the player itself shines underneath the white plastic case, just above the control wheel. The amber light tells you the Shuffle is charging up. (If the amber light is blinking, the iPod Shuffle is telling you not to disconnect it from the computer because it's updating or working overtime as a USB flash drive; see page 71 for more on how to enlist your Shuffle as a USB drive.)

It takes about 2 hours to get the battery up to an 80 percent charge, and it takes 4 hours to fully charge the Shuffle battery. Make sure the computer doesn't slide into

Sleep mode while the Shuffle is charging, though, as this might interfere with the power transfer. A green light means the Shuffle is all charged up and ready to roll.

Most new computers these days come with the high-powered USB 2.0 ports the Shuffle needs, and you can often get a charge out of a USB 1.1 port on the back (or front) of the computer.

However, older, low-powered USB 1.1 ports (like those on non-powered USB hubs or at the end of a USB keyboard) probably won't charge your Shuffle. You can still transfer music and files from one of the low-powered ports, but you'll need to get a powered port when your Shuffle needs juice.

If you find your computer doesn't have USB ports with enough power, don't despair or resign yourself to the Returns department—accessories to the rescue! Apple makes a $30 USB power adapter that goes right between the Shuffle's USB connector and the electrical outlet in the wall.

Using the iPod Shuffle

Through a simple interface of colored lights, buttons, and a switch on the back, your iPod Shuffle responds to your commands and tells you what it's up to. The circular control ring on the front of the Shuffle (Figure 3-1) has the familiar ◄◄ and ►► buttons on the left and right sides that let you go backward or forward through the songs stored on the player. At the top and bottom of the ring are the volume controls: a plus sign (+) for louder and a minus sign (–) for softer.

The all-important ►❚❚ button is right in the center of the control ring. Push the button to play a song and push it again to pause the track. Tapping any of the controls on the front of the Shuffle causes the little green light within the case to flicker in acknowledgement that you're pushing its buttons.

Full-size iPods have a separate switch that deactivates all the buttons temporarily, keeping the iPod on or off and at the same volume even if the player's controls get bumped accidentally. There's no separate Hold switch on the Shuffle, but you can put it in Hold mode just the same by pressing the ►❚❚ button for 3 seconds. Turn off the Hold mode by pressing ►❚❚ again for another 3 seconds.

As shown in Figure 3-3, on the back of the iPod Shuffle is a wide plastic switch that can be adjusted to three positions:

- **Off.** To turn off the iPod Shuffle and conserve your battery charge, slide the switch up so that none of the green color underneath is showing.

- **Play in order.** To set the Shuffle to not shuffle your songs, slide the switch one notch to the middle icon, which looks like two arrows chasing each other in a circle. This setting plays your songs or audio book chapters in the order you arranged them on the playlist you loaded on the iPodlet.

- **Shuffle.** Slide the switch all the way down to let the iPod Shuffle do what it was named for: play your songs in random order.

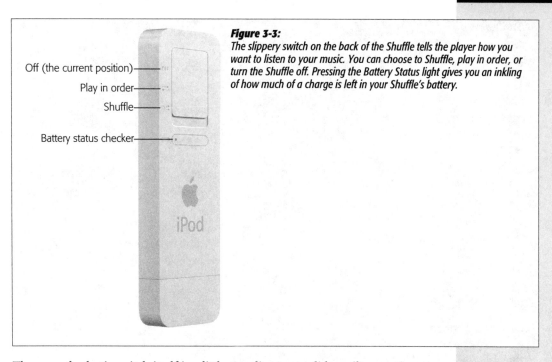

Off (the current position) —————

Play in order —————

Shuffle —————

Battery status checker —————

Figure 3-3:
*The slippery switch on the back of the Shuffle tells the player how you
want to listen to your music. You can choose to Shuffle, play in order, or
turn the Shuffle off. Pressing the Battery Status light gives you an inkling
of how much of a charge is left in your Shuffle's battery.*

The smooth plastic switch itself is a little too slippery to slide easily sometimes, so
you may need to wedge a fingernail on either side to shove it to the desired setting.
You might want to hold the Shuffle in one hand, flashlight-style, and move the
switch up or down with your thumb. This usually works well for popping back and
forth between Shuffle settings.

Below the switch is the Battery Status button, described in the box on page 66. The
small round headphones port is on the top of the iPod Shuffle, on the opposite end
from the USB connector.

You can either carry your iPod Shuffle in your pocket or wear it around your neck.
Apple includes two different covers to snap over the end of the USB connector: a
plain, unstrung plastic cap, and one that's attached to a lanyard so the Shuffle
hangs within easy reach around your neck. Forget about that old rule that says
you're not supposed to wear white after Labor Day—the iPod Shuffle is in fashion
year-round.

Transferring Music to the iPod Shuffle

Moving music to the iPod Shuffle is just as easy as moving it onto a regular iPod
(Chapter 2), and depending on your level of fussiness about what exactly goes onto
your iPod Shuffle, the music transfer can be even easier.

Like all iPods before it, the Shuffle was designed to work with Apple's iTunes software. If you're unfamiliar with iTunes or need a refresher course in ripping songs
into the digital tracks that iPods love, skip ahead to Chapter 5 to read all about it.
Tracks you've purchased from Audible.com (Chapter 6) or the iTunes Music Store
(Chapter 7) also work on the Shuffle.

Understanding the Shuffle's Light Show

Without a display screen, the iPod Shuffle has limited ways to communicate with you, and it accomplishes most of its messages with a series of colored lights flashing silently next to the control ring. A blinking amber light, for example, means that you should not unplug the Shuffle from the computer because it's either updating or hard at work as a USB flash drive (page 71). A steady amber light, on the other hand, means the Shuffle is in the process of charging its battery.

A steady green light while plugged into the computer means the Shuffle is fully charged. This same green light flashes briefly when you tap the ▶❚❚ button to start a song, and it blinks for a moment when you press the button again to pause the music.

If you see alternating green and amber lights blinking at you when you press any of the control buttons, the Shuffle probably needs to be reset (page 243).

The colored lights also tell you the Hold status of the iPod Shuffle. You can put the Shuffle into Hold mode by pressing down the center ▶❚❚ button for 3 seconds. The orange light blinks to indicate Hold is on. Press the same button for 3 seconds to release the Shuffle from Hold.

The green light blinks to indicate you have released your Hold.

If the iPod Shuffle is set to Hold and you press any of the buttons, the amber light will flash at you to let you know the Shuffle is not paying attention to any of your button thumping. When it's not set to Hold, you get a happy green-light flash when you press any of the buttons.

Because the Shuffle doesn't have a screen with a nice battery icon like other iPods, you can check your Shuffle's charge when you're out and about by pressing the Battery Status button on the back of the Shuffle (shown in Figure 3-3). The color of the tiny pinhead-size light on the button tells you the state of things:

• **Green** means you have a nice healthy battery charge.

• **Amber** means the battery is low.

• **Red** means the battery is extremely low.

• **No light whatsoever** means this baby needs to get plugged in for a few hours because there's no juice left.

The iPod Shuffle wasn't designed to be a complete repository for all your digital music. Because you can only store either 512 megabytes or 1 gigabyte of music at a time on the Shuffle, it's more like a short-range player that's there to provide you with a several-hours-of-life soundtrack between computer breaks.

But just as you can choose to let the iPod automatically mix up your songs or play them in the order you arranged them, you can also let the Shuffle pick a random sampling of tunes from your iTunes library—or, you can manually transfer precisely the tracks you want to take with you.

Loading Music the Automatic Way

You can't autosync your entire multigigabyte music library to your Shuffle, but you can Autofill your iStick with iTunes. Once you plug your player into the computer and iTunes recognizes it, a small panel appears at the bottom of the iTunes window (see Figure 3-4) and invites you to fill your iPod to capacity with the click of a button.

Figure 3-4:
The Autofill box appears at the bottom of iTunes when you plug in an iPod Shuffle. With Autofill, you tell iTunes where to collect the music–from the whole library or just a certain playlist. You can also tell it to grab songs in random order instead of the way they appear in iTunes and to concentrate on your most highly rated tracks.

You can snag songs from your entire library or just a particular playlist, and you can also opt to have the most highly rated songs in any collection get selected more often.

There's also a setting called "Choose songs randomly" in the Autofill box. Turning this checkbox on means iTunes moves over the songs in whatever order it feels like moving them, instead of transferring them in the same order they appear in the iTunes Library or a selected playlist.

Once you've Autofilled for the first time and then return for another batch of songs, you can turn on the checkbox next to "Replace all songs when Autofilling" (Figure 3-5) to have iTunes wipe the first batch of songs off the Shuffle and substitute them with new tracks. If you don't turn on the checkbox to replace the songs, iTunes just keeps autofilling from the selected music source until the Shuffle is stuffed.

Figure 3-5:
Checkboxes in the Autofill section of the iTunes window give you some control over how the Shuffle is filled. If you like completely replacing the randomly selected songs each time you plug in your Shuffle, turn on the checkbox next to "Replace all songs when Autofilling" to get a whole new mix.

If you've got iTunes Music Store songs in the mix, make sure your computer is authorized to play them (page 182); otherwise, you'll get a bleat box from iTunes (Figure 3-6) saying it couldn't move unauthorized tracks that were selected for Autofilling.

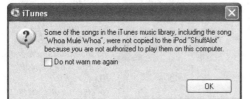

Figure 3-6:
Make sure your computer is authorized to play iTunes Music Store purchases or you'll get a message like this on your screen when using Autofill. See Chapter 7 for information on using the iTunes Music Store and its songs.

Once iTunes has filled up the Shuffle, you'll see the "OK to Disconnect" message in the iTunes status display (the info box at the top of the iTunes window). Click the Eject button next to your Shuffle's icon in the Source list to disconnect it, and then unplug the player from the computer.

Using Autofill can sometimes tie up iTunes for several minutes. If you want to stop an Autofill in progress, click the small X in the iTunes status display (Figure 3-7) to put on the brakes.

Figure 3-7:
X (circled) marks the spot to click if you need to stop iTunes in the middle of an Autofill.

Manually Adding Music to the iPod Shuffle

If you want the power over what goes on your Shuffle, you can opt for manual updating instead of letting iTunes choose the songs. As with any other iPod on manual control, you can drag songs and playlists from your iTunes library windows and drop them on the Shuffle's icon in the Source list to add them to the player (Figure 3-8).

When you've clicked on the Shuffle's icon in the Source list, you can arrange individual songs into the sequence you wish to hear them. The info down at the bottom of the iTunes window tells you how much space you're consuming on your Shuffle if you want to max it out manually with chosen playlists, albums, and songs.

You can also mix and match your song-loading methods. Start by dragging a few favorite playlists over to the Shuffle, and then click Autofill to finish the job. Just make sure the "Replace all songs when Autofilling" checkbox isn't turned on (Figure 3-5) or iTunes will wipe off all those tracks you personally added.

While regular hard drive iPods set to manual update can collect songs from multiple computers—say, your work and home PCs—the stubborn Shuffle is much

Figure 3-8:
You can also drag over your favorite albums, songs, and playlists and drop them on the Shuffle's icon in the Source list to manually add them to the player.

more monogamous and demands to be associated with only one computer at a time, as shown in Figure 3-9.

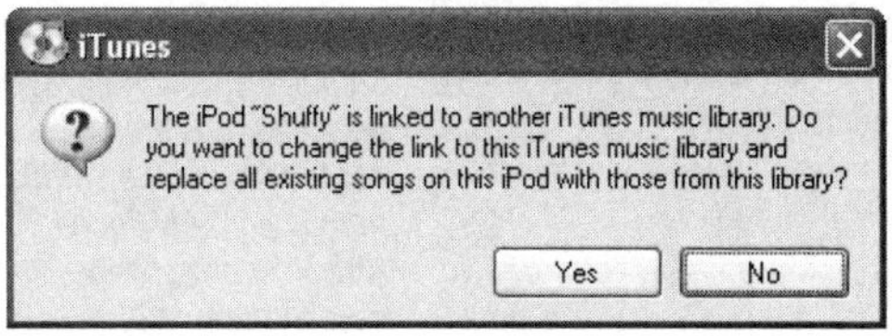

Figure 3-9:
The Shuffle stays true to only one computer at a time and will erase all the current tracks in its memory if you click Yes here. Clicking No makes iTunes ignore the Shuffle so you can't add music to it.

This can be a drag if you have different music on each machine. But if you're into the whole random-selection thing, you can autofill your Shuffle from either computer's music library and even go back and forth between a PC and a Mac.

And if you're feeling adventurous, there are ways to peek inside the Shuffle and snag the hidden music files. First, open the iPod Preferences box (Figure 3-10) and make sure iTunes isn't set to open automatically when the Shuffle is connected. Then, flip back to page 49 to read about the iPod_Control folder and the hidden world deep inside your iPod.

Tip: Although most people tend to think of the Shuffle as a finger-size jukebox of tunes in random order, it can also handle spoken-word content like audiobooks and podcasts. Chapter 6 explains it all.

The Virtual Shuffle

Thanks to a nifty setting in the iPod Preferences box, you can add songs to your Shuffle even if it's not currently connected to your computer. The Shuffle's icon stays in the iTunes Source list (as shown on the left in Figure 3-11), even if you have another iPod attached.

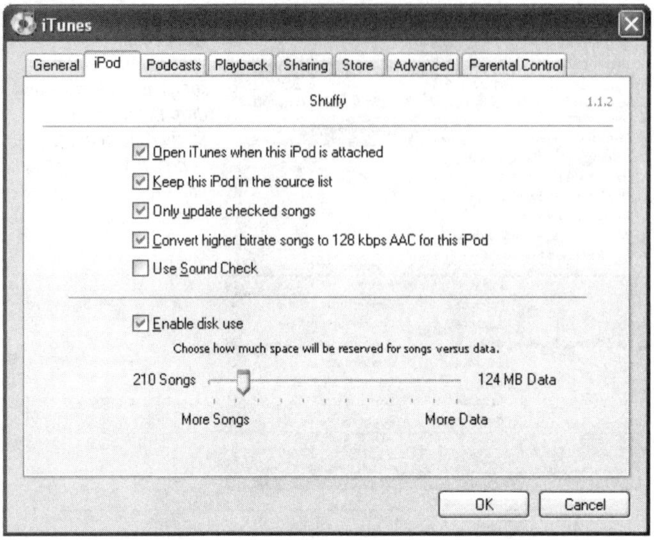

Figure 3-10:
You can make a number of adjustments to your Shuffle's behavior in the iPod Preferences box. For example, you can set the Shuffle to always show in iTunes, compress big tracks into small ones, and even turn it into an everyday USB flash drive for storing files and folders.

Figure 3-11:
With the iPod Shuffle set to always show in the Source list, you might see all your iPods hanging out together. (The Shuffle here is named "Podlet.") After you drag songs over to the virtual Shuffle, the titles are marked with a gray dot in the iTunes window, indicating they'll be synced to the Shuffle next time you plug it into the computer.

With the Shuffle's icon always in your Source list, you can drag over songs from iTunes to it. The next time you plug in the actual Shuffle to the computer, it syncs up all those new songs you added in its absence. When you drag a song to the Virtual Shuffle, a small gray dot appears next to its name (Figure 3-11) to let you know that it's headed for Shuffleville the next time you plug in the player.

To set up your Shuffle That's Always There (Even When It's Not), plug it into the computer's USB port and select the Shuffle's icon in the iTunes Source list. Click the iPod icon button at the bottom of the iTunes window to open the iPod Preferences box, and turn on the checkbox for "Keep this iPod in the source list," as shown in Figure 3-10.

Converting Songs to Fit on the iPod Shuffle

The Shuffle plays tracks in the AAC, MP3, Audible, and WAV formats, but it can't play the super-large, uncompressed AIFF or Apple Lossless formats. (If that sentence stopped you cold, skip ahead to Chapter 4 for a discussion of file formats and bit rates—and what they all mean to a new iPod owner.)

But just because that 60-megabyte AIFF file won't play on the Shuffle, doesn't mean that the song itself can't. You can instruct iTunes to convert an AIFF or Apple Lossless file into a svelte AAC copy specifically for the Shuffle.

Just open the iPod Preferences box when your Shuffle is connected (Figure 3-10), turn on the checkbox next to "Convert higher bitrate songs to 128 kbps AAC for this iPod," and click OK. This sends an AAC copy of the song to the Shuffle but leaves the original AIFF or Apple Lossless file just the way it was back in your iTunes Library.

You may want to turn this setting off if you have MP3 files encoded at higher bit rates (like 160 or 192 Kbps) that you want to transfer to the Shuffle because they'll get converted to the 128 Kbps AAC format and may not sound as good. There's nothing to stop you from flicking on this setting when you're working only with AIFF files and then turning it off when you want to copy over more MP3 songs.

Deleting Songs from the iPod Shuffle

When you've tired of the Shuffle's current contents, you can easily take off the old music and put on some new stuff.

If you're driving an automatic Shuffle, you can do this by clicking the Autofill button again (just make sure the "Replace all songs when Autofilling" checkbox is turned on; see Figure 3-5).

If you're taking the manual approach to Shuffledom, connect the Shuffle and then click its icon in the Source list to call up its contents in the main iTunes window. Click the song titles you want to remove and hit the Delete key.

Now you have room for fresh hot tunes.

Using the Shuffle as a USB Flash Drive

You know those cute little USB flash drives that fit in your pocket and let you haul around documents and files that are too fat to fit on a floppy? Your iPod Shuffle can do that, too—and still bring along dozens of songs to boot. It's two Widgets in one!

Configuring the Shuffle in iTunes

To set up the Shuffle for its part-time job as a USB drive, connect it to the computer and open its Preferences box, as described in Figure 3-10. Turn on the checkbox next to "Enable disk use." (You do the same thing to set up a regular iPod as an external hard drive, as explained in Chapter 9.)

On the Shuffle, you have to decide here how much space to allow for data files and how much space you want to preserve for music. Adjust the slider, as shown in Figure 3-12, to fit your needs and divide up the Shuffle's real estate between work and play. Click OK, and you're off to the rat races.

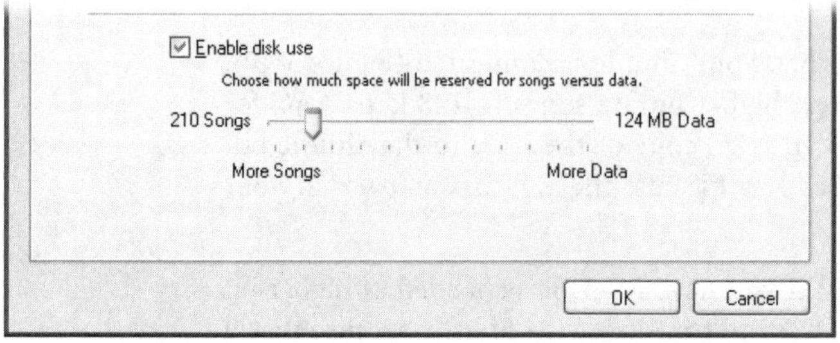

Figure 3-12:
With the slider at the bottom of the iPod preferences box, you can decide which is more important to your iPod Shuffle— room for music or room for documents, files, and other stuff to carry along from computer to computer.

There may come a time when you need more room for music or vice versa; when that time comes, go back to the iPod Preferences box and readjust the slider.

Moving Files to and from the Shuffle

Once your Shuffle has been configured to work as a USB drive, it shows up on the computer as another external drive, either in the My Computer area in Windows or on the Mac's desktop (Figure 3-13). Once you see the Shuffle's icon, you can drag and drop files to your heart's content, just like the music player was any old flash drive, floppy disk, external drive, or other form of portable media.

Because the computer now considers the Shuffle to be an external drive, you must treat it respectfully and properly eject the player before unplugging it. Blithely yanking the Shuffle out of the USB port will annoy the computer enough to flash an alert box at you about not unplugging the drive correctly. Worse yet, you could damage the files on the Shuffle.

When you have the Shuffle connected to the computer and see the amber light blinking gently on the front of the player, it's in use as an external drive. Don't unplug the Shuffle when the amber light is blinking.

There are several ways to unhitch the Shuffle from the computer and keep every-one happy:

• **The Eject button in iTunes.** Find the Shuffle's name in the iTunes Source list and click the Eject button next to its name.

• **The Safely Remove Hardware feature in Windows.** Way down yonder in the Windows system tray is the Safely Remove Hardware icon, which looks like a green arrow floating above a Lego brick. Click the icon, and then select the Shuffle from the list of attached devices to eject it safely from your computer.

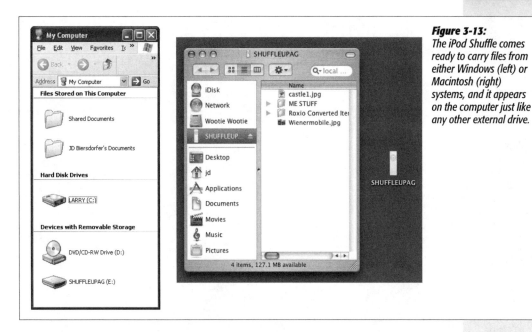

Figure 3-13:
The iPod Shuffle comes ready to carry files from either Windows (left) or Macintosh (right) systems, and it appears on the computer just like any other external drive.

- **The Mac's Drag-to-Trash Tradition.** Over the ages, countless floppies, CDs, Zip disks, and DVDs have been ejected from Macintosh computers everywhere by clicking the item's desktop icon and then dragging it across the screen to the Trash. This works for the Shuffle, too.

Once the amber light stops blinking, it's safe to pull the Shuffle out of the USB port.

If you plan to frequently use your Shuffle as a shuttle for files along with music, you may want to turn off the setting that makes the computer open iTunes every time you plug in the iPod Shuffle. That way you'll avoid the constant nag alert about the iPod being linked to another iTunes Library.

Start by opening the Shuffle's Preferences box, and when you get there, turn off the checkbox next to "Open iTunes when this iPod is attached."

The Shuffle is great for taking along valuable files and just enough music to get you through the day, but it's also a wonderful way to listen to your favorite podcasts and audiobooks—after all, when was the last time you could fit a whole hardback novel into your front shirt pocket and still have room left over for your bus pass and a Snickers bar? For more on using spoken-word content on your Shuffle, shuffle on over to Chapter 6.

Part Two:
iPod: The Software

2

Digital Audio Formats

Recorded music has appeared in a variety of shapes and sizes over the decades, including fragile discs spinning at 78 rpm, vinyl records in colorful sleeves that were artworks in themselves, pocket-size cassette tapes, and futuristic-looking compact discs. But no music format ever exploded into the public consciousness as quickly and widely as the bits of computer code known as *MP3 files.*

The MP3 format makes it possible to compress a song into a file small enough to be uploaded, downloaded, emailed, and stored on a hard drive. That feat of small-ness set off a sonic boom in the late 1990s that continues to reverberate across the music world today.

This chapter tells all about MP3 and other music formats, including the main iPod-approved format: AAC (Advanced Audio Coding), a copy-protected file type that makes Apple's iTunes Music Store possible.

Introduction to Digital Audio

The era of modern digital audio began in the early 1980s. A new, small, shiny for-mat called the audio compact disc, developed by Sony and Philips, began to appear in music stores alongside tapes and vinyl records. Unlike *analog* tapes and LPs, audio CDs stored music in *digital* form, and produced a bright, clean sound with pristine clarity. (Some audiophiles still prefer the "warmer" sound of vinyl, not to mention the expansive canvas that records provided for detailed album artwork, but many have accepted the CD.)

1985 was a pivotal year for the CD. The format's popularity got a huge boost from its first big seller, *Brothers in Arms* by Dire Straits, and a variation on the audio CD technology called CD-ROM (Compact Disc, Read-Only Memory) edged into the computer market as a way to play multimedia files and interactive programs.

When CD Met PC

Over the years, a CD drive became a standard component of a computer. On most audio CDs, songs are stored in a format called CD-DA (Compact Disc, Digital Audio), which is essentially the same thing as the AIFF format (page 82).

On a Windows PC, if you inspect the contents of a music CD, you see a screenful of names like Track01.cda. These turn out to be nothing but 1 KB files that point to the hidden audio tracks, as shown in Figure 4-1. Mac OS X displays the audio tracks in all their hefty glory as AIFF files, right in the Finder window (it even shows you song titles, if it can find them after a quick bit of Internet searching).

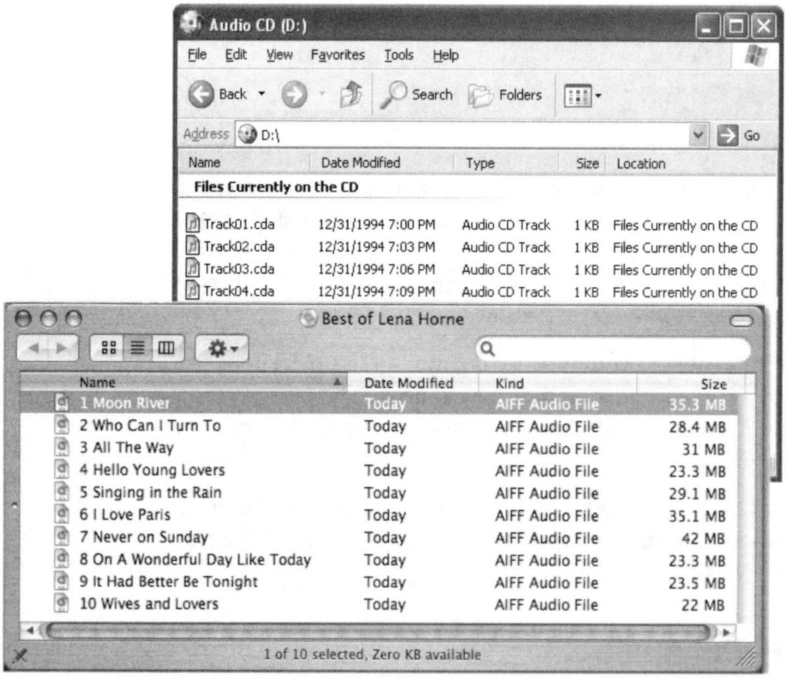

Figure 4-1:
Left: Here's what a desktop window looks like for a music CD inserted into a Mac: just like an MP3 playlist, except these AIFF files are much larger. Your computer can play these high-quality files, but they eat up a lot of hard drive space.

Right: Audio files are more bashful when a disc is inserted into a Windows drive. The tracks on this CD remain hidden behind tiny pointer files; you can lure them out only with CD-extraction software.

Even if you can't see the audio files, you can still *extract* them from the CD with software. "Extracting audio tracks" may sound like an uncomfortable medical procedure, but it means copying them from the CD to your hard drive in a computer-readable format. You may also hear the term *ripping* CDs, which is the same thing.

And while you're digesting new-millennium terminology: Once the music files are on your Mac or PC, you *encode* them into a compressed audio format like MP3 or AAC so that more music fits on a CD that you burn—or on a music player like the iPod.

Compressed Audio Formats

Up until a few years ago, the MP3 format was the only game in town for playing quality song files on your computer, whether downloaded from the Internet or taken from CDs. MP3 still dominates the Internet, but other formats—like Ogg Vorbis (an audio format favored by Linux fans and the open source software crowd; details at *www.vorbis.com*)—have dedicated fans, too.

Ogg Vorbis isn't on the list of iPod-compatible formats, but many others are, including MP3, AAC, AIFF, Apple Lossless, and WAV. Here's a brief explanation of each Podworthy format.

MP3

Suppose you copy a song from a Lena Horne CD directly onto your computer, where it takes up 35.3 MB of hard disk space. Sure, now you could play that song without the CD in your CD drive, but you'd also be out 35.3 megs of precious hard drive real estate.

Now, say you put that Lena Horne CD in your computer and use your favorite encoding program like iTunes to convert that song to an MP3 file. The resulting MP3 file still sounds really good, but it only takes up about *3.2 MB* of space on your hard drive—about 10 percent of the original. Better yet, you can burn a lot of MP3 files onto a blank CD of your own—up to 11 hours of music on one disc, which is enough to get you from Philadelphia to Columbus, Ohio on I-70 with tunes to spare.

How it works

MP3 files are so small because the format's compression algorithms use *perceptual noise shaping*, a method that mimics the ability of the human ear to hear certain sounds. Just as people can't hear dog whistles, most recorded music contains frequencies that are too high for humans to hear; MP3 compression discards these sounds. Sounds that are blotted out by louder sounds are also cast aside. All of this space-saving by the compression format helps to make a smaller file without severely diminishing the overall sound quality of the music.

New portable MP3 player models come out all the time, but many people consider the iPod's arrival in 2001 to be a defining moment in the history of MP3 hardware.

Note: MP3 is short for MPEG Audio, Layer 3. MPEG stands for Moving Pictures Experts Group, the association of engineers that also defined the specifications for the DVD video format, among others.

AAC

The Advanced Audio Coding format may be less than a decade old (it became official in 1997), but it has a fine pedigree. Scientists at Dolby, Sony, Nokia, AT&T, and those busy folks at Fraunhofer, collaborated to come up with a method of squeezing multimedia files of the highest possible quality into the smallest possible space—at least small enough to fit through a modem line. During listening tests, many people couldn't distinguish between a compressed high-quality AAC file and an original recording.

The Law of the Digital Music Land

Years before the iPod was even a twinkle in Steve Jobs's eye, the Recording Industry Association of America sued the makers of the first portable MP3 player. RIAA felt that the player—the soon-to-be-released Rio PMP300 from Diamond Multimedia—could serve as a tool for pirating copyrighted songs. Diamond eventually won the case. The court found that the Rio itself violated no federal music-piracy laws, paving the way for dozens more MP3 players to hit the market.

The Audio Home Recording Act of 1992 says that you can make copies of your own legally purchased music for your personal (noncommercial) use. Even though MP3 players didn't exist yet, the court ruled in the Rio case that consumers have the right to move the music they own onto a playback device—as long as it's for personal use.

The arrival of the MP3 format changed the way people listened to—and shared—their music. Before MP3, nobody thought much about copyright law when they dubbed a song mix to give to a friend or a romantic prospect. (After all, the exchange of the mix tape/CD has been an important part of the young American courting ritual for years.)

But the small size of MP3 files, mixed with the power of the Internet, ripped the lid off of a 55-gallon drum of worms. With music being passed freely all over the world and CD sales dropping (maybe as a result of MP3 sharing, maybe because of unrelated factors), industry groups like RIAA have begun looking for new ways to block digital music copying. They're also taking a highly litigious interest in Internet services that make sharing MP3 files easy.

In 1999, a file-sharing service called Napster got a lot of attention from music fans and lawyers alike. The Napster software, authored by a teenager named Shawn Fanning, let music lovers search out and share MP3 files with anybody else on the Internet running the same program—which turned out to be millions of people. Napster traffic became so heavy that at some universities, it actually created a drag on their networks, and resulted in a Napster ban.

While Napster gave people a chance to sample a wide range of music for free, it also sent RIAA on a legal mission to shut down the file-sharing service. RIAA eventually prevailed, and in 2002, Napster went to that great Web site in the sky.

(Napster, in its original form, died that day. But in October 2003, it returned in the form of an iTunes Music Store wannabe where music shoppers could legally download tracks for less than a buck apiece. In a further effort to ape Apple, Napster 2.0—as this Windows-only, pay-to-play service was dubbed—even began selling its own iPod clone.)

Although early attempts to squash other file-sharing services like Grokster and KaZaA in 2003 were first rebuffed by the courts, the RIAA succeeded in shutting down Grokster in 2005, and the group is looking into a new technology that can prevent CD tracks from being copied onto computers at all. RIAA has recently begun filing lawsuits against Internet service providers to find out the names of customers who use file-sharing services or host music-swapping sites and suing the individuals directly.

Mind you, MP3 files themselves are not illegal. Ripping tracks from CDs that you've purchased over the years for playing on your iPod is legal. Downloading MP3s offered freely by bands and musicians just wanting to be heard is also legal.

Copying copyrighted music that you didn't pay for is not legal, and that's why you can be sure we haven't heard the last from the RIAA.

What's so great about AAC on the iPod? For starters, the format can do the Big Sound/Small File Size trick even better than MP3. Because of its tighter compression technique, a song encoded in the AAC format sounds better (to most ears, anyway) and takes up less space on the computer than if it were encoded with the same quality settings as an MP3 file. Encoding your files in the AAC format is how Apple says you can stuff 15,000 songs onto a 60 GB iPod.

Note: You can think of AAC as the Apple equivalent of WMA, the copy-protected Microsoft format used by all online music stores except Apple's. For better or worse, the iPod doesn't recognize copy-protected WMA files.

The AAC format can also be copy protected (unlike MP3), which is why Apple uses it on the iTunes Music Store (see Chapter 7). The record companies would never have permitted Apple to distribute their property without copy protection.

Tip: Real Networks, with its own online music store, has a media-player program called RealPlayer 10.5 that can be used to wiggle your home-ripped tracks and RealPlayer Music Store purchases onto your iPod. Apple, of course, has changed the iPod's software at least once to block RealPlayer from nosing around its iPods and would prefer that you do your 99 cents-a-song downloading from its iTunes Music Store *only* (Chapter 7).

Because the iPod can play several different audio formats, you can have a mix of MP3 and AAC files on the device if you want to encode your future CD purchases with the newer format. If you want to read more technical specifications on AAC before deciding, Apple has a page on the format at *www.apple.com/mpeg4*.

Note: AAC is the audio component of MPEG-4, a new video format that's designed to get high-quality video compressed enough to travel over computer networks (even pokey old modem lines) and still look good onscreen.

Other Podworthy File Formats

The iPod was designed to handle AAC and MP3 formats the most efficiently, but it's not limited to them. Here are the other types of music files you can play on an iPod.

WAV

WAV is a standard Windows sound format, going all the way back to Windows 95. (Most Macs can play WAV files, too.) Windows fans download WAV recordings for everything from TV-show snippets to start-up sounds and other system alert noises. A WAV song usually sounds better than the same song in MP3—but it takes up more room on the iPod.

WMA (Windows Only)

If you've spent years ripping hundreds of audio tracks onto your PC using Windows Media Player, you must have had quite an emotional crash when you discovered they wouldn't work with iTunes or play on your iPod.

Fortunately, iTunes can convert them into AAC, MP3, or whatever iTunes format you specify (see page 93). The fine print: They must be *unprotected* WMA tracks (that is, not songs you bought from other online stores like Napster 2.0, Music-Match, or Wal-Mart—and not files for which you deliberately turned on, for some reason, Media Player's copy-protection option). And the conversion doesn't work unless your PC has Windows Media Player Series 9 or later installed. (If not, amble over to *www.microsoft.com/windows/windowsmedia* to download the software.)

When you install iTunes on your Windows PC, the iTunes Setup Assistant automatically offers to add your WMA files to your iTunes library (see Figure 2-2 back yonder in Chapter 2). If you didn't grab the chance at that moment, you can convert the WMA tracks at any time by dragging a folder full of them onto the Library icon in the iTunes Source list, or by choosing File → Add to Library and selecting the songs from your My Music folder. A dialog box appears, offering you the option to skip out if you suddenly change your mind.

Once the tracks are in iTunes-happy formats, you can not only play them on your desktop computer, but also download them to your iPod.

Note: The next two formats mentioned—AIFF and Apple Lossless—do *not work* on the iPod Shuffle. You first need to convert them to other formats like MP3 or AAC before trying to copy them to the Shuffle. Although they are high in sound quality and some audio purists prefer them, the song files in the AIFF or Apple Lossless formats can be gargantuan. At 40 or 50 megabytes per song, you'd barely be able to fit just one album on a small Shuffle anyway.

AIFF

Speaking of big file sizes, the AIFF standard (Audio Interchange File Format) can create sound files that sound spectacular—in fact, these *are* the audio files on commercial music CDs—but they hog hard drive space. For example, if you stick Prince's *Purple Rain* CD into your computer, double-click the disc icon, and drag the song file for "Let's Go Crazy" onto your desktop, you'll soon have a 46.9 MB AIFF file on your hard drive. Although the sound fidelity is tops, the files are usually 10 times bigger in size than MP3s.

Apple originally developed the AIFF standard, but AIFF files play on other operating systems, too.

Note: If you insist on putting monster-size files like AIFFs on your iPod, you'll have to worry about running out of battery power as well as disk space.

A modern iPod comes with a 32 MB memory chip. Yes, it serves as skip protection because it stores 25 minutes worth of MP3 or AAC music. But it also serves as a battery-life enhancer because the hard drive stops spinning whenever the music plays from the memory buffer.

If you have big song files on the iPod, the memory buffer holds less music. When it runs out of music data, the iPod has no choice but to read from the hard drive, which runs your battery down much faster.

Apple Lossless

The tradeoff with encoding your digital music files in compressed audio formats like MP3 and AAC is that while you can shrink the file, the sound quality of the resulting file is not as good as the original. This is because some of the audio data is discarded during the compression (mostly stuff you can't really hear well anyway). Because of this, formats like AAC and MP3 are referred to as *lossy.*

For some people with less discerning audio tastes, this is not a problem because the sound quality is almost as good as a CD, and besides, you can fit thousands of tracks on your iPod. But for true audiophiles with impeccable taste and bionic ears, the lossy formats make music sound thin, tinny, and terrible.

Before iTunes 4.5, WAV and AIFF were the formats of choice for most hard-core audio fans. Music in these formats sounded better because they were *lossless*—no audio data was discarded when the track was ripped from a CD. As noted in the previous AIFF discussion, though, the files did take up a big honkin' amount of hard drive space.

With its new Apple Lossless Encoder (available in the iTunes Preferences box, as shown in Figure 4-2), Apple has attempted to get the best of both worlds: great sounding files that take up about half the space of an uncompressed CD track. Yes, instead of 40 megabytes of precious hard drive space per song, you only have to pony up 20 megabytes for an Apple Lossless track.

To use the Apple Lossless format on your computer and iPod, you'll not only need at least iTunes 4.5, but also QuickTime 6.5.1 and iPod Update 2004-04-28 or later. If you've just purchased an iPod, these requirements aren't a problem, but if you've been iPodding for a few years and haven't updated your copy of iTunes, QuickTime, or your iPod itself, you have some work to do. QuickTime, Apple's all-purpose multimedia software, is included in the iTunes for Windows download package at *www.apple.com/itunes/download/*, and out-of-date Mac owners who didn't get the new version with Mac OS X Software Update can get it at *www. apple.com/quicktime/download*. For instructions on grabbing the latest iPod Update, see page 269.

Note: The Apple Lossless format only works on 2003-and-later iPods, including the iPod Mini. Owners of the pre–dock iPods that came out in 2001 and 2002 are at a loss for Apple Lossless.

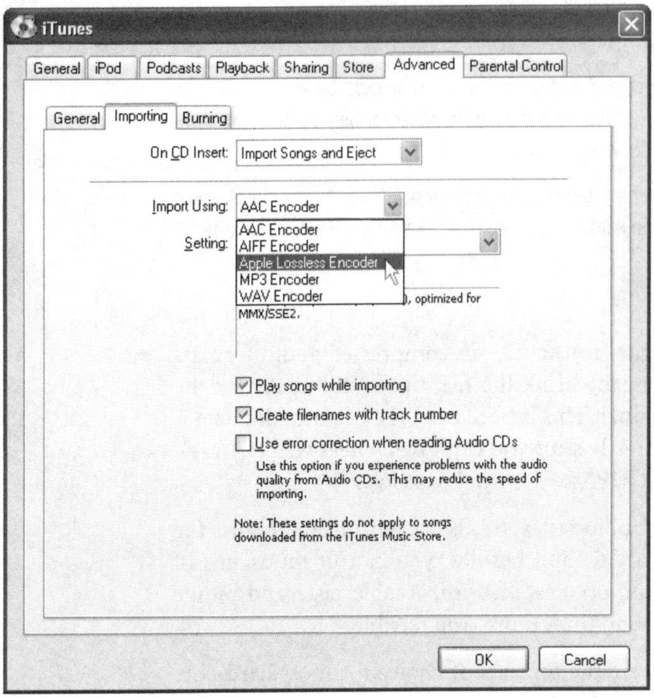

Figure 4-2:
There's more detail in the next chapter, but in case you're curious now, the iTunes Preferences box is where you go to choose your import format. (Press ⌘-comma on the Mac or Ctrl+comma in Windows to get there.)

Audible

You can listen to more than just music on your iPod; you can also listen to the spoken word. Not books on tape, exactly, but more like books on MP3—courtesy of *www.audible.com*. There's a lot to say about audio books on the iPod. If you just can't wait to find out more about audio books, skip on ahead to Chapter 6.

Bit Rates

Bit rate may sound like one of those unbelievably geeky computer terms (which it is), but it plays a big role in how your music sounds when you snag a song from a CD and convert it to MP3 or AAC format. When it comes to sound quality, all digital audio files are not created equal.

The bit rate has to do with the number of *bits* (binary digits—tiny bits of computer data) used by one second of audio. The higher the number of bits listed, the greater the amount of data contained in the file, and the better the sound quality.

Note: Eight bits make a byte. So why are audio files measured in kilo*bits* (thousands of bits) and not the more familiar kilo*bytes?*

Force of habit. Geeks measure size and storage capacity in bytes, but network speeds and data-transfer speeds have always been measured in bits. When you encode an MP3 file, the transfer and compression of the audio data into the new format is measured in kilobits.

Files encoded with lower bit rate settings—like 64 kilobits per second—don't include as much audio information from the original sound file. They sound thin and tinny compared to a file encoded at, say, 160 Kbps.

Just as you can't compare megahertz ratings across different chip families (like Pentium III vs. Pentium 4), you can't compare bit rates between AAC and MP3 files. A 128 Kbps AAC file generally sounds much better than a 128 Kbps MP3 file. In fact, tests by the group that developed the AAC standard found that a 96 Kbps AAC file generally sounds better than a *128* Kbps MP3 file. (Your ears may differ.) As a bonus, the AAC version takes up much less space on your hard disk and iPod. You probably don't want to encode AAC files lower than 128 Kbps, though, as the sound quality will begin to suffer noticeably.

For both formats, the higher the bit rate, the larger the file size. For example, an MP3 file encoded at 160 Kbps sounds a heck of a lot better than one recorded at 96—but it takes up over twice as much disk space (1.5 MB vs. 700 KB).

For MP3s, most people find that 128 Kbps is a good compromise of file size and sound quality. At that rate, MP3 files take up roughly one megabyte of space per minute of music. The 128 Kbps rate is considered high quality for the AAC format, which is why iTunes comes factory set to 128 Kbps. (Songs for sale in the iTunes music store are 128 Kbps AAC files, too.)

You're not stuck with the 128 Kbps rate for your own home-ripped tracks. If you're a classical music fan and want to hear every nuance of a symphony, go for 160 or even 192 Kbps. On the other hand, if you're listening to garage rock while strolling city streets, 96 Kbps may sound fine—giving you plenty of room on the iPod.

To make this kind of change, choose iTunes → Preferences on the Mac (Edit → Preferences in Windows), and click the Advanced tab and then the Importing tab.

Once you change your encoding preferences, you can use iTunes to quickly convert a track into the format you've just chosen. Click the track you want to change and choose Advanced → Convert Selection in iTunes. But while this will quickly convert the song, it's often not the best thing for maintaining audio quality, especially when converting between lossy formats like MP3 and AAC. To get the best possible sound out of your new chosen format, rerip the CD again with your adjusted settings.

Tip: The iPod can also play files encoded in the MP3 *VBR* (Variable Bit Rate) format, in which sophisticated software has adjusted the song's bit rate *continuously* along the length of the song. The song winds up using more data during sonically complex parts of a song (higher bit rates) and lower settings during simpler parts that require less data. By constantly adjusting the bit rate within the song, an MP3 VBR file conserves space more efficiently than a song encoded at a high bit rate all the way through.

To set up iTunes for MP3 VBR, go to Preferences, select Advanced → Importing → MP3 Encoder. From the Setting pop-up menu, choose Custom to find the option for VBR encoding.

---

iTunes for Macintosh and Windows

Apple's iTunes software—the ultimate jukebox program for Macintosh and Windows—supplies the software yin to the hardware yang of the iPod. It plays and organizes your music, copies music from your CD collection onto your hard drive, updates your podcasts, and burns new CDs with music in a sequence you like. It's also an online music store where you can buy a favorite song or music video, legally, for a buck or two, with just a few mouse clicks.

Introduction to iTunes

As the MP3 music craze of the late 1990s swept across the globe, software programs for playing the new music files on the computer began to pop up around the Internet. Many Windows fans fondly remember WinAmp as their introduction to MP3 software; early adopters on the Mac side likely recall programs like SoundApp, SoundJam MP, and MacAmp.

When iTunes debuted in January 2001, Apple reported that 275,000 people downloaded it in the first week. The iTunes software proved to be a versatile, robust, all-around music management program made exclusively for Macintosh. And it was *free.*

Even in that first version of iTunes, Mac fans could import songs from a CD and convert them into MP3 files; play MP3s, audio CDs, and stream Internet radio; create custom playlists; burn audio CDs without having to spring for extra CD burning software; zone out to groovy animated laser-light displays in the iTunes window while songs played; and transfer music to a few pre–iPod, Mac-friendly portable MP3 players.

When the iPod arrived in October 2001, iTunes 2 accompanied it, now with iPod synchronization, an equalizer for enhancing different types of music, a crossfade feature, and the ability to burn MP3 CDs.

Note: Although iTunes 6 is the latest and greatest version of the program, as of this writing, it only works with version Mac OS X 10.2.8 or later and Windows 2000 or later. If you're running Mac OS 9, you'll have to stick with iTunes 2. (Earlier versions of the Mac OS don't work with iTunes or the iPod.) Most of the iTunes features listed in the remainder of this chapter—and throughout the book—refer to iTunes 6.

Over the years, iTunes has evolved into a multimedia jukebox used by millions of people every day, from preschoolers to professional disc jockeys. On the music-management side, you can use the program to sort, rate, and edit every track in your music library and even add album artwork and lyrics to your song files. The latest incarnation of iTunes now plays video files and also lets you subscribe, download, and update podcasts automatically (those free episodic audio and video shows full of news, sports, and pop-culture commentary) for playback on your computer or iPod.

With *two million* songs within its virtual doors (and counting), and more than 11,000 audio books, 20,000 podcasts, and 3,000 videos, the iTunes Music Store is big enough to rate its own chapter in this book—Chapter 7. Apple has also opened versions of the iTunes Music Store around the world, with localized electronic storefronts for music-hungry customers across the globe, from the United Kingdom and the European Union to Japan and Australia.

iTunes 6, which arrived in October 2005, works only with Mac OS X 10.2.8 (make that Mac OS X 10.3.9, if you plan to use the video offerings) and later or Windows 2000 and later. The current version offers some juicy features:

- The AAC format, which can make music sound just as good as the MP3 format but without taking up as much precious space on your Mac, PC, or iPod.

- The option of Apple Lossless encoding for better-sounding files that take up half the space of their corresponding full-bodied CD tracks.

- A music-sharing feature that lets you blast your music *from* any Mac or PC on your home network, *to* any other—without any setup or configuration. (You can thank Apple's Bonjour network-discovery software for this feature; it's built into Mac OS X 10.2 and later, and it's provided to Windows by the iTunes installer.)

- The ability to burn your music collection to a blank DVD, which can hold 4.7 gigabytes of files.

- A place in the main iTunes window to display videos, artwork, or images—like scanned album covers—as your songs play.

- A Search bar that lets you filter your massive multimedia collection and find that one particular podcast or song in a jiffy.

- A Smart Shuffle option that gives you more control over iTunes's definition of "randomness" when it's deciding how to mix up your music.

- Printing functions that make creating CD jewel cases and song lists a one-click breeze.

- A way to save those On-The-Go playlists you made on your iPod when you were out and about.

- A menu command to search out duplicate copies of songs in the iTunes library.

- For owners of color-screen iPods, the power to transfer digital photo libraries to the iPod (Chapter 6), letting the little jukebox work double-duty as a shiny white wallet for photos on the little or big screen.

- Easy management controls to keep your podcast subscriptions up to date on both your 'puter and your 'Pod.

- For the iPod Shuffle, a convenient Autofill button that lets iTunes randomly fill up the tiny player with as many songs from the iTunes library as will fit on the svelte little stick. (See Chapter 3 to learn about using the iPod Shuffle for music and more.)

Many of the features in iTunes 6 also require Apple's QuickTime 7.0.3 software or later. (If you need to update iTunes or QuickTime, Apple keeps an area of its Web site devoted to news, updates, and downloads for QuickTime at *www.apple.com/quicktime/* and iTunes 6 at *www.apple.com/itunes.*)

A Quick Tour

The area at the center top of the iTunes window—the status area—tells you what song is playing, who's playing it, which album it came from, and how much playing time remains. To the left are volume and song navigation controls; to the right is a search box for hunting down or looking up specific singers or songs. Figure 5-1 presents a guided tour of the controls and functions on the iTunes screen.

The Source panel at the left of the iTunes window displays all of the audio and video sources you can tap into at the moment. If you have a CD in the computer's drive, for example, it shows up in the Source list, as will a currently connected iPod.

Clicking a name in the Source column makes the main song-list area change accordingly, like this:

- Click the Library icon and see all the music, videos, and other stuff in your iTunes library.

- Click the icon of a CD you've inserted; the disc's track list appears.

- Click a playlist (page 122); the contents of that music mix appear in the window.

- Click the Podcasts icon to see all the shows you've subscribed to, how many episodes you have on tap, and to get a link to more podcasts in the iTunes store.

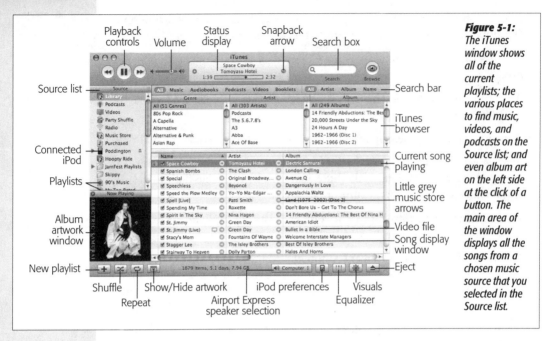

Figure 5-1:
The iTunes window shows all of the current playlists; the various places to find music, videos, and podcasts on the Source list; and even album art on the left side at the click of a button. The main area of the window displays all the songs from a chosen music source that you selected in the Source list.

- Click the Videos icon to see your own personal movie collection, right in iTunes.

- Click the Radio icon for a list of Internet radio stations, or the Party Shuffle icon to—well, see the box on page 112.

- Click the Music Store icon; you jump to Apple's online music emporium where you can browse, preview, and buy songs and videos (Chapter 7).

- Click one of those little gray arrows next to a song and find yourself transplanted into the album page for the song in the Music Store; Option-click an arrow and you go to the song's album in your own iTunes collection.

Tip: You can show or hide the Video and Party Shuffle icons in the Source list by visiting the General pane of iTunes's Preferences dialog box. If you're tired of accidentally landing in the Music Store after tripping over one of those gray arrows with your mouse, you can turn the Music Store link arrows off here, too.

The most recent editions of iTunes can also fill up the bottom of the window with a snapshot look at what's going on in the iTunes store. If you can't bear the temptation, find the blatant capitalism infuriating, or simply want maximum window space for your own music and movies, choose Edit → Hide MiniStore.

As shown in Figure 5-1, the iTunes window is brimming with tools for managing your music, all of which are described in detail starting on page 113. But first you'll need some music to work with. The next section explores one of the most popular uses for iTunes—ripping (copying) digital audio files from compact discs.

Hacking the iTunes Link Arrows

Wish the standard link-arrow setting took you to your own library and not to the Music Store? So did other people. It took less than a day for the wizards at the Mac OS X Hints Web site (*www.macosxhints.com*) to post a permanent fix for Mac OS X jockeys. Here's how.

1. Quit iTunes if it's open.

2. In Mac OS X, go to Applications → Utilities → Terminal.

   Double-click the Terminal program to open a text-based window into your system's innards.

3. In the Terminal window, type the following command on one line and press Enter.

   ```
   defaults write com.apple.iTunes
   invertStoreLinks -bool YES
   ```

4. Restart iTunes.

You have just flip-flopped the link arrow behavior; a single click takes you to your own library, and Option-click takes you out to the Music Store. If you want to change back, retype the command above, but exchange NO for YES.

Window Fun

Don't be misled by the brushed-aluminum look of the iTunes window. In fact, you can push and pull the various parts of the window like taffy.

- You can resize the panes within the iTunes window. Look for a shallow dot between panes; it denotes strips that you can drag to resize adjacent panes.

- The main song list is separated into columns, which you can sort and rearrange. Click a column title (like Artist or Album) to sort the list alphabetically by that criterion. Click anywhere in the column title to change the direction of the black triangle and reverse the sorting.

- Change the order of the columns by dragging them. For example, if you want to have Album right next to the song name, drag the word Album horizontally until it's next to Name.

- To adjust the width of a column, drag the vertical divider line on its right side.

- To resize all the columns so that they fit the information in them precisely, right-click (or Control-click if you have a Mac) any column title and choose, from the shortcut menu, Auto Size All Columns. Double-clicking on the vertical column lines automatically resizes them to fit the text as well.

- To add more columns (or less), right-click (or Control-click) any column title. From the pop-up list of column categories (Bit Rate, Date Added, and so on), choose the name of the column you want to add or remove. Column names with checkmarks are the ones that are currently visible.

Tip: Want to track your own listening habits? Turn on the Play Count in iTunes Options. Now you can see just how many times you've played "I Want You Back" by the Jackson 5 since you ripped that CD of old Motown gems to your hard drive. Checking out the Top 25 Most Played playlist in the Source window (page 90) can also let you know where your ears have been lately.

• If you intend to make a *lot* of adjustments to your list of columns, though, it's much faster to make the changes all at once. Choose Edit → View Options to produce the dialog box shown in Figure 5-2, where you can turn columns on and off en masse.

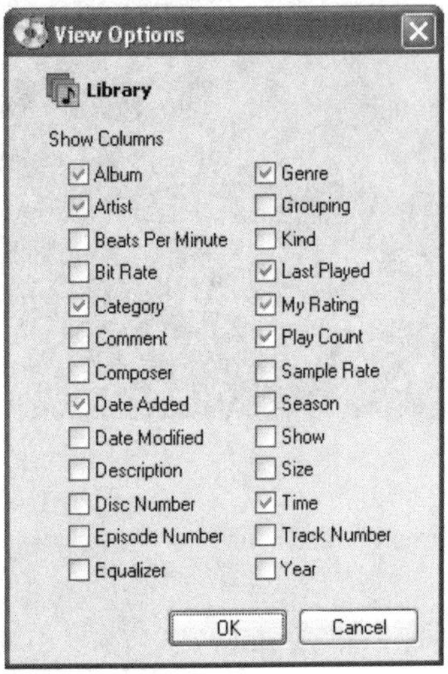

Figure 5-2:
The View Options box from the iTunes Edit menu lets you see as many—or as few—categories for sorting your music as you can stand.

Minimizing the window

Lovely as the iTunes window may be, it can take up a heck of a lot of screen real estate. When you're just playing music while you work on other things, you can shrink iTunes down to a svelte display panel that takes up a fraction of the size of the full window.

In fact, iTunes can run in three size modes: small, medium, or large. Here's how you pull this off:

• **Large.** This is what you get the first time you open iTunes.

• **Medium.** You can switch back and forth between large and medium by clicking the green zoom button at the top- or middle-left corner (or choosing Window → Zoom). If you use iTunes for Windows, press Ctrl+M or choose Advanced → Switch to Mini Player to get the medium-size window.

• **Small.** If your desktop isn't big enough for even the small iTunes window, shown in Figure 5-3 at lower left, try taking it down a notch. To create the mini bar shown at lower right in Figure 5-3, start with the medium-size window. Then drag the resize handle (the diagonal lines in the lower-right corner) leftward. To expand it, just reverse the process.

Tired of losing your mini-iTunes window among the vast stack of other open windows on your screen? In iTunes, you can make it so that the iTunes mini-player is

Figure 5-3:
And what size music would you like today? You can choose large, medium, or small. (Press Ctrl+M in Windows to get the medium size, which you can then scrunch up into the small player by dragging the resize handle.) Only the large version has the space to serve as command central for MP3s, Internet radio, visual effects, album artwork, and watching videos and movie trailers in the iTunes Music Store (Chapter 7).

always visible on top of all your other open documents, windows, browsers, and other screen detritus. Just open the iTunes Preferences box (⌘-comma on the Mac or Ctrl+comma in Windows), click the Advanced tab, and turn on the checkbox next to "Keep Mini Player on top of all other windows." Now you won't have to click frantically trying to find iTunes if you get caught listening to your bubblegum-pop playlist when you thought nobody was around.

Ripping CDs into iTunes

Ripping a CD means "converting its recordings into digital files on the computer." (Too bad recording-industry executives didn't know that when they accused Apple's "Rip, Mix, Burn" ad campaign of promoting piracy, evidently equating "Rip" with "rip off.")

With the proper iTunes settings, ripping a CD track and preparing it for use with the iPod is fantastically easy. Here's how to go about it.

Phase 1: Choose an Audio File Format

Before you get rolling with ripping, decide which format you want to use for your music files: MP3, AAC, AIFF, WAV, or Apple Lossless. To make your selection, choose iTunes → Preferences → Advanced (Mac) or Edit → Preferences → Advanced (Windows), click the Importing tab, and, from the Import Using pop-up menu, choose the importing format you want. See Figure 5-4.

GEM IN THE ROUGH

Arbitrary Groupings

The Grouping column heading (in iTunes 4.2 and later) lets you override the usual sorting criteria and keep together a bunch of songs of your own choosing. (If you don't see the Grouping column, right-click or Control-click *any* column heading and choose Grouping so that a checkmark appears next to its name.)

Many classical albums, for example, contain different symphonies, concertos, and other musical forms, all on one disc. How can you make sure that all of Mozart's *Concerto for Piano No. 5 in D Major (K 175)* stays together and doesn't get mixed in with concertos 6 and 8 from the same CD?

Easy. Select all the "songs" that belong together (by ⌘-clicking on the Mac, or Ctrl+clicking on the PC). Then, choose File → Get Info. iTunes asks if you're sure you want to edit the file information for all of the selected pieces at once; yes, you do.

In the Grouping field of the Get Info box, type *Piano Concerto 5* (or whatever group name you want). Now, when you click OK, you return to the main iTunes list.

To sort your list by grouping name, so that grouped pieces appear consecutively in the list, just click the word Grouping at the top of the column.

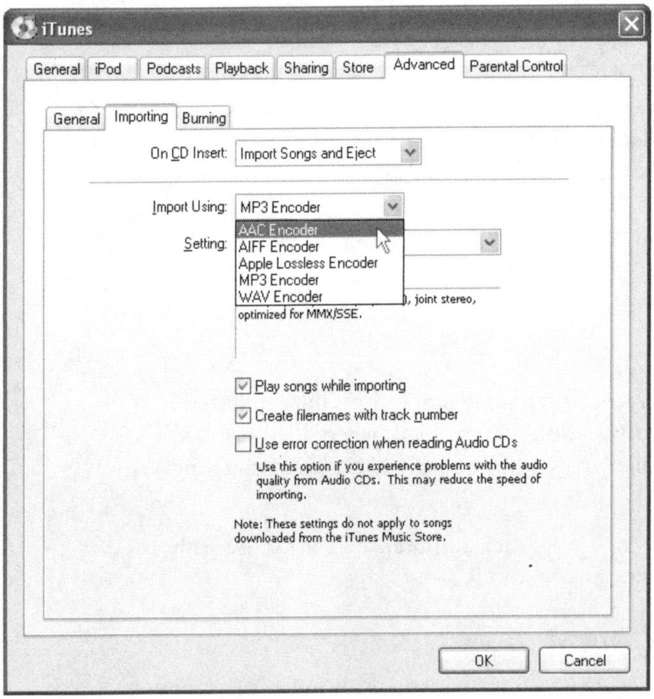

Figure 5-4:
The Importing preferences box is where you tell iTunes which file format and bit rate it should use when ripping tracks from a CD. Turning on "Create filenames with track number" arranges the songs you import in the same order in iTunes as they were on the CD—even if you don't choose to rip every song on the album.

Chapter 4 provides a detailed overview of most of these formats; most people use either the familiar old MP3 (.mp3) format or the spunky new AAC (.m4a) option. To recap: AIFF and WAV offer better sound quality than MP3 and AAC, but they result in larger file sizes. AAC usually creates files that take up about the same size but have the same sound quality of an MP3 file recorded at a higher *bit rate* (page 84).

Tip: Before you stack up the CDs next to the computer for an afternoon of ripping, you may want to test your format preferences by ripping test songs in various formats. Let your ears tell you which format and bit rate sounds best to you.

Phase 2: Download Song Names and Track Information

When you first insert a music CD into a Mac or PC, you may be disappointed to discover that, to the computer, the album is named "Audio CD," and the songs on it are called "Track 1," "Track 2," etc. It turns out that most audio CDs don't include any digital information about themselves. So, if you don't do anything to solve the problem, after you've ripped, say, seven CDs into iTunes, you'll find that you have seven songs called Track 1, seven songs called Track 2, and so on—not the easiest way to organize your music.

There are two ways to remedy the problem: You can type the information in manually or let iTunes go on the Internet to find out for itself.

The manual method

After you load up a CD, you can type in all of the song information for each track. To do so, click the track's name once to highlight its row and then a second time to open up the renaming box. Edit away.

Tip: You can edit the information in the Artist, Album, or Genre columns the same way.

Box Full of Buttons

The round button up in the top-right corner of iTunes changes depending on what you're doing. Here's what each one means and when you see it.

The Browse button appears when you click the Library icon to look through your collection or shop in the iTunes Music Store.

This version of the Burn CD button shows up when a playlist is selected in the Sources area or you have a separate playlist window open onscreen.

If you've taken iTunes up on its offer to burn a CD by clicking on the Burn Disc button shown above, this icon appears as the disc-burning process begins.

The Import button indicates that you've inserted a CD into your computer and are ready to rip some songs into your iTunes library.

When the iTunes Visualizations are turned on, clicking the Options button lets you adjust the frame rate and other visual settings.

To check for podcast updates or new radio streams available in the iTunes Radio area, click the Refresh/Update button.

You should consider this purely theoretical information, however; you'd be nuts to go about naming your CDs and tracks this way. Read on.

The online way

If you have an Internet connection, iTunes will make full use of it and automatically go fetch the names of the CDs songs when you insert the disc. (The Preferences box, shown in Figure 5-5, lets you control how iTunes hadles the CDs you feed it.) Behind the scenes, it's consulting a massive, comprehensive CD Database (CDDB), maintained by a company called Gracenote (*www.gracenote.com*). After iTunes sends information from the disc to the Gracenote CDDB servers, the database identifies the album and sends back the song titles and other data for iTunes to display.

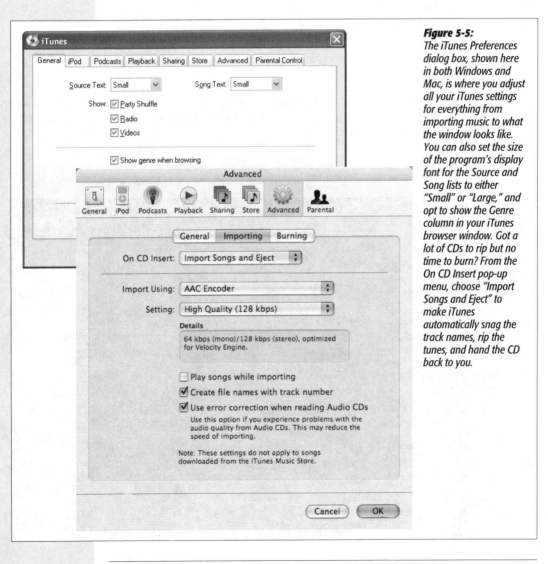

Figure 5-5:
The iTunes Preferences dialog box, shown here in both Windows and Mac, is where you adjust all your iTunes settings for everything from importing music to what the window looks like. You can also set the size of the program's display font for the Source and Song lists to either "Small" or "Large," and opt to show the Genre column in your iTunes browser window. Got a lot of CDs to rip but no time to burn? From the On CD Insert pop-up menu, choose "Import Songs and Eject" to make iTunes automatically snag the track names, rip the tunes, and hand the CD back to you.

(Firewall software may interfere with downloading CD track information. If you suspect that problem, ask your administrator or family geek to confirm that your computer's Internet settings are correct.)

If you aren't connected to the Internet when you're ripping music, you can always get the song titles later when you're back online. Just choose Advanced → Get CD Track Names.

Phase 3: Convert the Song to a Digital Audio File

Once the songs on the CD have been identified, the song and artist names, time, and other information pops up in the main part of the window, as shown in Figure 5-6. Each song has a checkmark next to its name, indicating that iTunes will convert and copy it onto the computer when you click the Import button.

Figure 5-6:
When you click Import CD, iTunes converts selected songs from the CD to MP3, AAC, AIFF, Apple Lossless, or WAV files on your hard drive (depending on what you've selected in Preferences). The status bar at top shows the song being imported, the amount of time left, and the speed of the conversion. Songs in progress sport a wavy line in an orange circle.

If you don't want the entire album—who wants anything from Don McLean's *American Pie* album besides the title track?—you can exclude the songs you *don't* want by removing the checkmark next to their name. Once you've picked your songs, click Import CD in the upper-right corner of the screen.

Tip: You can ⌘-click (Mac) or Ctrl+click (Windows) any box to deselect all checkboxes at once. To do the reverse, ⌘-click (or Ctrl+click) a box next to a list of unchecked songs to turn them all on again. This is a great technique when you want only one or two songs in the list; turn *all* checkboxes off, then turn those *two* back on again.

Another way to select a single song is to click it in the iTunes window and then choose Advanced → Convert Selection to MP3 (or whatever format you've chosen for importing). You can also use this menu item to convert songs that are *already* in your library to different audio formats.

As the import process starts, iTunes moves down the list of checked songs, ripping each one to a file in your Home → Music → iTunes → iTunes Music folder (Mac) or My Documents → My Music → iTunes → iTunes Music (Windows). Feel free to

---

switch into other programs, answer email, surf the Web, and do other work while the ripping is under way.

Once the importing is finished, each imported song bears a green checkmark, and iTunes signals its success with a little melodious flourish. Now you have some brand new files in your iTunes music library.

Tip: Getting iTunes for Windows to play nice with all of the various types of CD players available for PC hardware is no easy task. If you're gnashing your teeth in frustration because iTunes won't recognize the disc you're trying to import, try using the program's built-in CD checkup feature. Choose Help → Run CD Diagnostics. There's no guarantee it'll fix your wagon right there, but there are more CD troubleshooting tips for Windows folks at *www.apple.com/support/itunes/windows/cddiagnostics/*.

Phase 4: Add Cover Artwork and Lyrics

Songs you download from the iTunes Music Store (Chapter 7) often include artwork—usually a picture of the album cover. iTunes displays the pictures in the lower-left corner of its main window.

But you shouldn't have to be a slave to the artistic tastes of some faceless, monolithic record company; you can install any art you like for any song. If Pachelbel's *Canon in D* makes you think of puppies, you can have baby dachshund photos appear in the iTunes window every time you play that song. (Picking artwork for a track takes on a new importance if you want to burn a CD of songs and use the handy template for a jewel-case insert that iTunes offers; see page 128 for more about *that*.)

The only stipulation is that the graphic you choose must be in a format that Quick-Time can understand: JPEG, GIF, PNG, TIFF, or Photoshop, for example. Just keep in mind that the bigger the image size, the bigger the overall file size of the audio file and the more hard drive space you fill up.

Adding an image to an individual song: drag-and-drop method

To add an image file to a song you're listening to in iTunes, click the Show/Hide Song artwork button at the bottom of the iTunes window. The artwork pane appears. As shown in Figure 5-7, faint gray words appear in the pane, telling you exactly where to drag the image file. Just drag any graphics file right off of the desktop (or any other folder) and into this space to install it there.

Tip: If you find an image on the Web that you love, right-click (or Control-click) it, and choose "Download Image to Disk" to save it to your hard drive (the wording depends on your browser). Most browsers nowadays let you drag images off of the Web page onto your desktop, too. Either way, you can drag the resulting graphic into the iTunes artwork pane.

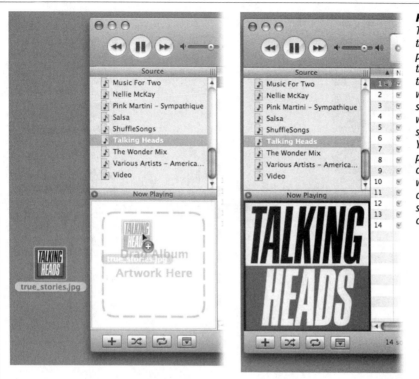

Figure 5-7:
To copy a picture into the iTunes artwork pane, just drag it into the designated spot in the corner of the window (after you've selected the song you want to illustrate). And speaking of cover art: You can print out a perfectly sized CD jewel-case insert, complete with song list, by choosing File → Print, selecting a format, and clicking the Print button.

Adding an image to an individual song: dialog box method

Instead of dragging a graphic off of your desktop, you may prefer to use the Get Info dialog box, where at least you can inspect the image before accepting it. Figure 5-8 shows the way.

Tip: You can even install *multiple* graphics for an individual song. Just drag multiple images into the artwork pane; thereafter, you can click through them with the arrows at the top of the Selected Song bar. If you use the Get Info dialog box shown in Figure 5-8, you can click Add, and then ⌘-click (Mac) or Ctrl+click (Windows) the multiple graphics files to achieve the same result.

If you decide you want to get rid of any artwork or change what's attached to your songs, click the track and press ⌘-I (Ctrl+I). Click the Artwork tab, then click the art in the window. Click the Delete button to remove the image.

Adding an image to an entire album

To select the same art for *all* the songs on an album (or by the same artist), saving yourself a little time, open the iTunes browser (page 90) by clicking the eyeball icon at the top right of the screen. Click the name of an artist or album in the browser, and then press ⌘-I (Mac) or Ctrl+I (Windows) to open the Multiple Song Information box. (You'll see a worrisome alert box from iTunes asking if you're sure about editing multiple items. Click Yes.)

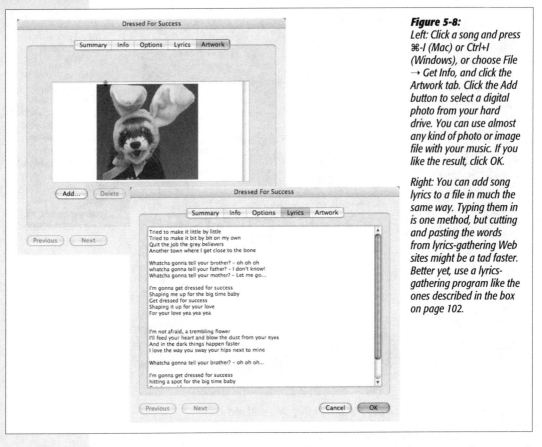

Figure 5-8:
Left: Click a song and press ⌘-I (Mac) or Ctrl+I (Windows), or choose File → Get Info, and click the Artwork tab. Click the Add button to select a digital photo from your hard drive. You can use almost any kind of photo or image file with your music. If you like the result, click OK.

Right: You can add song lyrics to a file in much the same way. Typing them in is one method, but cutting and pasting the words from lyrics-gathering Web sites might be a tad faster. Better yet, use a lyrics-gathering program like the ones described in the box on page 102.

In the Multiple Song Information dialog box (Figure 5-9), turn on the Artwork checkbox, and then double-click in the white area. In the window that opens, navigate to and select the image file you want to use for all the songs on the album, and then click OK. (Of course, you can also drag a graphic right off your desktop into this white box.) You'll see a progress bar as iTunes applies the artwork and any other group settings you've chosen for the files.

Click OK, confirm your decision one last time, and then enjoy the new album art.

Tip: On the Mac, you can apply the same image over and over again into all the songs in the same *playlist.* Visit *http://malcolmadams.com/itunes* and download a copy of the "Selected Artwork to All in Playlist" AppleScript. The next time you have an image that you want to associate with all the songs on a particular playlist, just fire up Doug's AppleScript (see page 227).

Finding and adding lyrics

With iTunes 5 and later, you can store a song's lyrics inside the song file just as you do with album art. To add lyrics to a song, select it in the iTunes window and press

---

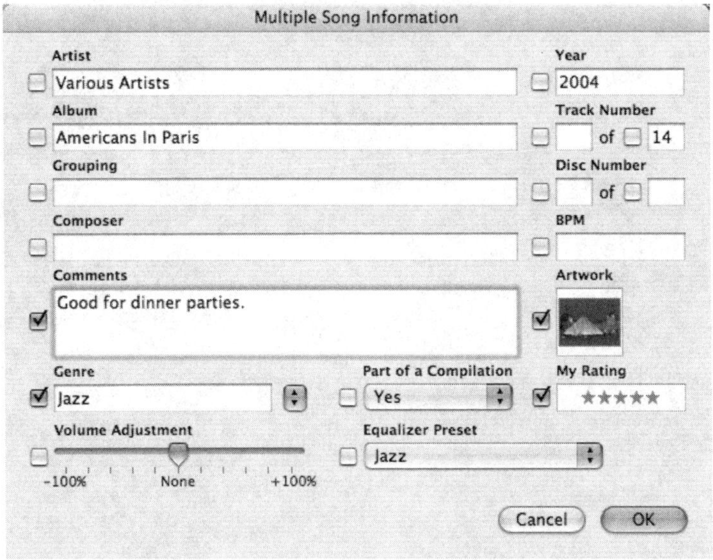

Figure 5-9:
The Multiple Song Information box can save loads of time by letting you change information in one fell swoop in the Artist, Album, or Genre category. For example, assign the Equalizer's "Classical" preset to all your Classical genre tracks or adjust the title of a mislabeled album to all the songs at once.

⌘-I on the Mac, or Ctrl+I in Windows, to call up the song's Info box. Then click the Lyrics tab.

Note: Some types of files you can use with iTunes don't support the lyrics function. AAC and MP3 are just fine for lyrics, but QuickTime and WAV files can't handle words, so you need to convert that WAV of "Jumping Jack Flash" if you want to have a gas, gas, gas with lyrics.

Here, you can either meticulously type in the verses to the song or look them up on one of the hundreds of Web sites around the Net that are devoted to cataloging song lyrics. Once you find your words, getting them into the iTunes Lyrics tab (shown in Figure 5-8) is merely a cut 'n' paste job away. If you want to add the lyrics to all the songs on an album or have several to do on the same playlist, click the Next button at the bottom of the window to advance to the next song to save yourself repeated keystrokes invoking the Get Info command.

When Apple added the lyrics feature to iTunes, though, people who program figured out much easier ways to lasso lyrics off the Web. Shareware programs like iLyric for Mac OS X (available at *www.versiontracker.com*) or Lyrics Search Base for Windows XP (*www.100share.com/song_lyrics.html*) give you a window full of words for thousands of popular songs that can be pasted into iTunes easily.

Getting Other Files into iTunes

Not all sound files come directly from the compact discs in your personal collection. As long as a file is in a format that iTunes can comprehend (MP3, AAC, AIFF, WAV, WMA, Apple Lossless, or Audible on the music side; and MP4, MOV,

Widget's Way with Words

Widgets are colorful mini-applications that work in the Dashboard area of Mac OS X and can round up all kinds of information for you—from weather reports to streaming video of the pandas at the San Diego Zoo. For those not using Mac OS X 10.4, there's Yahoo Widget Engine (formerly known as Konfabulator), a program for Windows and older Mac systems that has its own collection of Widgety wonders that can be downloaded for free at *widgets.yahoo.com*.

There are a few Widgets that can automatically copy the words to a song right into its iTunes file, including pearLyrics, which ran into some legal trouble but can still be found at *www.macupdate.com*. Another option is Toru Yano's Sing That iTune! Widget. Mac OS X 10.4 users can find it at *www.apple.com/downloads/dashboard/music/singthatitune.html*, while Windows and older Mac folks can find the Yahoo Widgets version at *widgets.yahoo.com/gallery*.

Once you install Sing That iTunes!, the little Widget peeps out on the Web and brings back any lyrics it can find for the track you're currently playing in iTunes. The Widget displays the lyrics on its front panel, but once you spin it around by clicking the tiny "i" in the bottom corner, there's a checkbox to turn on that will automatically embed those lyrics right into the song's file in iTunes.

Both the Dashboard and the Yahoo version of the Sing That iTune! Widget have a great little time-saver: In case the Widget can't locate the words to your song itself, there's a Search Google option that takes you right into a full-blown

browser search for lyrics sites that hold the information you seek. Flip the Widget around by clicking the "i" on the Mac edition or right-click it for the Yahoo version to get to the Google Search option.

Depending on the state of the software, the Yahoo version of the Widget may not embed the lyrics in iTunes like the Mac Dashboard version, but right-click on the Widget and you'll find a setting in its Preferences area to add iPod Note Reader tags to lyrics so you can take them along as Notes.

If you find typos in the lyrics the Widget retrieves, you can fix them and save them by right-clicking and selecting Save Changes from the menu; the Save Lyrics button on the Dashboard Widget does the same thing.

Both versions of Sing That iTune! save lyrics as text files stored in your computer in (My) Documents → Sing That iTune! folder. From here, you can drag them over to your iPod's Notes folder the next time it's connected to the computer so that you can view them later on the iPod's screen. If you don't know about Notes, page 201 explains how to use them for all sorts of iPod reading.

Owners of iPod Nanos and the video-playing iPods don't have to work that hard: If you've added lyrics to a song file and you're now playing it on your iPod, tap the center button three times to see the lyrics displayed on screen; tap twice if you didn't add any album artwork to the song file. The whole world is now your karaoke bar!

---

or M4V for iPod-friendly video), you can add it to the iTunes music library by any of several methods.

Note: The AAC format includes a copy-protection feature that MP3 doesn't have. Songs you buy from the iTunes Music Store and music encoded from your own CDs with iTunes work, but you may have trouble playing or moving other copy-protected AAC files (like those bought from LiquidAudio.com, for example).

- On the Mac, you can drag a file or folder full of sound or video files onto the iTunes icon on the Mac OS X Dock to add the music to the library. In Windows, hover the mouse over the iTunes taskbar button without letting go of the song files; when the program window opens, drop the songs on the iTunes window. (The taskbar gets cranky if you try to drop files directly onto the iTunes button.)

- You can also drag the files or folders straight into the iTunes window.

- If menus are your thing, choose File → Add File to Library, as shown in Figure 5-10. In the resulting dialog box, locate and click the file you wish to add, or ⌘-click (Mac) or Ctrl+click (Windows) several files in the list to highlight them all at once. Click Choose to bring it, or them, into iTunes.

Tip: You can set up your computer to auto-eject the CD when it's finished ripping—a great help if you plan to copy a bunch of CDs to your hard drive, assembly-line style. In iTunes, choose iTunes → Preferences (Mac) or Edit → Preferences (Windows). Click the Advanced icon or tab and then, on the Importing tab, where it says, On CD Insert, choose "Import Songs and Eject." From now on, each CD spits out automatically when it's done.

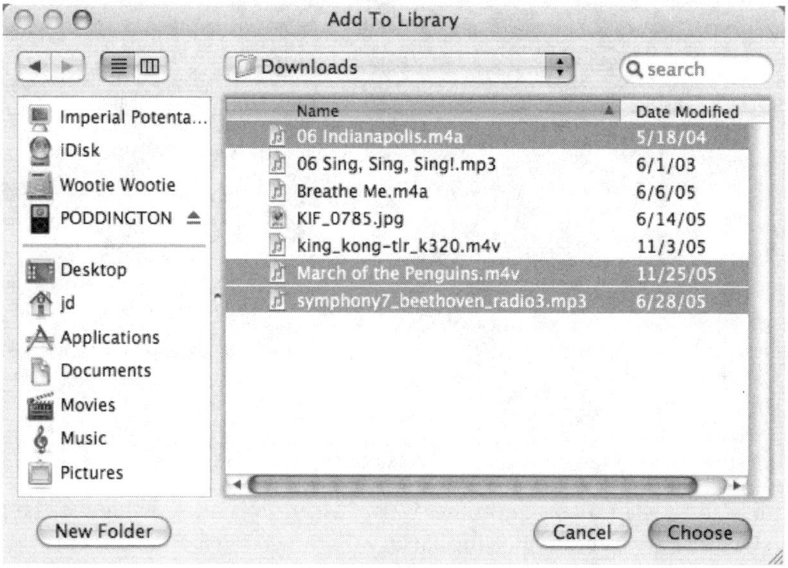

Figure 5-10:
The freely downloadable Clutter program is a great way to quickly beef up your album cover art collection. Clutter's Now Playing window (center) gives you easy access to basic iTunes controls like pause, previous, and next track. And after you've dragged a few covers to your desktop, click any of them to jump to that album.

Tip: If you want the song files you're adding to get copied into your iTunes Music folder from wherever they happen to be on your hard drive, choose iTunes → Preferences → Advanced → General on the Mac, or Edit → Preferences → Advanced → General in Windows, and make sure the checkbox next to "Copy files to iTunes Music folder when adding to library" is turned on. If it's not, the files are added to the iTunes database, but they stay in their current locations on your system.

Can't remember where the song file is stored after you've added it to iTunes? Click the track in the iTunes window and press ⌘-R on the Mac (Ctrl+R in Windows) to have the actual song file reveal itself onscreen from wherever it was stored.

Adding Videos

As described in Chapter 7, the Music Store now sells videos and TV shows that download right to your iTunes library. You can also add your own home movies,

---

Artwork Made Easy

If you have a scanner, the original CD, and a large amount of free time, you can scan in album cover artwork yourself.

Alas, life is too short already. If that scenario doesn't appeal to you, there are plenty of places around the Web to download pictures of album covers that have been previously scanned and are just hanging out for you to copy.

Amazon.com and AllMusic.com have comprehensive selections, as do most sites that sell CDs. That's still a lot of manual effort, though: looking up an album, Control-clicking or right-clicking its artwork, choosing Copy from the shortcut menu, and finally pasting it into iTunes.

Fortunately, a great little free Mac OS X program called Clutter (Figure 5-11) can spare you even that effort. (You can download it from *http://sprote.com/clutter*.) After you launch Clutter while playing a song in iTunes, it recognizes the song and automatically downloads an image of the album cover from Amazon.com.

The album cover art appears both in Clutter's Now Playing window and the Dock. You can also drag the image onto your desktop to create a sea of tiny, floating album-cover windows, as shown in Figure 5-11. When you click a cover, iTunes jumps to that album and starts playing it.

If you want to add any of your Clutter covers to your iTunes tracks, choose File → Copy Cover to iTunes to quickly apply the artwork to your selected iTunes track. Clutter is a Mac OS X program, and Fetch Art for iTunes (available at *www.versiontracker.com*) is another art-picking app for Mac, but Windows fans have a few options themselves.

One artsy bit o' shareware is the iTunes Art Importer (*www.yvg.com/itunesartimporter.shtml*), a floating panel that rides shotgun alongside iTunes and snags album artwork from Amazon for tracks you've selected in the iTunes window. With the click of a button, the program downloads the art and applies it to your tracks so that you don't have to do it manually. Album Cover Finder, a $9 shareware program from Amphonic Designs (*www.albumcoverfinder.com*), fills up your iTunes library with album art all at once, and it works with Windows XP and Mac OS X.

A Web-based service, art4iTunes (*www.art4itunes.com*) also seeks out album covers on your behalf. You just need to export the desired song list in the plain text format from iTunes (choose File → Export Song List to get rolling) and upload the file with a form on the Web site. The art4iTunes site rounds up the appropriate album covers from the tracks on your list and displays them so that you can then drag and drop them right into iTunes.

downloaded movie trailers, and other bits of video to iTunes, as long as the files are in QuickTime-friendly video formats.

Note: QuickTime 7, required for watching videos in iTunes 6, uses new video compression technology called the H.264 codec to squeeze a whole lotta DVD-quality picture into a relatively small file size, giving video files a sharper image and more definition onscreen. The videos you buy from the iTunes Music Store are encoded with H.264 (also known by its more formal name, MPEG-4, Part 10); you can read more about it (and see samples of the technology at work) at *www.apple.com/quicktime/technologies/h264.*

Compatible video formats include QuickTime Movie and MPEG-4 and have one of these file extensions at the end of its name: .mov, .m4v, or .mp4. Other common video formats like .avi or Windows Media Video (.wmv) won't play in iTunes, but you can always convert them to acceptable form with Apple's $30 QuickTime software or any of the dozens of video-conversion programs floating around the Web, like Digital Media Converter (*www.deskshare.com/dmc.aspx*) or some of those mentioned on page 139.

Figure 5-11:
Select the file you'd like to add to your expanding iTunes library with the File → Add File to Library command. If the files you want to add aren't in iTunes-friendly formats, sites like Hit Squad (www.hitsquad.com) and MP3-Converter (www.mp3-converter.com) can help you find shareware that can convert different audio formats.

Adding video files to iTunes is just like adding music files. You can drag the file's icon from your desktop and drop it on the iTunes Library icon or use the File → Add to Library command to locate and import your files. Once you get the videos into iTunes, you can play them in the iTunes window or copy them to your iPod; Chapter 6 has all the information on *that*.

Tip: Movie and music video files all get lumped in the Videos section of your iTunes library, but you can tag the two different types of files yourself to help organize your collection a bit better. To add either a Movies or a Music Video designation to a file, click its title in your iTunes window, choose File → Get Info → Options and use the menu next to Video Kind to label the file.

Adding Podcasts

You can find podcasts all over the Internet, and the iTunes Music Store has at least 20,000 of the most popular ones within easy reach of your mouse. You can find the Music Store's podcasts in a couple of ways: Either click the Podcasts icon in the iTunes Source list and then click the link for the Podcast Directory at the bottom of the window, or just zip into the Music Store from the Source list and click the Podcasts link on the main page. Either way, you're plopped right into the middle of iTunes Podcast Central. Flip to page 158 to see how simple it is to get podcasts into iTunes from the Store. But as well-stocked as the iTunes Music Store is, it doesn't have every single podcast out there.

Some Web sites have links to podcasts posted right on the page. These links, often noted with an orange tag labeled with "Pod," "RSS," or "XML" are links to that podcast's *feed*. Like news feeds that use RSS (Really Simple Syndication or Rich Site Summary, depending on which nerd you ask) to update your Web browser with the absolute latest headlines, blog entries, or other news, podcast feeds deliver the latest episode of your favorite audio or video shows right to your desktop.

To get one of these podcast feeds piping into iTunes, click the orange icon on the page. You may get a screen full of text, but the URL in the browser's address bar is the important thing here. Copy that address, then go to Advanced → Subscribe to Podcast in iTunes and paste the URL into the box, as shown in Figure 5-12. Click OK and then relax as iTunes takes care of the rest. Chapter 6 has more information on playing and managing podcasts.

Figure 5-12:
If you can't find a particular show in the iTunes Music Store, you can add it to your pile o' podcasts by choosing Advanced → Subscribe to Podcast and pasting the show's subscription URL (typically found on the program's Web page) into the box.

> **Subscribe to Podcast**
>
> URL:
>
> http://feeds.feedburner.com/808Talk
>
> Cancel   OK

Tip: If a certain podcast gets you so excited that you just have to share it with your friends immediately, click its title in your iTunes window and drag it to the desktop. This creates a Podcast Subscription File (*.pcast*) that you can attach to an email. Your recipients just need to drag the *.pcast* file into their copy of iTunes to sign up for the feed.

Deleting Songs and Videos

If you want to delete a video, song, or songs—like when you outgrow your Britney Spears phase and want to reclaim some hard drive space by dumping those tracks from the *Oops...I Did It Again* album—click the title in the Albums pane, select the songs you want to delete from the song list, and press Delete (Backspace).

Tip: Selecting songs works just like selecting files in the Mac Finder or in Windows. Select a swath of consecutive songs in the list by clicking the first, then Shift-clicking the last. Add or remove single additional songs to the selection by ⌘-clicking (Mac) or Ctrl+clicking (Windows).

When iTunes asks if you're sure you want to delete the music, click Yes. You'll usually be asked twice about deleting a song, the first time for deleting it from a list, the second time about deleting the music file from your iTunes music library altogether. If you want your hard drive space back, click Yes to both and then empty your Trash or Recycle Bin.

Dealing with Duplicates

Accidentally pulled more than one copy of the same song into iTunes and find yourself lamenting the wasted megabytes of precious hard drive space? In iTunes 4.7 and later, you can have the program seek out and round up duplicate songs— just click the Library icon or a playlist icon in the iTunes Source list, then choose Edit → Show Duplicate Songs.

After iTunes locates all the dupes, it shows them in its main window with a notice at the bottom that reads, "Displaying Duplicate Songs." Here, you can look through and delete extra copies you don't need. But before you start whacking away, make sure these are true duplicates—and not two versions of the same tune by different people, two separate performances (like a live and a studio version of the same ditty), or a version of the same song from its original album and one from a soundtrack compilation.

Once you have cleaned up your library, at the bottom of the iTunes window, click Show All Songs to clear out the list of duplicates and show your full collection in all its glory.

Playing Music

To turn your computer into a jukebox, click the triangular Play button in the upper-left corner of the iTunes window or press the Space bar. The computer immediately begins to play the songs whose names have checkmarks in the main list.

The central display at the top of the window shows not only the name of the song and album, but also where you are in the song, as represented by the diamond in the horizontal strip. Drag this diamond, or click elsewhere in the strip, to jump around in the song.

Or, just click the tiny triangle at the left side of this display to see a pulsing VU meter, indicating the current music's sound levels at various frequencies.

Tip: You can also control CD playback from the Mac's Dock. Just Control-click the iTunes icon (or click and hold it) to produce a pop-up menu offering playback commands—like Pause, Next Song, and Previous Song—along with a display that identifies the song currently being played.

As music plays, you can control and manipulate the music and the visuals of your Mac or PC in all kinds of interesting ways. As a result, some people don't move from their machines for months at a time.

Smart Shuffle

With its sometimes uncanny ability to randomly pluck and play songs that just seem perfect together from all around your music library, the Shuffle feature (page 35) has won over a huge number of fans, especially those who don't want to think about what to listen to as they noodle around on the Internet. But, sometimes, the

---

random shuffling can be a bit jarring, especially if you have a wide range of music crammed onto your hard drive and the buzzsaw screech of a classic punk track may not provide the sonic segue you were looking for after that delicate Vivaldi concerto.

But as shown in Figure 5-13, iTunes lets you control some of the unpredictability of your random song shuffling with the Smart Shuffle setting in the program's Preferences box. Just choose iTunes → Preferences on the Mac, or Edit → Preferences in Windows, and click the Playback tab in the box to get there. Within the Smart Shuffle area, you can tell iTunes to shuffle songs, whole albums, or groupings (often used by classical music fans to round up all the parts of a particular symphony on a disc full of multiple symphonies; see page 94).

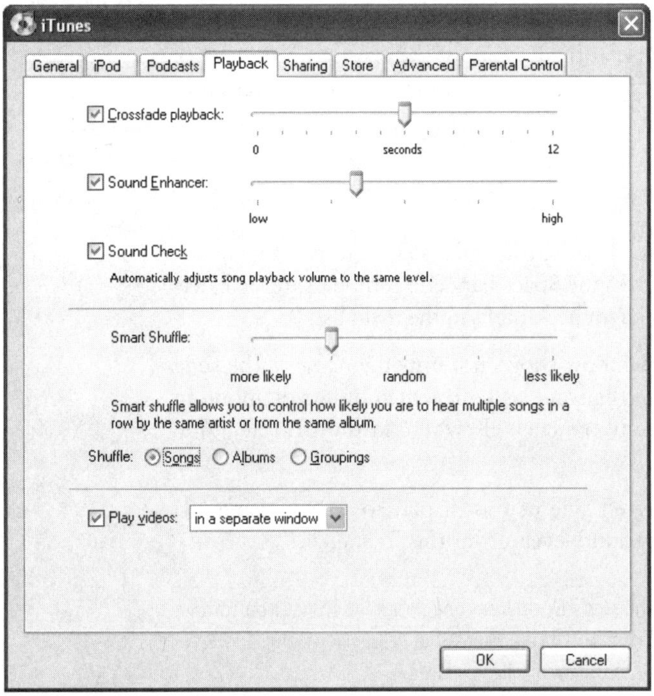

Figure 5-13:
Use the slider in the middle of the Smart Shuffle section to make it more or less likely that you'll hear consecutive songs by the same band as iTunes shuffles through your music library. If you find your shuffling has gotten a bit predictable, you can always come back to this box and change things up again.

You can also tinker with fate and use the slider bar in the box to increase or decrease the probability that iTunes will play tracks from the same album or artist back to back, instead of jumping all around your library. Just nudge the slider toward "more likely" or "less likely" to hear consecutive tracks from the same singer. This can be helpful, say, if you secretly hope to hear a few Gwen Stefani tracks in a row to get in a groove before iTunes moves on to something else.

Note: If you click the button for Albums or Groupings when adjusting your preferences in the Smart Shuffle area, iTunes will play all the songs on that album or within that grouping *in the order they appear on the album* without mixing up the tracks within the album or grouping. Once iTunes has played all the songs on the album or in the group, it will randomly start playing another whole album or song grouping.

Visuals

Visuals is the iTunes term for an onscreen laser-light show that pulses, beats, and dances in perfect sync to the music you're listening to. The effect is hypnotic and wild. (For real party fun, invite some people who grew up in the 1960s to your house to watch.)

To summon this psychedelic display, click the flower-power icon in the lower-right corner of the window (see Figure 5-14). The show begins immediately—although it's much more fun if you choose Visualizer → Full Screen so that the movie takes over your whole monitor. True, you won't get a lot of work done, but when it comes to stress relief, visuals are a lot cheaper than a hot tub.

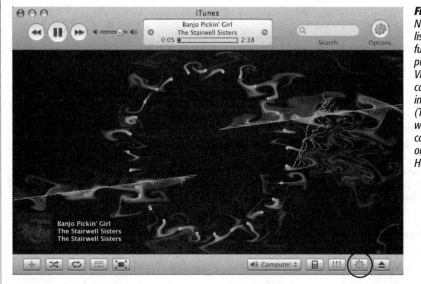

Figure 5-14:
No matter what you're listening to, the animated full-color patterns produced by the iTunes Visualizations feature can make it a more interesting experience. (This feature works really well with the original cast album from "Hair" or anything by Jimi Hendrix.)

Once the screen is alive with visuals, you can turn it into your personal biofeedback screen by experimenting with these keys:

Key	Function
?	Displays a cheat sheet of secret keystrokes. (Press it repeatedly to see the other shortcut keys.)
F	Displays, in the upper-left corner of your screen, how many frames per second iTunes's animation is managing—a quick, easy way to test the power of your graphics circuitry.

Key	Function
T	Turns frame rate capping on or off—a feature that limits the frame rate to 30 frames per second to avoid sapping your computer's horsepower when you're working in other programs.
I	Shows/hides info about the current song.
C	Shows/hides the current Visuals configuration (the name of the current waveform, style, and color scheme) in the upper-right corner of the screen.
M	Turns slide show mode on or off. In slide show mode, the visuals keep changing color and waveform as they play. (Otherwise, the visuals stick with one style and color.)
B	Turns on an Apple logo in the center of the Visuals screen.
R	Chooses a new waveform/style/color at random.
Q or W	Cycles through the various waveform styles stored in iTunes.
A or S	Cycles though *variations* on the currently selected waveform.
Z or X	Cycles through color schemes.
Number keys	Cycles through the 10 different preset, preprogrammed waveform/color/style configurations.
D	Restores the default waveform settings.

Note: These are the secret keystrokes for the *built-in* visuals. The Web is crawling with add-on modules that have secret keystrokes of their own.

Keyboard Control

You can control iTunes's music playback using its menus, of course, but the keyboard can be far more efficient. Here are a few control keystrokes worth noting:

Function	Keystroke (Windows)	Keystroke (Mac)
Play, Pause	Space bar	Space bar
Next song/previous song	Right arrow, left arrow	Right arrow, left arrow
Next source/previous source	Down arrow, up arrow	Down arrow, up arrow
Louder	Ctrl+up arrow	⌘-up arrow
Quieter	Ctrl+down arrow	⌘-down arrow
Mute	Ctrl+M	⌘-M
Fast-forward, rewind	Ctrl+Alt+right arrow, +left arrow	Option-⌘-right arrow, -left arrow
Eject	Ctrl+E	⌘-E
Turn visuals on	Ctrl+T	⌘-T
Turn visuals off	Ctrl+T or mouse click	⌘-T or mouse click
Full-screen visuals	Ctrl+F	⌘-F
Exit full-screen visuals	Ctrl+T, Ctrl+F, or mouse click	⌘-T, ⌘-F, or mouse click

The Graphic Equalizer

If you click the Graphic Equalizer button (identified in Figure 5-1), you get a handsome floating control console that lets you adjust the strength of each musical frequency independently (see Figure 5-15). (Mac fans can also press ⌘-2 or choose Window → Equalizer to get the console onscreen.)

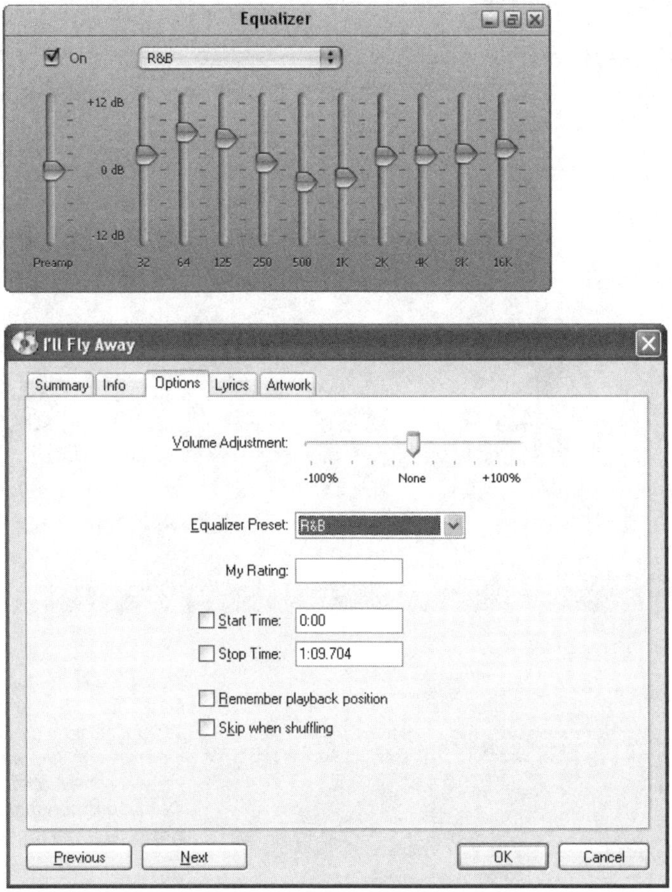

Figure 5-15:
Top: Drag the sliders (bass on the left, treble on the right) to accommodate the strengths and weaknesses of your speakers or headphones (and listening tastes). Or, save yourself the trouble by using the pop-up menu above the sliders to choose a canned set of slider positions for Classical, Dance, Jazz, Latin, and so on.

Bottom: You can also apply preset or customized equalizer settings to individual songs under the Options tab in the song's Get Info box (shown here in Windows).

To apply Equalizer settings to a specific selected song, press ⌘-I (Mac) or Ctrl+I (Windows), or choose File → Get Info and click the Options tab, shown at bottom in Figure 5-15.

You can drag the Preamp slider (at the left side of the Equalizer) up or down to help compensate for songs that sound too loud or soft. To design your own custom preset pattern with the Preamp and the other 10 sliders, click the pop-up tab at the top of the Equalizer and select Make Preset.

Tip: You can also make an Equalizer pop-up tab appear as one of the iTunes columns. Choose Edit → View Options and turn on the Equalizer checkbox.

UP TO SPEED

Party Shuffle On, Dude

The standard iTunes Shuffle feature can be inspiring or embarrassing, depending on which songs the program happens to play. Especially when your guests discover the Milli Vanilli tracks buried in the depths of your collection.

Party Shuffle lets you control which songs iTunes selects when it's shuffling at your next wingding. It also shows you what's already been played and what's coming up in the mix, so you'll know what to expect.

To use it, click the Party Shuffle icon on the iTunes Source list. (If you don't see it, visit the Preferences dialog box, click General, and turn on Party Shuffle.) Until you turn it off, iTunes will display a message each time that describes what Party Shuffle does.

Now, you see an extra panel at the bottom of the iTunes window, as shown in Figure 5-16. Using the pop-up menu, select a music source for the mix—either an existing playlist or your whole library. If you don't like the song list that

iTunes proposes, click the Refresh button at the top of the iTunes window to generate a new list of songs from the same source.

As in any iTunes playlist, you can manually add songs, delete them from the playlist, or rearrange the playing order. Party Shuffle may grab the same track multiple times, especially if you turn on "Play higher rated songs more often," so watch for unwanted dupes.

(The shortcut menu that appears when you Control-click or right-click a song lets you add it again into the Party Shuffle mix—or, if you're seized with a sudden inspiration for your mix, designate it to play that track next.)

Once you're satisfied, click the Play button and let the music play on. With plenty of upcoming tracks displayed, you can feel free to mingle with guests without having to worry about your less-favorite songs crashing the party mix out of the blue.

Figure 5-16:
Party Shuffle Central. Use the pop-up menus in the Display area to specify how many songs you want to see coming up in the mix, and how many recently played ones you want to see.

Preventing Ear-Blast Syndrome

No longer must you strain to hear delicate Chopin piano compositions on one track, only to suffer from melted eardrums when the hyperkinetic Rachmaninoff cut kicks in right after it. The Sound Check feature attempts to bring the disparate volumes into line, making the softer songs louder and gently lowering the level of the more bombastic numbers in the iTunes library. Audiophiles may nitpick about the Sound Check function, but it can be quite useful, especially for times—like bicycling uphill—when constantly grabbing at the iPod's volume controls on the remote or scroll wheel are inconvenient.

The first step to using Sound Check is to turn it on. In iTunes, open the Preferences box (⌘-comma on a Mac or Ctrl+comma on a PC). Click the Playback icon or tab and turn on the box for Sound Check.

You also need to turn on Sound Check on the iPod itself: From the iPod's main screen, choose Settings → Sound Check and click the Select button. The next time you connect the iPod to the computer, iTunes will make the audio adjustments so your synchronization session may take a little longer.

Playing Videos

Cranking up your iTunes movie theater is a lot like playing a song: Double-click on the title of the video you want to play and iTunes starts playing it. You can spot the video files in your Library by the small gray icon that looks like a TV screen next to their titles.

When you click on the Videos icon in the iTunes Source list, all of your movies, TV shows, and music videos are displayed together. You can use the last two icons on the Search bar (page 90) to show your video collection, respectively, as a series of text titles or as a set of thumbnails giving you a little picture preview of the video's contents.

With video, you get a few viewing options to choose from. You can play the video in the album artwork window, opt to have it open in a separate window floating above iTunes (see Figure 5-17), or you can watch it at full-screen size on your computer.

To pick your preferred screen size, open the iTunes preferences box at iTunes → Preferences → Playback (Mac) or Edit → Preferences → Playback (Windows). Make sure the checkbox next to "Play videos" is turned on and then make your decision with the drop-down menu.

You're not stuck with that decision forever, though. Even if you choose to just have the video play in the album artwork window, you can pop it into its own floating window by double-clicking on the album artwork window as it plays. You can also expand it to full-screen size by clicking the full-screen button underneath the album artwork window, as shown in Figure 5-17. (To shrink a video back down from the full-screen size, click it as it plays.)

iTunes Administration

At its heart, iTunes is nothing more than a glorified database. Its job is to search, sort, and display information quickly and efficiently. Here, for example, are some powerful managerial tasks it stands ready to handle.

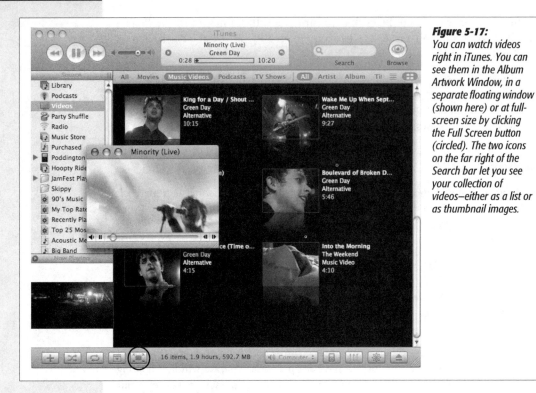

Figure 5-17:
*You can watch videos
right in iTunes. You can
see them in the Album
Artwork Window, in a
separate floating window
(shown here) or at full-
screen size by clicking
the Full Screen button
(circled). The two icons
on the far right of the
Search bar let you see
your collection of
videos—either as a list or
as thumbnail images.*

Searching for Songs

You can call up a list of all the songs that have a specific word in their title, album name, or artist attribution, just by typing a few letters into the Search box at the top of the window. With each letter you type, iTunes shortens the list of songs that are visible, confining it to tracks that match what you've typed.

And for even more searching precision, the iTunes Search bar appears at the top of the browser windows as you type. The left side of the Search bar lets you sort your results by category, like Music or Videos, and the right side lets you winnow down those results even more by letting you choose where the search keyword appears, like in the album's name or the podcast's title.

For example, typing *train* brings up a list of everything in your collection that has the word "train" somewhere in the song's information—maybe the title of the song, maybe a video by the band Wire Train, maybe the audiobook of Patricia Highsmith's *Strangers on a Train*.

But say you just want *song* names with *train* in the title for that mix you're making for your cross-country roadtrip. To filter those overall results down to just the song titles and weed out everything else, click the Music button on the left side of the Search bar and then click Song. Just the songs with *train* in the title are left standing, as shown in Figure 5-18.

Figure 5-18:
The Search box in the iTunes window can quickly find all the songs in the library that match the keyword you enter, and the buttons on the Search bar help you filter your results even more precisely. To erase the Search box so that you see all your songs again, click the little circled X button on the right side of the box.

You can also make the Search Bar appear even when you aren't using the Search box—for instance, if you wanted to quickly see how many Audiobooks you have and identify their authors. Choose Edit → Show Search Bar to make it appear when you want to use it. When you want to clean up your iTunes window, Edit → Hide Search Bar makes the extra layer of buttons go away again. Be sure to click the "x" in the Search box itself to clear any search terms out and have iTunes once again show you your entire collection.

The Browser

The Browse button is the eyeball in the upper-right corner of the iTunes window. (It appears only when the Library icon is selected in the Source list at the left side of the screen.) It produces a handy, supplementary view of your music database, this time organized like a series of columns (shown in Figure 5-19).

It's worth noting, by the way, that this two-panel Browser can become a *three-panel* browser, much to the delight of people who enjoy the phrase "drill down." Figure 5-20 has details.

Tip: Can't get back that full list of albums on the right Album pane after you've clicked a name in the Artist list in the left pane? Go to the top of the Artist list and click All. The complete album list reappears.

Critic's Corner

Although there's no way to give a song two thumbs up within iTunes, you can label each song in your collection with a star rating (one to five). Not only can you, too, now feel like a *Rolling Stone* record critic, but you can also use your personal rating system to spontaneously produce nothing but playlists of the hits.

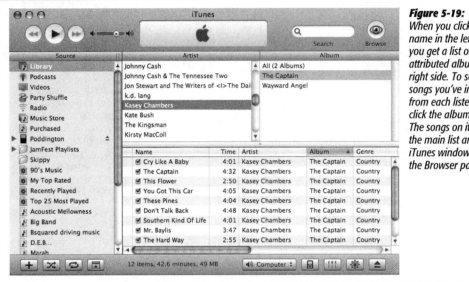

Figure 5-19:
When you click an Artist name in the left column, you get a list of all attributed albums on the right side. To see the songs you've imported from each listed album, click the album name. The songs on it appear in the main list area of the iTunes window, beneath the Browser panes.

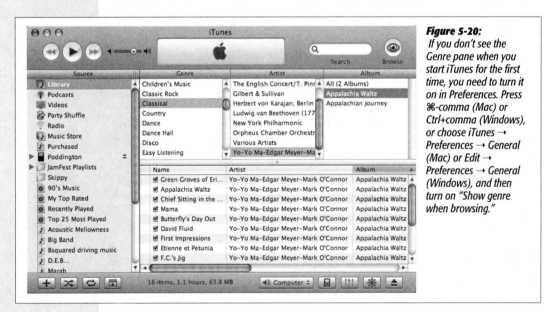

Figure 5-20:
If you don't see the Genre pane when you start iTunes for the first time, you need to turn it on in Preferences. Press ⌘-comma (Mac) or Ctrl+comma (Windows), or choose iTunes → Preferences → General (Mac) or Edit → Preferences → General (Windows), and then turn on "Show genre when browsing."

To add a rating to a song in the Song list window, first make sure the My Rating field is turned on in the iTunes Options box (⌘-J [Mac] or Ctrl+J [Windows]). Then proceed as shown in Figure 5-21.

Once you've assigned ratings, you can sort your list by star rating (click the My Rating column title), create playlists of only your personal favorites (page 122), and so on.

Tip: On the newer iPods, you can even rate songs on the go; your ratings will transfer back to iTunes. To rate a song on the iPod, start playing it and tap the Select button from the Now Playing screen until you see shadowy dots on screen. Use the scroll wheel to spin across the ghostly gray dots onscreen and transform them into the number of stars you feel the song deserves.

Editing Song Information

You have a couple of different ways to change song titles in iTunes—for example, to fix a typo or other incorrect information.

In the song list, click the text you want to change, wait a moment, and then click again to make the renaming rectangle appear. Type to edit the text, exactly as when you change a file name on the desktop.

Another way to change the song's title, artist name, or other information is to click the song in the iTunes window and press ⌘-I (Mac) or Ctrl+I (Windows) to bring up the Get Info box. (Choose File → Get Info if you forget the keyboard shortcut.) Click the Info tab (Figure 5-22) and type in the new track information. This is the way to go if you have several pieces of information to change.

Tip: Once you've got a song's Get Info box up on the screen, you can use the Previous and Next buttons to navigate to the other tracks grouped with it in the iTunes song list window. This way, if you want to rapidly edit all the track information on the same playlist, on the same album, in the same genre, or by the same artist, you don't have to keep closing and opening each song's Get Info box.

Converting Between File Formats

To get the conversion underway, choose iTunes → Preferences (File → Preferences on a PC) and then click the Importing button. From the Import Using pop-up menu, pick the format you want to convert to and then click OK.

Figure 5-22:
Top: The Info tab is where you can add, correct, and customize information for each song.

Bottom: Click the Summary tab for the lowdown on the song's bit rate, file format, and other fascinating technical details.

Note: If you're going from a compressed format like MP3 to a full-bodied, uncompressed format like AIFF, you shouldn't hear much difference in the resulting file. Quality could take a hit, however, if you convert a file from one compressed format to another, like MP3 to AAC. If you're a stickler for sound but still want the space-saving benefit of the AAC format, it's best just to set the iTunes preferences to encode in AAC (page 79) and rerip the song from the original CD.

Now, in your iTunes library, select the song file you want to convert and then choose Advanced → Convert Selection to AAC (or MP3, AIFF, or WAV, depending on what you just picked as your import preference). If you need to convert AIFF or Apple Lossless files before loading them onto your iPod Shuffle, this is one quick 'n' easy way to do it.

If you have a whole folder or disk full of potential converts, hold down the Option key (Mac) or Shift key (Windows) as you choose Advanced → Convert to AAC (or your chosen encoding format). A window pops up, which you can use to navigate to the folder or disk holding the files you want to convert. The only files that don't get converted are protected ones: Audible.com tracks and AAC songs purchased from the iTunes Music Store.

The song or songs in the original format, as well as the freshly converted tracks, are now in your library.

Joining Tracks

If you want a seamless chunk of music without the typical two-second gap of silence between CD tracks, you can use the Join Tracks feature to stitch together a sonic sampler in one big file. This feature is great for live albums or other CDs that run one song into the next.

To rip multiple songs as one track, pop in the CD you want to use, download the song information, make sure the list is sorted by track number, and then Shift-click to select the tracks you want to join during the ripping process. You can only join tracks that are in sequential order on the CD.

Once you've got the tracks selected, go to Advanced → Join CD Tracks. iTunes displays a bracket around the selected tracks and indents the names of the tacked-on ones. If you change your mind and want to separate one of the tracks from the group, select it and go to Advanced → Unjoin CD Tracks. (You can Shift-click to peel off multiple tracks from the group, too.)

Click the Import button to rip the selected songs to one big track.

Note: Trying to join up some tracks only to find the Join Tracks item dimmed out on the Advanced menu? Here's a troubleshooting checklist. First, make sure you've got the CD selected in the iTunes Source list because you have to perform joining while ripping. The songs to be joined need to be in the exact same ascending order as they are on the CD.

If it looks like they're in the right order but the Join Tracks command is still dimmed, go to the first column on the left of the iTunes song display window and click the top of the column. Make sure the top of the column is blue and the black triangle on top of it is pointing up. Now try Join Tracks again.

Changing Start and Stop Times for Songs

Most of the time, there's musical interest in every juicy moment of the songs that you download, buy, or rip from CDs. Every now and then, though, some self-indulgent musician releases a song with a bunch of onstage chitchat before the music starts. Or maybe you've got a live album with endless jamming at the end as a song plays out.

Fortunately, you don't have to sit there and listen to the filler each time you play the file. You can adjust the start and stop times of a song so that you'll hear only the juicy middle part.

As you play the song you want to adjust, observe the iTunes status display window; watch for the point in the timeline where you get bored. Say, for example, that the last two minutes of that live concert jam is just the musicians riffing around and goofing off. Note where *you* want the song to end.

FREQUENTLY ASKED QUESTION

A Trip to the Library

Where exactly does iTunes store its music library on my computer's hard drive? Can I move the music library if my hard drive starts to get full?

The music library is the program's personal database. It stores all of the songs you've imported into the program, as well as all of the playlists you created from those songs. This database file sits in your Home → Music → iTunes Music folder (Mac) or My Documents → My Music → iTunes → iTunes Music folder (Windows).

If you rudely drag the iTunes Music folder to a different place without telling iTunes, it will think the songs are gone. The next time you start the program, you'll find it empty. (While iTunes remains empty but calm, *you* may have heart palpitations as you picture your music collection vanishing in a puff of bytes.)

To move the iTunes Music folder to a new drive, just let the program know where you're putting it. Move the folder to the desired location, then choose iTunes → Preferences (Mac) or Edit → Preferences (Windows) and click the Advanced icon or tab. In the area labeled iTunes Music Folder Location, click the Change button, and navigate to the place where you moved the iTunes Music folder. Finally, click OK.

Exhale.

Then select the track you want to adjust. Choose File → Get Info to call up the information box for the song, and proceed as shown in Figure 5-23.

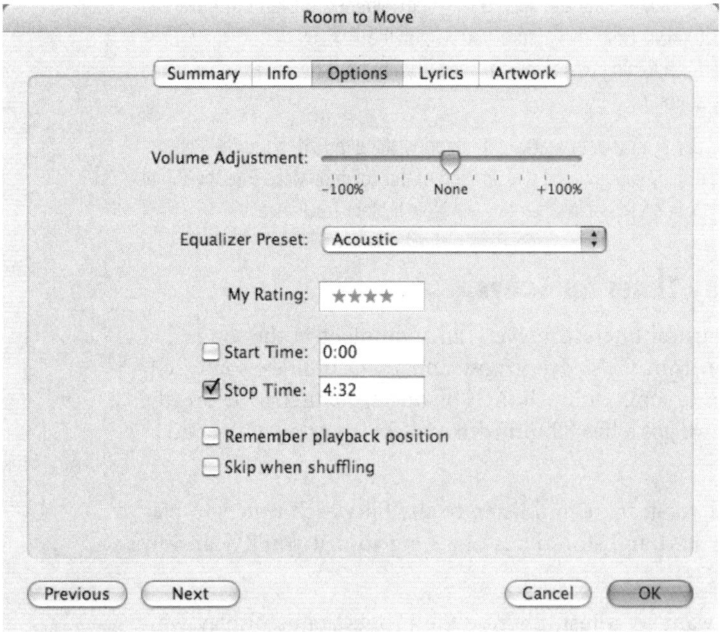

Figure 5-23: *Song too long for your taste? Click the Options tab and take a look at the Stop Time box, which shows the full duration of the song. Change the number to the length of time you want the song to run, as you noted earlier. iTunes automatically turns on the Stop Time box. Click OK to lop off those last two boring minutes of the song. (You can do the exact same trick at the beginning of a song by adjusting the time value in the Start Time box.)*

The shortened version plays in iTunes and on the iPod, but the additional recorded material isn't really lost. If you ever change your mind, you can go back to the song's Options box, turn off the Stop Time box, and return the song to its full length.

Tip: It's fun to wander around in iTunes as your music plays, and it's extremely easy to drift away from your current playlist. If you want to go directly back to the song that's currently playing, just click the curled arrow on the right side of the oval iTunes display window.

This handy icon, called the *snapback* arrow, serves as a one-click shortcut to the File → Show Current Song menu, or you can press the keyboard shortcut (⌘-L on the Mac; Ctrl+L in Windows). It only works when there's a song actually playing, but you can use it in your own collection or while traipsing around song previews in the Music Store.

Internet Radio

Not satisfied with being a mere virtual jukebox, iTunes also serves as an international, multicultural radio without the shortwave static. You can find everything from mystical Celtic melodies to American pop to programming from Japan, the Caribbean, Germany, and other spots around the globe.

Computers with high-speed Internet connections have a smoother streaming experience, but the vast and eclectic mix of musical offerings is well worth checking out—even if you have a dial-up modem. Just click the Radio icon in the Source list to see a list of stations, as shown in Figure 5-24.

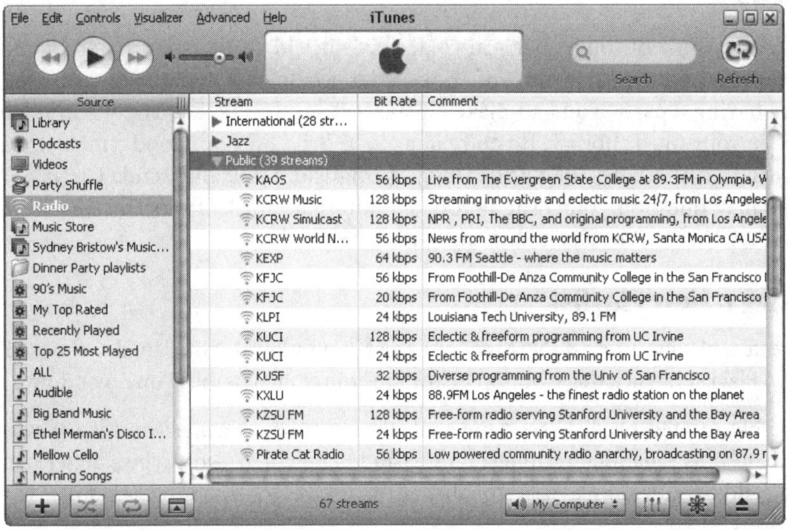

Figure 5-24:
The Radio list displays the categories and subcategories that can take you around the world in 80 stations with iTunes. Click the Refresh button to update the station list.

If you find your radio streams are constantly stuttering and stopping, choose iTunes → Preferences (Mac) or Edit → Preferences (Windows). In the Preferences dialog box, click the Advanced icon or tab and then click General. From the Streaming Buffer Size pop-up menu, choose Large. Click OK.

Having the buffer set to Large may increase the waiting time before the music starts flowing through your computer from the Internet, but it allows iTunes to hoard more music at once to help make up for interruptions caused by network traffic.

Once you've listened to all the stations listed in iTunes, hit the Internet. You can find more radio stations that stream around the Web at sites like *www.shoutcast. com* and play them through iTunes when you click the link to listen.

Tip: It's possible to save music streams to your computer's hard drive, although the practice dances dangerously close to copyright infringement. Programs like RadioLover (*www.bitcartel.com/radiolover*) and Streamripper X (*http://streamripperx.sourceforge.net*) for Mac OS X, or RipCast (*www.xoteck.com/ripcast*) and Audiolib MP3 Recorder (*www.audiolib.com/recorder*) for Windows, let you save radio streams as MP3 files. Audio Hijack for the Mac also lets you save streaming audio and comes with programs to help enhance the audio if you buy it as part of Roxio's $50 Boom Box software suite for the iPod (*www.roxio.com*).

If you really love radio, check out Griffin Technology's RadioSHARK, a fin-shaped USB attachment that plugs into your computer and lets you listen and record AM/FM radio broadcasts even if you're not at the computer. You can easily transfer the recorded files to your iPod so you can time shift your favorite shows right into your pocket. The RadioSHARK sells for $70 at *www.griffintechnology.com*.

Playlists

A *playlist* is a list of songs that you've decided should go together. It can be made up of pretty much any group of songs arranged in any order. For example, if you're having a party, you can make a playlist from the current Top 40 and dance music in your music library. If you're in a 1960s Brit Girl Pop mood, you can make a playlist that alternates the hits of Dusty Springfield, Lulu, and Petula Clark. Some people may question your taste if you, say, alternate tracks from *La Bohème* with Queen's *A Night at the Opera,* but hey—it's *your* playlist.

Making a New Playlist

To create a playlist, press ⌘-N (Mac) or Ctrl+N (Windows). You can also choose File → New Playlist or click the + button below the Source area of the iTunes window.

All freshly minted playlists start out with the impersonal name "untitled playlist." Fortunately, its renaming rectangle is open and highlighted—just type a better name. As you add them, your playlists alphabetize themselves in the Source window.

Once you've created and named this spanking new playlist, you're ready to add your songs. You can do this in several different ways.

If this is your first playlist, opening the playlist into its own window might make it easier for you to see what's going on. To do so, double-click the new playlist's icon in the Source list, which opens a window next to your main iTunes window. From here, drag the song titles you want over to the new playlist window. (You can also open the iTunes Music Store into its own window with the double-click trick.)

Another way to add songs to a playlist is by dragging tunes to the playlist's icon in the Source list from the main iTunes window (see Figure 5-25). You can also scroll through a big list of songs, selecting tracks as you go by ⌘-clicking on the Mac or Ctrl+clicking in Windows, and then choosing File → New Playlist From Selection.

Figure 5-25:
Making a playlist is as easy as dragging song titles from your library window to your new playlist window. The other way to fill a playlist is to drag tunes from the Songs window and just drop them on the new playlist's icon in the Source list. (If you have a lot of playlists, though, you risk accidentally dropping songs on the wrong icon.)

Don't worry about clogging up your hard drive. When you drag a song title onto a playlist, you don't *copy* the song; you're just giving iTunes instructions about where to find the files. In essence, you're creating an *alias* or *shortcut* of the original. You can have the same song on several different playlists.

Note: Anytime you see an exclamation mark next to a title in the iTunes song list, iTunes is alerting you that it can no longer find that song in its library. The song may have been moved or deleted by accident.

If you think you know where you moved it, double-click the song title and navigate to where you think the song is living. Once you find it, select the song file and click Choose.

Modifying a Playlist

If you change your mind about the order of the tunes you've selected for a playlist, just drag the song titles up or down within the playlist window to reorder them.

You can also drag more songs into a playlist or delete the titles from the list if you find your playlist needs pruning. (Click the song in the playlist window and hit Delete or Backspace to get rid of it. When iTunes asks you to confirm your decision, click Yes.) Remember, deleting a song from a playlist doesn't delete it from your music library—it just removes the title from your *playlist.* (Only pressing Delete or Backspace when the *Library* icon is selected gets rid of the song for good.)

Tip: If you want to mix up the songs on a playlist but don't feel like thinking about it, iTunes can do it for you. Click the Shuffle button at the bottom of the iTunes window. You'll hear your playlist songs in a random order.

Deleting a playlist

The party's over and you want to delete that playlist to make room for a playlist for next week's bash. To delete a playlist, click it in the Source list and press Delete (Backspace). (Again, this just zaps the playlist itself, not all the stored songs you had in it. Those are still in your iTunes Music folder.)

Tip: You make video playlists just like you make music playlists. Just create a new playlist and drag the desired video clips onto it. Although iTunes has a Videos playlist of its own in the Source list, you can't drag your own clips onto it to add them. If you drag them onto the Library icon to add them, however, they end up in the Videos area anyway.

Smart Playlists

Just as you can have iTunes vary your song order for you, you can also have the program compose playlists all by itself. Once you give it some guidelines, a *Smart Playlist* can go shopping through your music library and come up with its own mix for you. The Smart Playlist even keeps tabs on the music that comes and goes from your library and adjusts itself on the fly.

You might tell one Smart Playlist to assemble 45 minutes worth of songs that you've rated higher than four stars but rarely listen to, and another to play your most-often-played songs from the 1980s. Later, you can listen to these playlists with a turn of the iPod's control dial, uninterrupted and commercial-free.

To start a Smart Playlist in iTunes, press Option-⌘-N (Mac) or Ctrl+Alt+N (Windows) or choose File → New Smart Playlist. A Smart Playlist box opens: It has a purple gear-shaped icon next to the name in the Source list (a regular playlist has a blue icon with a music note icon in it).

Tip: When you press Option (Mac) or Shift (Windows), the + button for Add New Playlist at the bottom of the iTunes window turns into a gear icon. Click the gear button to get a new Smart Playlist to appear in the Source list, all ready for you to set up.

Now, you can give the program detailed instructions about what you want to hear. You can select the artists you want to hear and have iTunes leave off the ones you're not in the mood for, pluck songs that only fall within a certain genre or year, and so on. You can make a Smart Playlist using information from any field in the song's tag, like a collection of every tune in your library that's track 17 on an album.

Click the little + sign at the end of each line to keep adding criteria, or click the – sign to remove one. See Figure 5-26 for an example.

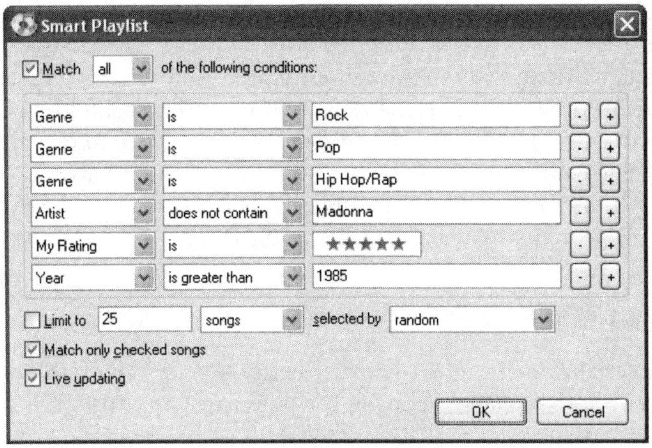

Figure 5-26:
This Smart Playlist seeks out all pop, rock, hip hop/rap tracks with a personal rating of five stars that were recorded after 1985 and that weren't sung by Madonna. By adding fields and adjusting the specifications for what type of music you're looking for, you can really come up with some highly intelligent Smart Playlists.

Then, provided the "Live updating" checkbox is turned on, iTunes will always keep this playlist updated as your collection, ratings, and play count changes, and so on.

A Smart Playlist is a dialogue between you and iTunes: You tell it what you want in as much detail as you want, and the program responds back with what it thinks you want to hear. Once you lay out the boundaries, iTunes pores through the current contents of your music library and generates the playlist.

Tip: If you find Smart Playlists are becoming an obsession, take a browser ride over to *www. smartplaylists.com*. There, you'll find many like-minded individuals exchanging tips, tricks, and tales about Smart Playlists, iTunes, and what they'd like Apple to add to the *next* version of the program.

Playlist Folders

If you like to have a playlist or five for every occasion, but find your iTunes Source list is getting out of control, iTunes gives you the power to tidy things up by storing multiple playlists inside convenient folders.

To add a folder to your Source list, click the Library icon in the Source list and choose File → New Folder. A new "untitled folder" appears on the list, inviting you to change its name to something more original. If you miss your chance to name it here, select it later and click the words "untitled folder" once to highlight them so you can type the real folder name you want to use. Once your new folder is set up, drag any playlists you want to store inside it onto the folder's icon to add them.

If the whole family shares one computer, folders can give each person a tidy receptacle to store his or her personal playlists. Folders are also great for storing a bunch of playlists that go great together, so when you select the folder, iTunes will play all the songs right down each playlist stored inside.

Tip: You can also use the Smart Playlists feature (page 124) to monitor new tracks added to playlists in your folders. To have a Smart Playlist keep tabs, use the drop-down menus in the Smart Playlist box to create a setting for "Playlist is" and then select the name of your folder from the drop-down list of playlists.

But while these Playlists folders are great for bring order to your iTunes Source list, they don't travel well, meaning you can't drag your folders over to your iPod and expect to see submenus of playlists to scroll though. If you do drag a folder onto your iPod, all the individual playlists inside it get mashed together into one giant playlist bearing the name of the folder they were stored in on iTunes. This may not matter to some people, but others may find it unbearably messy after all the effort that went into organizing things on the iTunes side of the fence.

Burning a CD or DVD

If want to record a certain playlist on a CD for posterity—or for the Mr. Shower CD player in the bathroom—iTunes gives you the power to burn. In fact, it can burn any of three kinds of discs:

- **Standard audio CDs.** This is the best part. If your computer has a CD burner, it can serve as your own private record label. iTunes can record selected sets of songs, no matter what the original sources, onto a blank CD. When it's all over, you can play the burned CD on any standard CD player, just like the ones from Tower Records—but this time, you hear only the songs you like, in the order you like, with all of the annoying ones eliminated.

Tip: Use CD-R discs. CD-RW discs are not only more expensive, but they may not work in standard CD players. (Not all players recognize CD-R discs either, but the odds are better.)

- **MP3 CDs.** A standard audio compact disc contains high-quality, enormous song files in the AIFF format. An *MP3* compact disc, however, is a data CD that contains music files in the MP3 format.

  Because MP3 songs are much smaller than the AIFF files, many more of them fit in the standard 650 or 700 MB of space on a recordable CD. Instead of 74 or 80 minutes of music, a CD-R full of MP3 files can store *10 to 12 hours* of tunes.

  Just about any computer can play an MP3 CD. But if you want to take the disc on the road or even out to the living room, you'll need a CD player designed to read both standard CDs and discs containing MP3 files. Many modern players can play both CDs and MP3 CDs, and the prices are not much higher than that of a standard CD player. Some DVD players and home-audio sound systems can also play MP3 CDs.

Note: You can't easily convert copy-protected AAC files into MP3 files, so you can't burn an MP3 CD from a playlist that contains purchased music. If you're determined to do that, certain workarounds are available. You could use certain frowned-upon utility programs from the Web. Or, you could burn the AAC files onto a CD and then rip *that* into iTunes, exactly as described earlier in this chapter. At that point, the songs are MP3 files.

- **Backup CDs or DVDs.** If your Mac has an Apple SuperDrive that can play and record both CDs and DVDs, you have another option. iTunes can also back up 4.7 gigabytes of your media collection at a time by copying it to a blank single-sided DVD. Most Windows computers with DVD burners can also burn DVDs with iTunes. (Even if you've burned video files on there, the disc won't play in any kind of player, of course; it's just a glorified backup disk for restoration when something goes wrong with your hard drive.) If you don't have a DVD burner, you can cook up a CD or three of backup files instead.

Note: Although earlier versions of iTunes would stop burning a long playlist once it got to the last full song it could fit on a disc, iTunes 4.2 and later versions ask you to insert another disc if it runs out of room on the first one, and then it picks up where it left off.

You pick the type of disc you want to make in the Preferences dialog box (Figure 5-27). Then proceed as follows.

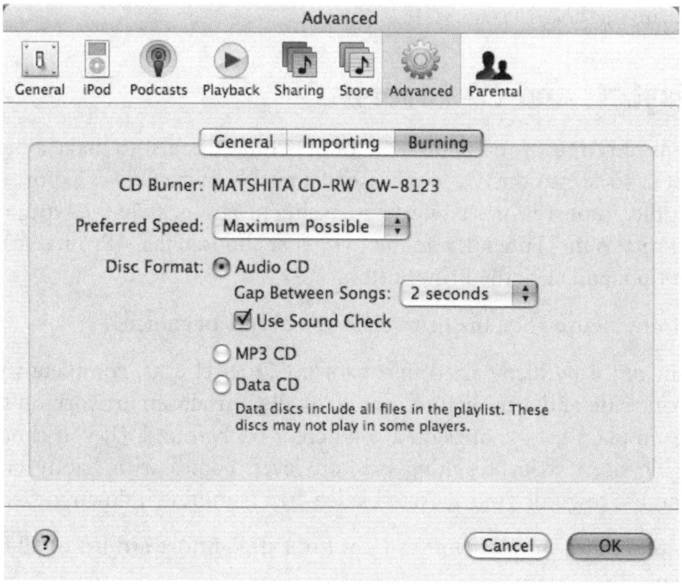

Figure 5-27:
Choose iTunes → Preferences (Mac) or Edit → Preferences (Windows), and then click Burning. Then select the recorder you want and what kind of CD to make: a standard disc that will play in just about any CD player, an MP3 CD for a computer's CD drive (and some newer home decks), or a backup just for safekeeping.

1. **Select the playlist you want to burn. Check to make sure you have all the songs you can fit, in the order you want them in.**

   Consult the readout at the bottom of the window, which lets you know how much playing time is represented by the songs in the playlist.

2. **When you're ready to roll, click the Burn Disc button at the top-right corner of the iTunes window.**

   The icon changes into a yellow-and-black graphic that resembles the symbol used for fallout shelters in the 1950s.

3. **Insert a blank CD into your computer's drive when prompted. Click the Burn Disc button again after the program acknowledges the disc.**

   iTunes prepares to record the CD, which may take a few minutes. In addition to prepping the disc for recording, iTunes has to convert the music files to the standard format used by audio CDs (if you're cooking up an audio disc to play in the car or home stereo).

   Once iTunes has taken care of business, it lets you know that it's now burning the CD. Again, depending on the speed of your computer and CD burner, as well as the size of your playlist, the recording process could take several minutes.

   When the disc is done, iTunes pipes up with a musical flourish. Eject the CD (by pressing the Eject key at the upper right of a Mac keyboard, for example) and label the top of the newly minted music storehouse with a magic marker (or your favorite method).

Printing Playlists and CD Covers

In earlier versions of iTunes, you had to do a lot of gymnastics just to make a nice-looking song list to tuck into the CD jewel case of a freshly burned disc: Export the playlist as a text file, import it into a word-processing program, style the type, and 6 hours later...*Print*. With iTunes 4.5 or later, you just choose File → Print, select a preformatted option, and click the Print button.

As you can see from Figure 5-28, the Print dialog box is *full* of choices.

- You can print out a perfectly sized insert for a CD jewel case, complete with song list on one side and a miniature mosaic of all your album artwork on the other—or just a plain list of songs on a solid color background. (If you choose to make a CD insert, your resulting printout even comes with handy crop marks you can use to guide your X-Acto blade when trimming it down to size.)

- If you want something simpler, you can opt for a straightforward list of all the songs on the playlist.

- You can also print out a list of all the albums that have contributed songs to your playlist, complete with album title, artist name, and the songs' titles and times for each track culled from that particular album.

Fast User-Switching in Mac OS X and iTunes

If you live in a household where multiple people use the same Mac, you've probably wanted to share music between accounts at some point but been thwarted because only one copy of iTunes with its one music library could be running at a time. Or someone has logged in behind your back when you got up to get a Coke and is now whining because iTunes is locked up in your account and can't be closed until you log in and quit the program.

But with iTunes and Mac OS X 10.3 and later, each user can have his or her own library and use iTunes even if the program's already open in another account. Users can also share music between different people on the same machine, so anybody who logs on with the Mac's Fast User-Switching feature can use shared music, just like people on the same subnet of the network can see and play shared music from an iTunes library (see below).

To set up a library or playlists for sharing, just choose iTunes → Preferences → Sharing. Turn on the checkbox

next to "Share my music," and select how much of your collection you'd like to offer up to your roommates. When other users have their iTunes preferences set to look for shared music, they'll see yours out there for the playing. You just have to make sure iTunes is open in each account that's sharing music in order to see the shared tracks.

Sharing music can get a little wacky if one account is playing a song and someone else logs in and starts playing a song in iTunes as well—you get both songs playing at once, with no way to turn off the first user's music from the second user's account. It's one way to get Elvis to duet with Usher but probably not the most listenable.

And, unfortunately for Windows XP users who are yelling "Hey! What about *our* Fast User-Switching???", these features only work on the Mac.

And if you don't want to print right there (or want to use that fancy color laser printer at work instead of your own smeary black-and-white inkjet), you can also save your document as a ready-to-print PDF or temporary file with all the text and images in place. There's also a choice of formats for black-and-white or color printers in the Print box pop-up menu.

Tip: Want to use one of your own personal photos for the cover of your CD case? Just add the artwork of your choice to a track (page 98) and when it comes time to make the case, select the track on the playlist with the personalized picture and choose File → Print → Theme: Single Cover to place your photo on the front.

Playing Songs Across a Network

If you've taken the trouble to set up a home network so your family can share a printer, an Internet connection, and so on, more treats await. With iTunes, you can share songs and playlists with up to five networked computers—Macs, PCs, or a mix of both. You could, for example, tap into your roommate's jazz collection without getting up from your desk, and she can sample the zydeco and tejano tunes from your World Beat playlists. The music you decide to share is streamed over the network to the other computer.

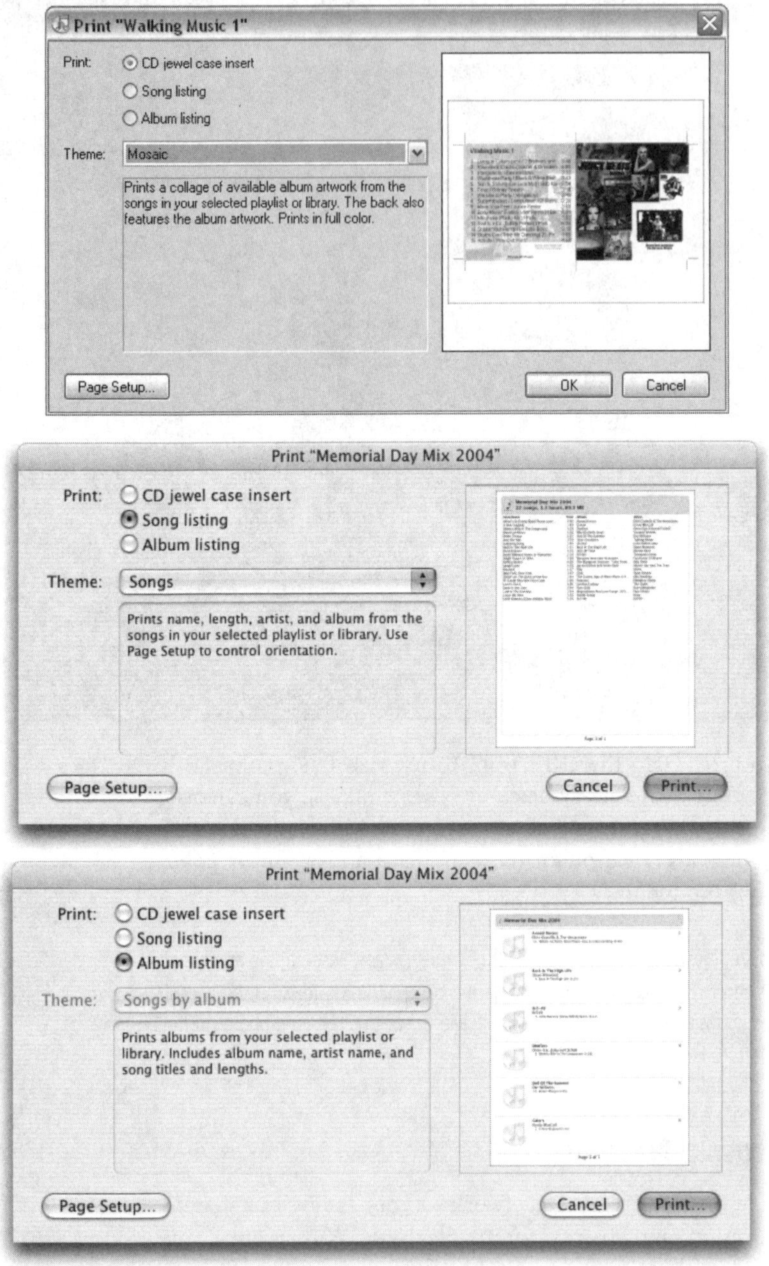

Figure 5-28:
The Print dialog box gently guides you though making a CD jewel-case insert (top), just printing out a basic list of songs (middle), or creating a catalog listing of all the albums on a mix (bottom). In Mac OS X, you can also fax a copy of your document to someone (click the Print button to get to the Mac's built-in fax option).

Note: In iTunes 4.0, you could even listen to music on Macs *elsewhere on the Internet,* as long as you knew their IP addresses (network addresses). It didn't take long for people to figure out how to exploit this feature and share music all over the Internet in sneaky ways that Apple had never intended.

In response to hysterical phone calls from the record companies, Apple removed this feature (and the Advanced → Connect to Shared Music command) in version 4.0.1. Now you can connect only to other machines on your own office or home network.

To share music across a network, the machines involved must meet a few requirements:

- The Macs on the network must use at least iTunes 4.5 and Mac OS X 10.2.4 or later. The Windows computers need iTunes 4.5 or later.

- The computers must be on the same *subnet* of the network. (If you don't know what that means, read on.)

- The iTunes Sharing preferences for each computer involved need to be configured properly.

Preparing to Share

The *subnet mask* (that is, the chunk of the network you're on) is identified by four numbers separated by periods, like this: 255.255.255.0. (Nobody ever said networking was user-friendly.)

To check the subnet number of a Macintosh, open System Preferences (under the menu) and click the Network icon. In Windows, choose Start → Control Panel, double-click the Network Connections icon, and right-click the icon for your connection. Then choose Properties from the shortcut menu. In the Properties box, click Internet Protocol, and then click Properties to see the subnet information.

Unless you are adept and agile when it comes to configuring and maintaining computer networks, this subnet information may not mean anything to you. But if all the computers on your network are connected to the same network router, odds are you'll all probably be on the same subnet. Computers behind different routers, say, across a big office complex network, probably won't be on the same subnet, so you may not be able to share your music with the guy in the accounting department after all.

Sharing Your Own Music

To "publish" your tunes to the network, choose iTunes → Preferences (Mac) or Edit → Preferences (Windows) and click the Sharing icon. Turn on "Share my music" (see Figure 5-29). You can choose to share your entire collection or just selected playlists.

Whatever you type in the Shared Name box in the Sharing preferences will show up in your friend's iTunes Source list. You can also require a password as a key to

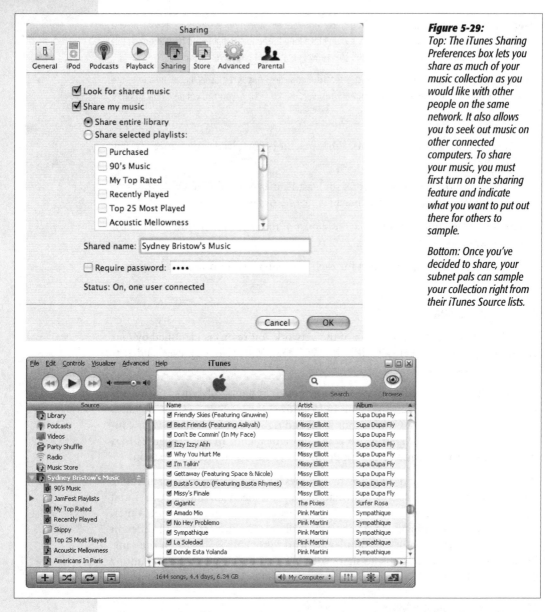

Figure 5-29:
Top: The iTunes Sharing Preferences box lets you share as much of your music collection as you would like with other people on the same network. It also allows you to seek out music on other connected computers. To share your music, you must first turn on the sharing feature and indicate what you want to put out there for others to sample.

Bottom: Once you've decided to share, your subnet pals can sample your collection right from their iTunes Source lists.

your own music library—a handy feature if you feel that your colleagues mooch off of you quite enough in other areas of life.

You can share AAC, MP3, AIFF, WAV, Apple Lossless files, and radio station links with your network buddies but not Audible files. And sharing means "streaming" here. You can listen to shared music, but you can't burn someone else's music files to a CD, copy them to an iPod, or add them to your own library.

Finally, remember that songs bought from the iTunes Music Store can play on a maximum of five machines. If you want to listen to such a song across the network, one that hasn't been authorized on your computer, you must first enter the Apple account name and user password that was used to purchase the song.

Listening to Someone Else's Tunes

It's easy to listen to somebody else's music collection; once it's been shared, their iTunes libraries generally appear right in your Source list, labeled with whatever name your benevolent buddy has chosen for the shared collection. (See Figure 5-29, bottom.)

Double-click the desired song to fire it up and play through your computer's speakers. (If your pal has put a password on the shared collection, you'll have to type that in before you can listen.)

Tip: Want to know if a certain song is shared? Select the title and press ⌘-I (Mac) or Ctrl+I (Windows), or choose File → Get Info. If the word "Remote" appears next to Kind in the Summary area, you're looking at a shared file.

If the other person's tunes aren't showing up, choose iTunes → Preferences (Mac) or Edit → Preferences (Windows) and click the Sharing icon. In the Sharing Preferences box (Figure 5-29, top), turn on "Look for shared music."

GEM IN THE ROUGH

Policing iTunes with Parental Controls

If you have small children and would like to restrict access to some of the things they can see in the iTunes Source list, the Parental Controls preferences gives you The Power. With Parental Controls turned on, you can prevent the icons for Podcasts, Radio, the Music Store, or Shared Music from appearing in the Source list to keep them away from tiny hands and ears.

You can also bar Music Store tracks and podcasts tagged with the "Explicit" content label from being previewed, purchased, or subscribed to by anyone using this copy of iTunes for Music Store shopping sprees. To take control of the Parental Controls, open the iTunes Preferences box by choosing iTunes → Preferences → Parental on a Mac or Edit → Preferences → Parental on a Windows machine.

Once you get inside the Parental Controls settings (see Figure 5-30), you can turn on the checkboxes to disable the features you want to lose. To make sure those pesky, computer-savvy kids don't sneak right back in and enable the features you've just disabled, click the lock icon at the bottom of the box to make iTunes request the computer administrator's password for any additional changes.

You need to have Windows XP or at least Mac OS X 10.3 in order to slap a password lock on the Parental Controls controls; Windows 2000 and Mac OS X 10.2.8 can only hide the items, but someone small and sneaky could come along and make them visible again in this same Preferences box ·because these older operating systems don't demand a password to make changes to the Parental Controls.

But, remember, disabling Podcasts in the Parental Controls area not only prevents the icon from showing up in the Source list, it prevents *you* from subscribing to and downloading any podcasts yourself.

Figure 5-30:
One big Parental Controls bummer: Disabling Podcasts in the Parental Controls area not only prevents the icon from showing up in your kid's Source list, it prevents you from subscribing to and downloading any podcasts yourself.

Turning Off Music Sharing

If you want a little privacy for your music collection, you can easily turn off the Sharing function. Just go back to the iTunes Preferences box (Figure 5-29) and click the Sharing icon. Turn off the "Share my music" box and then click OK to disable the feature until the next time you're feeling generous. Your playlists are no longer visible to other people on the network.

You can also temporarily disconnect your computer from a shared playlist by going to the bottom corner of the iTunes window and clicking the Eject button. (The Eject button changes its icon depending on what you're connected to; it allows you to unhitch an iPod, pop out a disc, or unlink your computer from a shared music library.)

CHAPTER 6

iPod Multimedia

You can listen to more than just music on your iPod; you can also listen to podcasts, audio books, recorded radio shows, and even certain magazines and newspapers read aloud for your listening pleasure. And if you've got a color-screen iPod (including the Nano), you can up your multimedia arsenal even further because you can use your iPod to look at digital photos on the go. If you have one of those video-enabled iPods, you can watch music videos, animated shorts, and TV shows from the iTunes Store, plus film trailers, home movies, and other digital videos in your collection. This chapter explores the iPod's other treats for your ears and eyes.

Watching Video

In October 2005, a longtime industry rumor came true: Apple finally launched the iPod's video-playing era. These new models (the fifth generation, if you're keeping score at home) can play videos on their gorgeous color screens, so you can while away office lunch hours, breaks between classes, and interminable bus rides by watching TV shows in the palm of your hand. This section shows you where to find video files and how to juggle them between computer and iPod, as well as how you can convert digital movies for screening on your own Shirt Pocket Cinema.

Finding Video for the iPod

When Apple rolled out the new video iPods, it made sure to serve up some video *content* for folks to play on the newfangled devices. As explained in Chapter 7, the iTunes Music Store now sells music videos, classic Pixar cartoons, and selected television shows, all for about $2 apiece. The store also hosts a collection of video podcasts for download.

In addition to video from the iTunes Music Store, you can add your own video files to your iPod, as long as the clips are in a compatible format, like the popular QuickTime and MPEG-4. You can tell if a video file is iPoddable by its file extension: Look for .mov, .mp4, or .m4v. Remember, though, that you can convert video from many other formats for iPod play, as explained on page 139. To add video files to the iPod, add them to iTunes first, just as you would a music track (page 101), and then use one of several synching options (page 139) to copy them over to the player.

Tip: The official movie site of many an upcoming film now features a downloadable trailer formatted just for the iPod. Browse through some of the links at *www.apple.com/trailers* to see what film previews are listed, and then click through to the film's own Web site to see if they offer an iPod download.

Of course, not long after the video iPod was unveiled, the hunt was on across the Web to find downloadable bits of video that would work on this fab new player. And after sitting next to geeks on commuter trains who had long ago figured out how to rip their *Babylon 5* DVD box sets and play the shows on their Sony PlayStation Portable (better known as the PSP), more than a few iPod owners began to explore how to do the same type of video conversion. (If you're interested in learning how, see page 139.)

Using Video Files on the iPod

Videos you buy from the iTunes Music Store (and other iTunes-friendly videos) appear in the Videos menu of your iPod after you copy them onto the device. To watch a music video, TV show, or other clip, scroll through the various Video submenus, (Video Playlists, Movies, Music Videos, TV Shows, and Video Podcasts) until you find something you want to watch.

Say you want to watch something in your Movies menu. As shown in Figure 6-1, you select Movies from the main Videos menu. The next screen lists all the files tagged as Movies on your iPod. (Page 105 explains how you can label and tag music and movie files on the iTunes side of the fence before you move them to the iPod.) Scroll to the movie file you want to watch and then press the Play/Pause button to start the show.

Here are the main iPod playback controls you use when viewing videos:

• **Press the Play/Pause button again to pause the program.** Pausing a video on the iPod works just like hitting Pause on a VCR or TiVo so you can go get more Doritos. Press the button again to pick up where you left off. (If your video files won't hold their place, see the tip on page 158 to help them remember their playback position.)

• **To increase or decrease the video's volume, run your finger along the scroll wheel.** This volume adjustment feature works just like it does to control the sound levels when listening to music files.

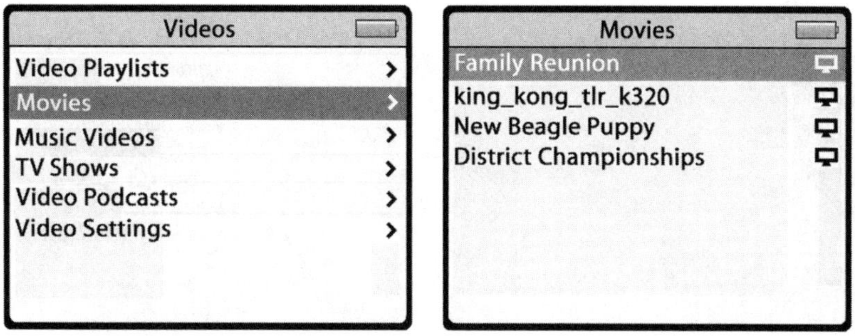

Figure 6-1:
Left: The Videos menu on the fifth-generation iPod shows all types of moving pictures you've stored on the device. Scroll to the category you want to peruse, press the Select button, and pick a file to watch from the listings.

- To fast-forward or rewind through part of a video, tap the Select button. A time code bar appears along the bottom of the screen. Use the scroll wheel to advance or retreat through the scene.

When your video ends, the iPod flips you back to the menu you were last on before you started watching your show. If you want to bail out before the movie is over, press the Menu button.

Note: Some video files come in a letterboxed format that create a thin, horizontal strip of picture across your iPod's display. If you're not into widescreen HamsterVision, visit the Video Settings area of the Videos menu (seen on the left side of Figure 6-1) and change the Widescreen option to Off. The sides of your video may get squished as the picture expands to fill the iPod's screen, but you can see the action in the center of the screen a bit better.

Once you've got some video files on your iPod, you're not limited to just watching them on the small screen, either. Page 147 has the details on how to display video and photo slideshows stored on your iPod on your TV screen with an AV cable.

Converting Your Home Movies

All those home movies you edited on your computer, or dubbed into digital files from old tapes, can also find new life on your iPod. You simply export a copy of each file as an MPEG-4 or QuickTime-compatible movie with a screen resolution of 320×240 pixels, which is the size that works best on the iPod. Most popular consumer video-editing programs for Windows, like Pinnacle Studio and Ulead's Video Studio, can export movie files to the MPEG-4 format.

Mac OS X fans who've got iMovie HD can export their film projects right out of that program to the iPod 320×240 format from the File menu. To do so, with your finished iMovie project on screen, choose File → Share. Click the QuickTime tab in the resulting box, choose Expert Settings from the "Compress movie for" pop-up menu, and then click Share.

In the next dialog box (Figure 6-2), choose "Movie to iPod (320×240)" from the Export menu, and then pick a place to save the file. Click Save, and then get a snack—the video compression usually takes several minutes.

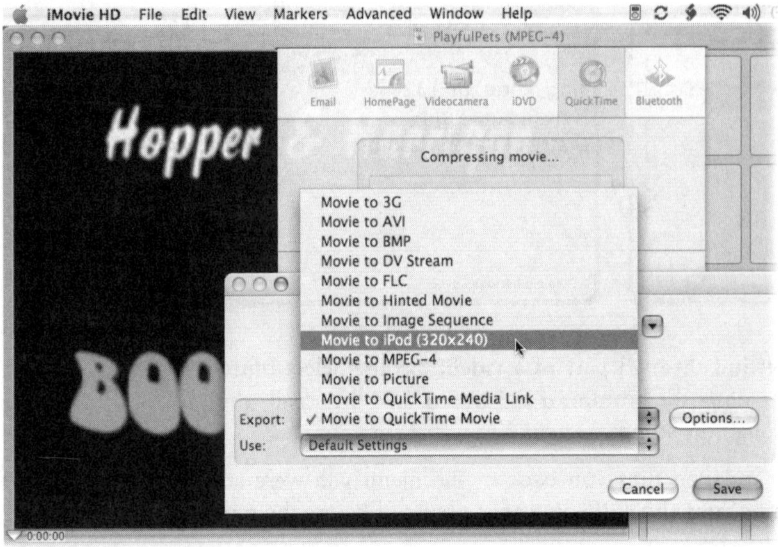

Figure 6-2:
With iMovie HD, you can export your cinematic masterpiece right into a version that both plays and fits on your iPod's screen. (Overpriced popcorn and stale Goobers not included.)

This action saves a copy of your movie to an iPod-ready file and deposits it on your computer's desktop (or wherever you saved it). Next, just drag the new movie file into the iTunes library or use the File → Add to Library menu command to get the movie into iTunes. Once you connect your iPod, you can drag the movie over to the player's icon in the Source list to add it, or just sit back and let the iPod automatically update itself as per your sync settings (page 139).

Tip: You can use iTunes itself to convert some videos into an iTunes-friendly format (make sure you're using at least iTunes version 6.0.2.) To do so, add the video to your iTunes library, right-click the track's name, and then, from the shortcut menu, choose "Convert Selection for iPod."

The program grinds away, converting your videos into H.264 mini-movies (page 104) that are 320 pixels wide, which is just the right width for iPodvision. Depending on your computer's power, it may take a while for iTunes to plow through the conversion, but you'll see a progress bar in the status display window giving you an idea of how much farther the program has to go.

If you have a copy of QuickTime 7 Pro on your computer, there's also a menu option for iPod export. Just open the movie you want to convert with QuickTime 7 Pro, then choose File → Export and select "Move to iPod (320×240)" from the menu in the Export box.

Note: QuickTime 7 Pro is the full version of the QuickTime player program that comes with iTunes. The Pro version works on Mac OS X and Windows 2000 or XP, and costs $30 at *www.apple.com/quicktime*.

Video-conversion programs

A flurry of programs designed to convert all kinds of video files into iPod movies surfaced in the video iPod's wake. In addition to the commercial programs, several shareware titles also appeared. Here are a few:

- **iVideoToGo.** InterVideo, maker of DVD copying and playback software, has a $30 conversion program for Windows that converts DVD movies and just about any other video format for iPod compatibility (*www.intervideo.com*).

- **PQ DVD to iPod Video Converter.** This $35 program for Windows converts TiVo recordings, DVD video, DiVX, Windows Media Video, RealMedia and AVI files to the iPod's video format (*www.pqdvd.com/dvd-to-ipod-video-converter.html*).

- **Videora iPod Converter.** With this freeware, you can gather up all those .avi and .mpg video clips stashed away on your PC and turn them into iPod video clips. Find it at *www.videora.com/en-us/Converter/iPod*.

- **Podner.** Mac OS X owners can convert their movies, even those in .avi and DiVx formats, with this $10 shareware program (*www.splasm.com/products/productpodner.html*).

- **HandBrake.** Mac folks wishing to convert DVD movies and other files for the iPod quickly adopted this easy-to-use bit of freeware. You can get it at *http://handbrake.m0k.org* and various shareware archives around the Web.

If you already use a TV tuner card and your computer's hard drive to record television shows with products like SnapStream's Beyond TV ($150 at *www.snapstream.com*) or Instant TV from ADS Technologies (prices vary; *www.adstech.com*), you should be able to export and convert these recordings to iPod-ready files with one of the above programs as well. If you're on a Mac, you can use the EyeTV EZ for Mac from Elgato Systems ($150 at *www.elgato.com*) and export 320 × 240 MPEG-4 files right from the EyeTV software.

Tip: TiVo, the wily digital video recorder that reads your mind and records your television shows, is also getting into the iPod video picture. The company is working to enhance its TiVoToGo software (which moves recorded shows off the TiVo box and onto the Windows computer), so it can also move recorded shows right onto the iPod. TiVo also clams to be developing a Mac version of the software. Visit *www.tivo.com* for more information.

Synching Videos

Chapter 2 gives you the lowdown on synching your music files, which is probably the first type of entertainment most new iPod owners attempt. Synchronizing the video files in your collection works the same way, except you click a different tab in the iPod Preferences box (Figure 6-3) to get to those settings. Once you're there, just click to select your preferred synchronization mode.

Ripping (Off) Your DVDs

Plenty of programs let you yank a DVD movie off its disc and convert it into an MPEG-4 file for the iPod. But using these tools puts you in a legal gray area, as you're technically violating the disc's copyright protection technology, which is protected under the Digital Millennium Copyright Act of 1998. Commercial DVDs are typically encrypted to prevent anyone from copying the video files from the disc and passing them around. (If these legal matters intrigue you, give a read to *www.copyright.gov/legislation/dmca.pdf*.)

Many DVD owners, however, feel that since they paid for the disc, they own the right to do whatever they want with

it, including play it on an iPod. Like MP3 and AAC files encoded from commercial compact discs, many people feel that copying DVD movies falls under the fair-use rights consumers are entitled to if they legally purchase the work.

Although the movie industry has yet to go after programmers writing DVD decryption and conversion programs with a Napster-style smackdown lawsuit, it may still happen. In any case, if you convert your own commercial DVD movies for use on your iPod, keeping them between you and the iPod is much more ethical than dispensing someone else's copyrighted material on the Internet.

Figure 6-3:
Once inside the iPod's Preferences box, click the Videos tab, and then click what you'd like to synchronize from your collection. For example, you can have the iPod suck down just your movie trailers and TV shows, if those are the only videos you want to watch on the go.

One thing to remember, though: If you have the iPod set to manually update your music (page 47), you have to likewise manually copy your video files by dragging the ones you want to watch over to the iPod's icon in the iTunes Source list. If you have the iPod set to automatically update everything, or to just update selected playlists, you can also choose to automatically update all or just some of your video playlists as well.

Tip: Got a friend or a relative who wants an iPod but doesn't want to set it up, rip any music, or tinker with an iTunes library? Send your pal to LoadPod (*www.loadpod.com*), a company that specializes in filling up new iPods with the CD collections of new owners who are too busy (or too nervous) to do it themselves. The company recently added a DVD-conversion service as well for the owners of video iPods who'd like to bring along mini-movies on their travels.

Displaying Photos

So, you've done it. You, the Devotee of Displaying Digital Photos (or perhaps you're the Coveter of the Color Screen), have ponied up the extra cash and purchased an iPod Photo, a video iPod, or iPod Nano with a vibrant color screen. No longer must you haul out crumbling photo albums, since you can show off your shots on the iPod. And, if you have a full-size iPod, you can hook it up to the television with an AV cable and present your pictures on the big screen.

What You Need for iPod Photos

In addition to a computer that meets the system requirements for iTunes 6 (or later) and your iPod model, you need a few other things to get your pictures syncing up a storm:

• **Compatible photo management software for the Mac or Windows—or a folder of photos on your hard drive.** The iPod and Nano can sync with several popular photo programs that you may already have. On the Mac, there's iPhoto 4.0.3 or later. Windows mavens can grab pictures from Adobe Photoshop Album or the more versatile Adobe Photoshop Elements.

You can also transfer pictures from a folder of photos on your computer, like the iPhoto Library folder for those who are a few iPhoto versions behind, or My Pictures on the Windows side of the fence.

• **Digital photographs in the proper format.** Most of the common photo formats used by digital cameras, Web pages, and email programs are acceptable to iTunes, along with a few others:

— On the Mac, you can use JPG and GIF files, as well as images in the PICT, TIFF, BMP, PNG, JPG2000, SGI, and PSD formats.

— In Windows, JPG, GIF, TIF, BMP, PSD, SGI, and PNG files work for the iPod.

Note: You can't pull in pictures from a locked volume like one of those photo-stuffed compact discs the drugstores give you when they process your film. To move those pictures to your iPod, import them into your photo program of choice or copy them to the photo folder on your hard drive first.

Getting Pictures onto the iPod

Okay, so you've got the right iPod, the right version of iTunes, and a bunch of pictures in iTunes-friendly formats on your hard drive. How do those photos get from your hard drive to the iPod? They get there like the music does—through iTunes.

But first, you should set up your iTunes preferences to copy the photos you want to carry around, like so:

1. **Connect the iPod to your Mac or PC with its cable.**

   Once the iPod shows up in the iTunes Source list, click its icon to select it.

2. **At the bottom of the iTunes window, click the iPod Options button.**

   The Preferences box appears, as shown in Figure 6-4, right.

3. **In the iPod Preferences panel, click Photos.**

   To have the iPod automatically synchronize pictures the way it synchronizes your music, select "Synchronize photos from" in the Photos box, and then choose your photo program's name (like iPhoto or Photoshop Elements) from the pop-up menu.

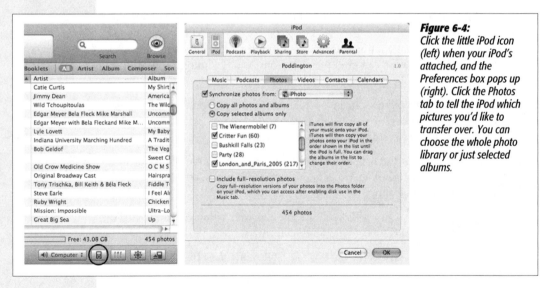

Figure 6-4:
Click the little iPod icon (left) when your iPod's attached, and the Preferences box pops up (right). Click the Photos tab to tell the iPod which pictures you'd like to transfer over. You can choose the whole photo library or just selected albums.

If you don't use any of these programs and just want to copy over a folder of photos on your hard drive, select "Choose folder" from the pop-up menu instead and then navigate to the desired folder. You can sync just the photos in your chosen folder, or include the photos tucked away in folders *inside* your chosen folder, too.

Select the "Copy all photos and albums" option if you want every single image in your photo program's library to get hauled over to the iPod. (If you don't want those bachelorette-party snaps or other embarrassing pictures to get copied, opt for the "Copy selected albums only" choice and then pick just the particular collections you want from your image program.)

Now, whenever you connect the iPod, it syncs the photo groups you've designated and also picks up any new pictures you've added since you last connected it. During the process, iTunes displays an "Optimizing photos…" message in its status window, as shown in Figure 6-5.

Figure 6-5:
When you synchronize your pictures to the iPod, iTunes optimizes them so they'll look extra good on the TV screen.

Don't let the term "optimizing" scare you: iTunes hasn't taken it upon itself to touch up your photographic efforts. The program is simply creating versions of your pictures that look good blown up to TV-screen size and tucking away the copies away on your hard drive before it adds them to the iPod.

Note: Although you can manually drag your music files to the iPod to add fresh material when you see it in the iTunes Source list, you can't add picture files or photo folders that way. Unless you have the iPod Camera Connector (page 328) jacked into your digital camera, you have to transfer the images you want using iTunes synchronization.

Copying photos at full resolution

When iTunes optimizes your photos for iPoddification, it streamlines the images a bit for faster travel instead of copying the big, full-resolution files. But if you want, you can copy the full-size photo files to transfer them to another computer—good news if you're a professional photographer.

Note: As you can tell from Figure 6-6, you can sync the pictures between only one computer (or user account) and your iPod at a time.

To snag the big pictures, connect the iPod and select it in the iTunes Source list. Make sure you've set up the iPod as a hard disk (page 204). Click the iPod Preferences box (Figure 6-4, left), and then click Photos and turn on the "Include full-resolution photos" checkbox. After you sync, full-resolution copies of the photos sit happily in the Photos folder on the iPod's hard drive when you connect it to another computer. (The Photos folder also has a subfolder called Thumbs that's full of iPod-optimized images all scrunched up in special .ithmb files, but you really can't do much with them in this form aside from admiring the file extension.)

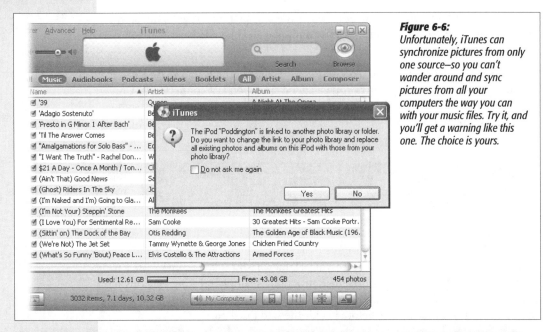

Figure 6-6:
Unfortunately, iTunes can synchronize pictures from only one source—so you can't wander around and sync pictures from all your computers the way you can with your music files. Try it, and you'll get a warning like this one. The choice is yours.

GEM IN THE ROUGH

Album Art on the iPod

For many people, the glory days of album art may have passed when the 12-inch vinyl record finally succumbed to the invasion of the compact disc. The multiple personalities on the cover of *Sgt. Pepper's Lonely Hearts Club Band* or the sleek simplicity on the front of a Fleetwood Mac album just don't have as much impact when shrunk down to a CD cover size—or smaller.

But even at minuscule size, the album artwork is helpful for quickly recognizing the source of a particular song, and that same artwork that comes with each and every track you buy from the iTunes Music Store can now be displayed in glorious living color alongside the song information on the iPod or iPod Nano's color screen. Tap the Select button while the song is playing and the iPod will display a full-screen version of the art. And it's not just album artwork that shows up when the songs play—it's any image you've attached to your song files that will show up on the iPod screen.

If you want your iPod to show off your artwork as you play your tunes, connect it to your computer and click its icon when it shows up in the iTunes Source list. At the bottom of the window, click the iPod Preferences button (it's the one with the iPod icon). When the Preferences box pops up, click the iPod icon or tab if it's not selected already. On the Music tab, turn on the checkbox next to "Display album artwork on your iPod." Click OK to close the iPod Preferences box.

If you get tired of all the extra visual stimulation on the iPod's screen, you can always connect the player and reverse the process. And don't worry—ditching your art on the iPod doesn't strip it out of your iTunes files, so you'll still be able to see those Barbie-sized album covers when you crank up your desktop playlists in iTunes.

Viewing Pictures on the iPod

Once you've got those photos freed from the confines of your computer, you'll probably want to show them off to all your pals. To get to the goods, choose Photos → Photo Library on the iPod's main screen. Or, if you opted for different photo albums when you set up your synchronization preferences (page 142), scroll to the name of the album you want to view and press the round Select button.

The iPod pops up a screen filled with tiny versions of the pictures in the group you just selected (Figure 6-7). Use the scroll wheel to maneuver the little yellow highlight box, and then zoom along the rows until you get to the picture you want to see. If you have hundreds of pee-wee pix to plow through, tap the Previous and Next buttons to advance or retreat by the screenful.

Figure 6-7:
When you open a photo library or album on the iPod Photo, you get a screen full of thumbnail versions (well, a chihuahua's thumbnail, perhaps) of your photos. Scroll to the one you want to see, and then press the Select button to call up a full-sized version on the iPod's screen.

Highlight the photo and press the Select button to call up a larger version that fills the iPod screen. Press the Previous and Next buttons on the click wheel to move forward or backward through the pictures in the album. Press the Menu button to go back to the screen of tiny photos.

Preparing the iPod for a Slideshow

Setting up a photo slideshow takes all that clicking work out of your hands and frees you to admire the pictures without distraction. To run a slideshow on the iPod itself, you need to set up a few things, like how long each photo displays and what music accompanies your trip to Disneyland.

Start by choosing Photos → Slideshow Settings. You'll see a whole slew of options to shape your slideshow experience, all of which are listed below and explained in detail on page 26.

- Use the Time Per Slide menu to set the amount of time each photo is displayed on screen, from 2 to 20 seconds. You can also choose to move to each new image manually with a tap of the click wheel.

- Use the Music menu to pick one of the iPod's playlists to serve as a soundtrack for your slideshow, if you want one. You may even want to compose a playlist in iTunes just to use with a particular slideshow. If you've already got music assigned to the photo album in iPhoto, choose the From iPhoto option at the top of the menu.

- As with your music, you can also repeat and shuffle the order of your photos. You can also add fancy Hollywood-style scene transitions by choosing Photos → Slideshow Settings → Transitions. Pick from several dramatic photo-changing styles, including "Push across" and "Wipe from center."

- To make sure the slideshow shows up on the iPod's screen, set the TV Out setting (toward the bottom of the screen) to Off, which keeps the signal in the iPod. (Nano owners don't have to worry about this step.) Or you can select Ask, so that each time you start a slideshow, the iPod politely inquires whether you intend to run your photos on the big or small screen.

Playing the slideshow

Once you've got your settings just the way you want them, select the album or photo you want to start with, and then press the Play/Pause button on the click wheel to start the show. Press the Play/Pause button again to temporarily stop the show; press it again to continue.

Your choice of music, transitions, and time per slide all match what you chose in the Slideshow settings, but if you get impatient, you can also use the Previous and Next buttons on the click wheel to manually move things along.

Tip: Want to know how much of your iPod's drive is filled up with your music, videos, and photos? Just go to the main screen and choose Settings → About to see a list of just how many songs, how many videos, and how many photos you have—and how many gigabytes you have left.

Displaying Photos and Videos on a TV

Music is more fun when you share it—see Chapter 10 for a variety of ways to share your tunes on any iPod model—and so is digital photography. With a photo slideshow, you can take your friends on a personalized tour of your best shots, complete with a musical soundtrack. And with the right hookup, you can even watch your iPod's digital videos on a TV set, making the iPod the tiniest TiVo ever.

Connecting the iPod to the television set

To get those iPodded photos and movies dancing across your TV screen, you must connect the two together with a special AV cable for the iPod. This cable (shown in action in Figure 6-8) has a miniplug connector on one end and a three-headed bouquet of silver tipped RCA-style connectors on the other. You can buy the iPod AV cable for $19 in stores that sell iPod merchandise or at *http://store.apple.com.*

Figure 6-8:
One quick cable connection and your iPod is ready to take over the room. The stereo miniplug end of the iPod AV cable goes into the iPod's headphones port or the Line Out jack on the back of the dock. The three-headed, color-coded end of the cable plugs into the corresponding color-coded input jacks on the TV set, as shown here.

If you look closely at the RCA end of the cable, you'll see a different color on the back of each plug: Red, White, and Yellow. These tints aren't there to jazz up an otherwise drab white cable with a splash of color, though. They actually correspond to the input ports on your television set.

On traditional RCA cables, here's what each color means:

- **Red** is the right-channel sound signal.
- **White** is the left-channel sound signal, but it also carries mono sound.
- **Yellow** is the video signal.

Most television sets manufactured in the past few years have a set of these tri-color jacks somewhere. If you're lucky, the manufacturer put them on the front of the set so you don't tangle yourself in the wires and dusty tumbleweeds behind your home entertainment altar.

Take your special iPod AV cable and match up the colored plugs to the colored jacks on your TV set. Connect the stereo miniplug end of the cable to the iPod, either to the headphone port or to the Line Out jack on the back of the iPod's dock. Your iPod is now connected to your TV.

Apple strongly recommends that you use its own shiny, white AV cable that happens to cost $19—and that you not use a cheaper cable from, say, Radio Shack. Apple claims that most other cables aren't compatible with the iPod. Frugal and persistent iPod owners quickly proved otherwise, finding ways to pipe iPod video into their TV using non-Apple cables by switching around the colored plugs that transmit the iPod's audio and video signals. One popular workaround goes like so:

- Red cable plug into yellow TV jack.

- Yellow cable plug into white TV jack.

- White cable plug into red TV jack.

AV cables from different manufacturers may behave differently, though, so it may take more tri-color fiddling around to get the iPod's picture on the TV.

Note: Some television sets have only two ports—white and yellow. The white jack carries a mono sound signal, which is how you can get audio *and* video on one of those two-jack televisions.

Using the S-Video option

Apple has sold a variety of white plastic docks for its iPods since 2003, and now offers a $39 Universal iPod Dock available with audio and S-Video ports on the back. The S-Video jack is the round one on the right side of the dock (Figure 6-9). If you already know what S-Video is, you're probably an AV geek with a complete set of cables for every occasion. For the uninitiated, S-Video stands for Super Video. It does the same things as a standard AV cable, but many people believe it gives a clearer, sharper picture.

Figure 6-9:
That round port on the back of the iPod dock is the S-Video jack. When connected to the S-Video jack on a television set with an appropriate S-Video cable (not included with the iPod), a superior picture often results.

So, if you have an S-Video port on your television, you can use an S-Video cable to connect the S-Video port on the TV to the S-Video port on the iPod's dock. Purchase an S-Video cable at your local electronics store, since Apple doesn't include one with the iPod—or with the dock for that matter.

The S-Video cable carries only the video signal to the TV, so if you want to groove to your tunes while you show off your photos, you need to make an audio connection between the two units as well. You can use the red and white plugs on the iPod AV cable to carry the sound—leave the yellow video plug unconnected since you're getting your image onscreen through the S-Video cable.

You can also buy a separate audio cable from Apple to run from the iPod to the TV. One option that solves all your AV dilemmas here is the Monster iTV Link cable (Figure 6-10), which sells for $40 at *http://store.apple.com*. It gives you S-Video and audio in one.

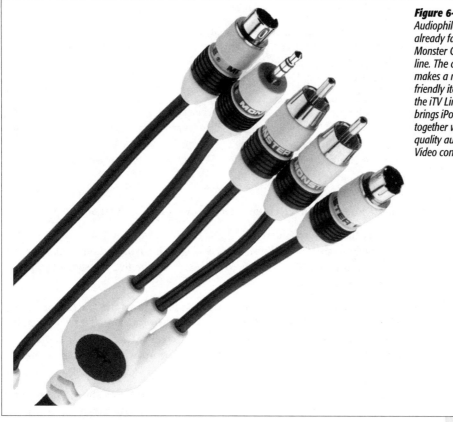

Figure 6-10:
Audiophiles are probably already familiar with Monster Cable's product line. The company also makes a number of iPod-friendly items, including the iTV Link Cable that brings iPod and television together with high-quality audio and S-Video connections.

Tip: Got a box full of old Mac equipment up in the attic but no S-Video cable? Take a look for the old-style Mac ADB cables with the little round connectors. These cords, which used to link keyboard to computer back before USB came along, can pinch-hit for an S-Video cable.

Playing Your Slideshow or Videos on the TV

Once you've linked your color screen iPod to your TV, you're almost ready to start the show. You just need to adjust a few more things on the iPod, as follows:

1. **Choose Photos → Slideshow Settings → TV Out → On.**

   The On option tells the iPod to send the slideshow out to the TV screen instead of playing it on its own screen. (You can also set it to Ask, if you want the iPod to pester you about what screen to use when the time comes.) For video output, choose Videos → Video Settings → TV Out → On.

2. **Select your local television broadcast standard.**

   If you're in North America or Japan, choose Photos → Slideshow Settings → TV Signal → NTSC.

   If you're in Europe or Australia, choose Photos → Slideshow Settings → TV Signal → PAL.

   If you're in an area not listed above, check your television's manual to see what standard it uses or search the Web for "world television standards." If you're working with video here instead of photos, select your TV signal in Videos → Video Settings.

Note: NTSC stands for National Television System Committee, and PAL is short for Phase Alternating Line. The main difference between the two standards is the number of lines that comprise the onscreen picture: NTSC uses 525 lines on screen to make up the picture, while PAL uses 625 lines. PAL images are generally sharper and better looking compared to NTSC, much to the dismay of Australians vacationing in the United States.

---

3. **Turn on your TV and select the video input source for the iPod.**

   You select the input for the iPod's signal the same way you tell your TV to show the signal from the DVD player or VCR. Typically, you press the Input or Display button on your TV's remote to change from the live TV signal to the new video source.

Now, cue up a slideshow on the iPod (page 146) and press the Play/Pause button. Your glorious, breathtaking photographs—scored to the sounds of your selected music, if you wish—appear on your television screen. (Because television screens are horizontal displays, though, vertical shots end up with black bars along the sides.)

Your preselected slideshow settings (page 26) control the show, or you can advance it manually with your thumb on the click wheel. Although just one photo at a time appears on the TV screen, if you're driving the iPod, you can see not only the current picture, but the one before it and the one after, letting you narrate your show with professional smoothness: "OK, this is Shalimar *before* we had to get her fur shaved off after the syrup incident…"

If you're showing a video, select the file you want to display on the TV from your Videos menu, and then press Play/Pause.

Presentations on Your iPod

Okay, we all know now that the iPod can display slideshows on a TV screen, right? But what about other types of slideshows, like those presentations that are an unavoidable part of daily corporate or student life?

With a little finagling, you can get your presentations up and running on the iPod, eliminating the trouble of hauling your laptop into the conference room. (And when your part of the meeting is done, you can unhook your iPod and discretely play a few rounds of Solitaire while the boring stuff continues.)

To make these portable presentations, you start by creating them in a program that can export the slide files to one of the iPod's accepted photo formats, like JPG. Both Microsoft PowerPoint for Windows and Macintosh (the presentation software favored by both third graders *and* chief marketing officers everywhere), and Keynote, Apple's own slide-making software for Mac OS X, can handle this chore.

Note: Some slides look better when exported to the iPod than others. Be prepared to fiddle with the export and font settings in either program to get the results you desire.

Microsoft PowerPoint

After you've written, designed—and, most importantly, *proofread*—your presentation in PowerPoint, you're ready to begin the steps for iPoddification.

1. **With the saved presentation on the screen, choose File → Save As.**

   This action opens the Save As dialog box.

2. **Select "JPEG File Interchange Format (*.jpg)" from the menu. Then save the JPEG files into a folder on your hard drive.**

   Make sure you're saving every slide and not just the one visible as a JPEG file. PowerPoint for Windows nags you with a message reminding you to export all your slides, but you need to click Options to get to that same setting in the Macintosh version (Figure 6-11).

3. **Connect your iPod and open its Preferences box (see page 93).**

   In the "Synchronize photos from" menu, select the folder of slides you just saved and click the Copy All Photos option.

The next time you update your iPod, the presentation slides go along for the ride. Once on the iPod, just hook it up and run it like a regular photo slideshow (page 154).

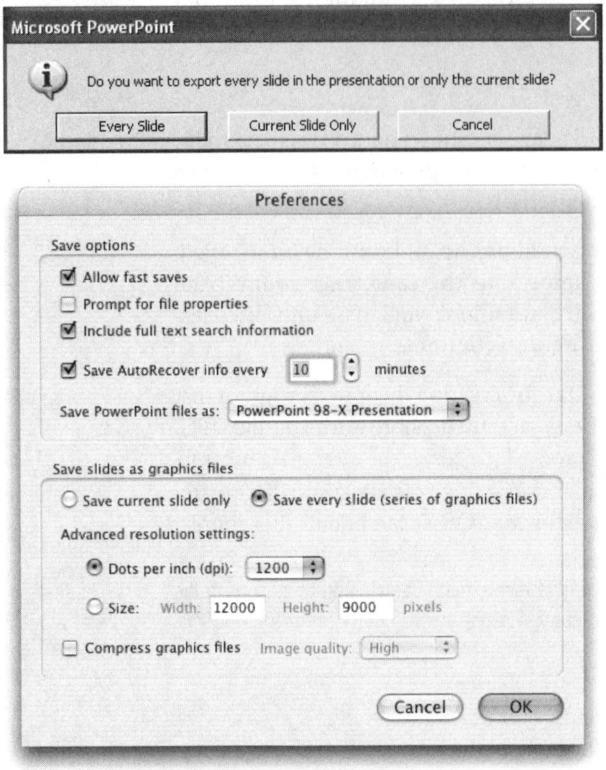

Figure 6-11:
Microsoft PowerPoint varies a bit between its Windows (top) and Macintosh (bottom) versions when it comes to saving presentations as JPEG files. Be sure to save your whole presentation as a collection of JPEG files and not just the selected slide.

Keynote

Apple's Keynote software gives Mac owners a product all their own when it comes time to whip up a presentation. The program can import PowerPoint files as well.

1. **Open a Keynote or PowerPoint file, and then choose File → Export. In the dialog box that opens, click the QuickTime button, and then click Next.**

   The next window gives you some QuickTime export options.

2. **In the Playback Control area, choose Interactive Slideshow; in the Format section, choose Full Quality, Large; finally, click Export.**

   Keynote exports the slideshow to a QuickTime file on your Mac. To play it on the iPod, you must export it to a series of JPEG files.

3. **Open the exported file in QuickTime. Then choose File → Export.**

   Another screenful of export options awaits.

4. **In the Export panel, turn on "Movie to Image Sequence," and then click the Options button next to it. Select JPEG as the format, and set "Frames per second" to 1.**

   When you're done, click OK to export the slides to a folder on your hard drive.

5. Connect your iPod and open its Preferences box (see Figure 6-4, left). Then, in the "Synchronize photos from" menu, select the folder of slides you just saved and click the "Copy all photos and albums" option.

As with PowerPoint, when you update the iPod, your converted Keynote presentation makes the leap to the player's hard drive alongside your music, photos, and other files.

iPresent It

Mac OS X offers yet another option for presentation relocation, thanks to iPresent It, an $18 shareware program that appeared on the Web less than a month after the original iPod Photo's arrival in 2004. The industrious Michael Zapp, who also has several other iPod-centric programs, created the software, which works with Mac OS X 10.3 and later. You can find it at *www.zapptek.com* or on the "Missing CD" page at *www.missingmanuals.com*.

Once you've downloaded and opened iPresent It, just click the + button in the program's window (Figure 6-12) to add a PowerPoint presentation, PDF file, or Keynote presentation exported as a PDF file to the list. Then, pick iPhoto or the folder you use for syncing your pictures to the iPod, and then click Create Slideshows. iPresent it does the rest.

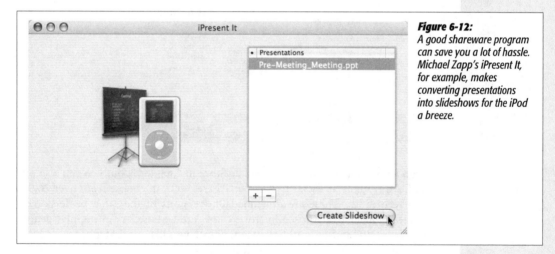

Figure 6-12:
A good shareware program can save you a lot of hassle. Michael Zapp's iPresent It, for example, makes converting presentations into slideshows for the iPod a breeze.

When you're all done presenting, hook up your iPod, fire up iPresent It, and use the minus sign (–) button to remove any presentations you never want to see again.

Listening to Audio Books

Narrated stories have been a popular form of entertainment since the days of old radio serials, but audiobooks are finding legions of new fans in the digital age. Why haul a two-pound book around when you can download the audio version to your iPod and have someone read it to you?

Audible

One of the easiest ways to get audio books and similar entertainment is from Audible.com, which offers a huge selection. You can buy Audible files right at the iTunes Music Store (Figure 6-13), where more than 11,000 titles nestle alongside all those Phish and Weezer albums.

Figure 6-13:
You don't have to surf to Audible.com to find Audible content. The iTunes Music Store has more than 11,000 Audible titles in stock. (You can find out what else is in the Store in the next chapter.)

You can learn all about the iTunes Music Store in Chapter 7, but you can also buy direct from Audible at *www.audible.com*. There, you can choose from over 26,000 spoken recordings. These are downloadable versions of the same professionally produced audio books you see in stores—the latest bestsellers in popular genres, children's books, and even old science fiction faves, like Neal Stephenson's *Snow Crash*. You'll also find periodicals such as *The New York Times* and *The Wall Street Journal*, plus speeches, lectures, and language instruction.

Buying from Audible.com

To buy audio books and other items from Audible, you need to set up an account on the company's Web site, much like you do with other e-commerce sites like Amazon and Expedia. Once you sign up, you can decide if you want to try one of Audible's subscription plans—billed monthly to your credit card—or just buy books when you feel like it. (Audible members get perks like discounts and special offers from the company, though.)

Using content from Audible on your iPod requires just three things (well, four, if you count money):

- **An Audible account.** Go to *www.audible.com* and create an Audible account for yourself, complete with address and billing information.

- **Audible's free software.** Once you create your account and log in, click the Device Center link on the main Audible page (if you didn't specify which portable player you use during your account-creation trip). The Device Center has information and software for just about every kind of MP3 player, iPods included. Mac fans can just use iTunes instead of the Audible software, but Windows people needs the small Audible Download Manager program, available on the Device Center page.

- **An iPod.** Shuffle, Nano, ancient 5-gigabyte Original iPod—any model will do.

When you go through the steps and download a book or periodical from Audible, the software you installed downloads and moves the purchase into iTunes, as shown in Figure 6-14. If you use Windows, you must install the helper program. On the Mac side, iTunes takes care of things as long as you've configured the program properly: Choose iTunes → Preferences → Advanced → General and click the Set button next to "Use iTunes for Internet music playback."

Tip: Want to jump ahead in a big long audio book on your iPod but have no idea where you'll land? Tap the Select button while the file is playing and the progress bar changes to display little vertical lines. These are chapter marks for the audio book—just nudge the scroll wheel to skip to the next chapter.

The Audible format

Audible.com files that come from its Web site (*not* from the iTunes Music Store) use the .aa file name extension. You can't convert .aa files to MP3, but you can burn them to an audio CD to play on the stereo—and, of course, you can copy them to your iPod. The files show up in iTunes just like any other track in your library (Figure 6-15), but you must type in your Audible account name and password in order to first use them.

Audible files are copy-protected, so certain limits apply. For example, you can play Audible tracks on three different Windows-based computers or two Macs. You can use Audible on two different iPods, but burn it only once to a CD.

Note: Audio books and other spoken-word files purchased through the iTunes Music Store come in a copy-protected version of the AAC format with the file extension .m4b and have different usage rules and rights, as explained in the next chapter.

Otherwise, audible files work just like plain old audio files. The iPod even remembers where in the audio book you stopped listening, so you can pick up where you left off. Better yet, these little electronic bookmarks get synchronized between iTunes and iPod, so if you're listening to a chapter of a book on your iPod while

---

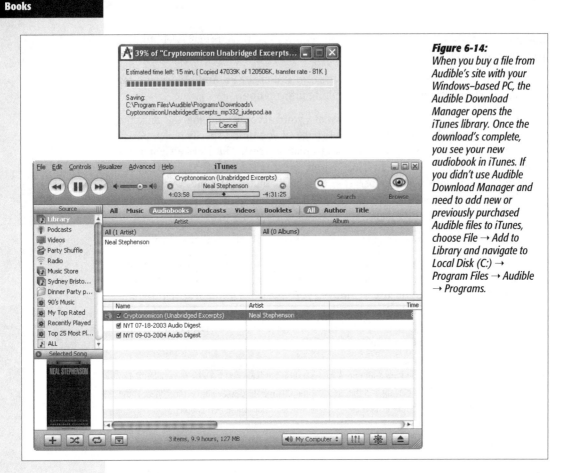

Figure 6-14:
When you buy a file from Audible's site with your Windows–based PC, the Audible Download Manager opens the iTunes library. Once the download's complete, you see your new audiobook in iTunes. If you didn't use Audible Download Manager and need to add new or previously purchased Audible files to iTunes, choose File → Add to Library and navigate to Local Disk (C:) → Program Files → Audible → Programs.

walking home from work, you can connect the iPod to your computer to transfer the bookmark. Then you can continue listening at your desk, in iTunes, without missing a sentence.

Most recordings from Audible.com come in a variety of sound resolutions, from low-fi, AM radio-like sound to a really good MP3 quality. Once you set up an Audible account, you can specify that your audio player is an iPod, and the site will offer you a choice of compatible resolutions when you check out. The resolutions that work on the iPod are Audible's Formats 2, 3, and 4. The higher the number, the better the audio quality—which also means a bigger file to download and hog up your hard-drive space.

Audio Books on the iPod Shuffle

Don't let its featherweight form factor fool you—the iPod Shuffle has enough memory inside to store and play your favorite audio books from Audible and iTunes. But because the Shuffle is in its own little world compared to the rest of iPoddom, keep a couple things in mind when using your spoken-word files on this flash-memory player:

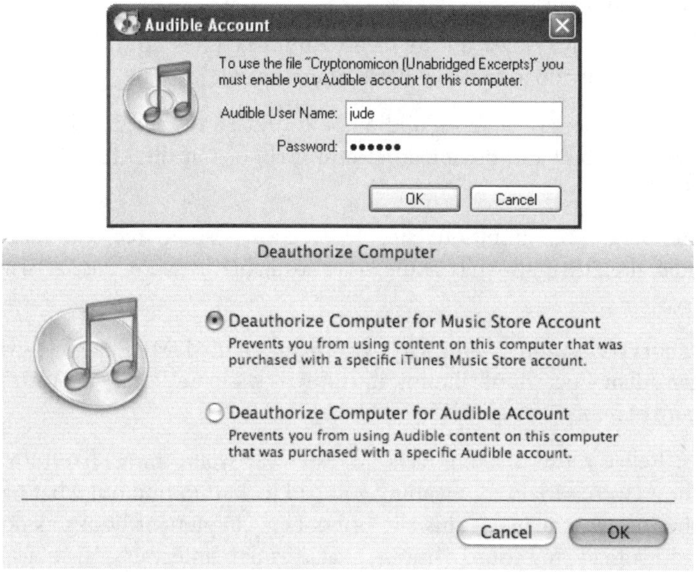

Figure 6-15:
If you've maxed out the number of computers you can authorize to play Audible content, you must deauthorize one of the existing machines before adding a new one. You do so the same way you authorize or deauthorize a computer for iTunes Music Store purchases: In iTunes, choose Advanced → Deauthorize Computer (bottom).

- **Add audio books manually.** To listen to an audio book from Audible or the iTunes Music Store on an iPod Shuffle, you must drag the book file onto the player while it's plugged into your computer. The Autofill feature in iTunes doesn't snag audio books for you.

- **Don't set the Shuffle to shuffle.** Move the slider on the back of the iPod Shuffle to the "play in order" setting (page 64) to hear your audio books. Some book plots are hard enough to follow when they *are* in order, but the StickPod saves you the potential confusion—when the shuffle setting is on, the player skips audio books and just plays your music tracks.

UP TO SPEED (LITERALLY)

Adjusting the Speed of the Read

A nice, long audio book is a great way to spend time, but sometimes you want to listen faster than the narrator is speaking. Or sometimes, you wish he'd slow down.

If you bought your iPod in 2004 or later, you can take this matter into your own hands and adjust the speed. (Sorry, owners of older iPods: As of this writing, only iPods that arrived in the summer of 2004 or later have the speed setting.)

To change the reading speed on the iPod, go to Settings → Audiobooks. Three speeds are available here: Slower, Normal, and Faster. Scroll to the one you want to try and hit the Select button to choose it. These speed changes aren't permanent. If you don't like the way it sounds, just return to the Audio books setting and change it back.

Audio Books from Other Sources

Although it's a powerhouse player on the scene, Audible.com is not the only place to get audio books to download for your iPod. There's also:

- **Audiobooks.com.** A large e-tailer of audio books on CD, the site also has a section where you can buy and download electronic books in the MP3 format at *www.audiobooks.com*.

- **Project Gutenberg.** This ambitious site devoted to posting free text files of uncopyrighted literature also has some titles available as MP3 files at *www.gutenberg.org*.

- **AudiobooksForFree.** Another site for free uncopyrighted MP3 books—with lots of Edgar Allan Poe, Frank Baum, and other classic authors—is at *http://audiobooksforfree.com*.

- **Podiobooks.** Relive those thrilling days of yesteryear when things like movies and radio shows were serialized, meaning you had to *wait* to find out what happened on the installment plan. This site offers new chapters of books as podcasts that download to your computer at regular intervals. Visit *www.podiobooks.com* to sign up.

And of course, you can always rip your regular old audio book CDs into iTunes, just like your music CDs.

Tip: Tired of losing your place in a long audiobook, music video, symphonic movement, or other mega-file? With iTunes 5 and later, you can slip in a virtual bookmark that remembers where you left off, no matter where or when you stop.

To turn on a file's bookmarking function, click the title in the iTunes display window and choose File → Get Info → Options. Turn on the "Remember playback position" checkbox, and then click OK. If your iPod model has a click wheel (which includes most models born in 2004 and beyond), and you've updated it with the latest iPod firmware (page 269), your virtual bookmarks sync between iTunes and the iPod.

Podcasting

Just as Web logs, or *blogs*, let everybody publish their priceless musings on the Web (with help from a computer, an Internet connection, and the right software), *Podcasting* now adds the ability to speak those thoughts out loud, for others to download and listen to on their computers or portable devices. (The culturally savvy neologist who coined the term *podcast* was clearly a brand loyalist, but podcasts work on many a digital music player.)

Everyone from media pros like former MTV VJ Adam Curry to bloggers who find speaking more fun than typing serve up these recorded programs—usually in MP3 format—free on their Web sites. You can enjoy podcasts on a ridiculous variety of topics from agriculture to politics to daily life in Hawaii. What's more, most podcasts get frequent updates—sort of like new episodes of your favorite sitcom. By using software designed to snag and download podcasts (including iTunes), you can make sure you always have the most recent edition of your favorite podcast.

The Podcasts list in iTunes's Source list (Figure 6-16) shows all the podcasts you subscribe to. In the iTunes window, you can see podcast titles, along with current and past episodes that were released before you signed up. (Just click the Get button next to a grayed-out past episode to fetch a copy.)

Shows with new episodes that you haven't listened to yet have a blue dot next to them. If you decide you don't like a podcast all, you can stop future downloads by selecting it in the iTunes window and clicking Unsubscribe in the bottom-right corner, as seen in Figure 6-16. To add podcasts you might like better than that one you just ditched, click the Podcast Directory link on the bottom-left side of the window.

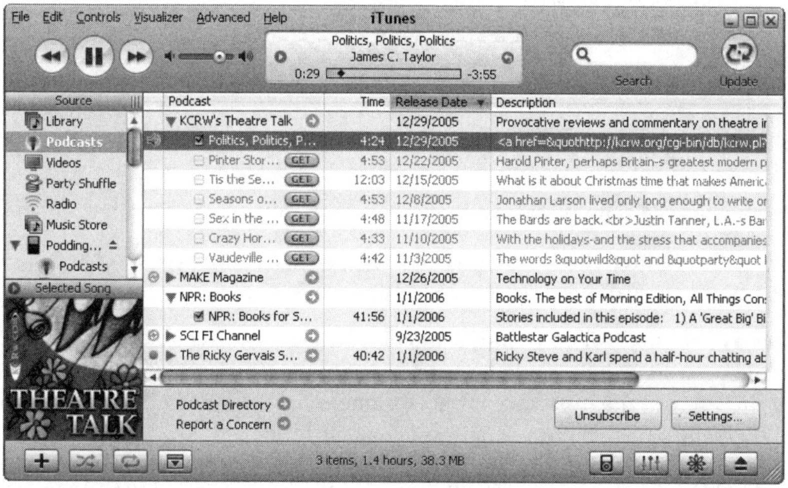

Figure 6-16:
By clicking the Podcasts icon in the iTunes Source list, you can see all the shows you've subscribed to. Along the bottom of the screen, you can look for more podcasts by clicking the podcast Directory Link, cancel subscriptions with the Unsubscribe button, and access podcast management preferences with the Settings button.

Adding podcasts to iTunes is easy—just a few clicks or maybe a cut 'n' paste job here and there (see page 174 for details). Once you start subscribing to podcasts, you're probably going to want to listen to them on your iPod. The next section tells you how to manage your existing podcast subscriptions in both iTunes and on the iPod.

Tip: Think you can do a better job than some of those yappy podcasters out there? Check out page 232 for tips on how to make your own podcasts and get them out there for the world to hear. Once your podcast is complete, submit it to the iTunes Music Store by going to the Podcasts area and clicking the link for "Submit a Podcast."

Managing Podcast Subscriptions

Once you sign up for a podcast (or six) in iTunes, you can tell the program how you want it to handle your shows. Choose iTunes → Preferences → Podcasts on the Mac or Edit → Preferences → Podcasts in Windows to get to the settings shown in Figure 6-17. (If you're already wandering around iTunes' Podcasts area, clicking the Settings button in the bottom-right corner opens Preferences in a jiffy.)

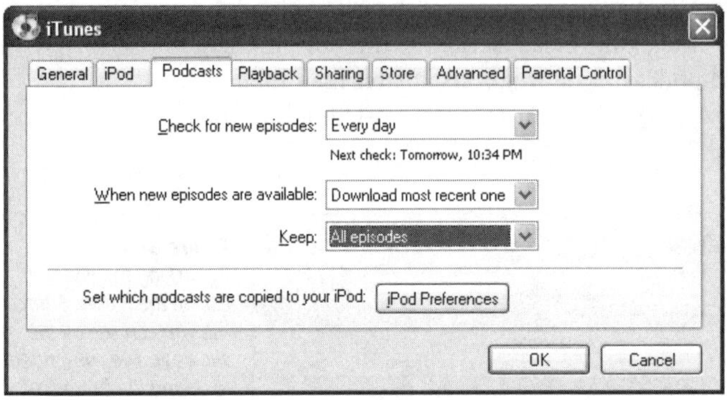

Figure 6-17:
The Podcast preferences box lets you tell iTunes precisely how you want it to handle podcasts for you. You can choose how often to check for update frequency, how many episodes to download, and how many to keep around.

Once you open the iTunes Podcast Preferences box, you can decide a few things:

• **How often iTunes checks the Internet for new episodes.** You can have it look every hour, every day, every week, or opt to check manually.

• **What iTunes does when it finds new episodes.** You can get all the episodes of a certain podcast (which could be a hefty download if its archive contains lots of old shows), just the most recent one, or ignore new material altogether because you're going to get whatever you want yourself.

• **How many episodes to keep around.** If hard drive space is at a premium (especially if you've discovered the joys of digital video), you can tell iTunes how many installments to hang onto. You can keep them all, just the unplayed or most recent shows, or the last 2, 3, 4, 5, or 10 episodes.

Underneath all these options for iTunes is a button for iPod Preferences. This button controls what happens when it's time to copy podcasts to your iPod. If you've already set up your music- and video-syncing preferences for the iPod (as explained back on page 45), the Podcasts tab of the iPod Preferences box looks comfortingly familiar (see Figure 6-18). Here, you can tell the iPod how to handle your podcasts: automatically update all of them, automatically update just a select few, or let you manually drag over the ones you want to take with you.

If you choose one of the automatic update methods, the Update pop-up menu at the bottom of the box wants to know how many episodes of each podcast should pop over to the Pod—all of them, just the ones you've turned on in the iTunes display window, the most recent ones, or just the shows you haven't yet listened to.

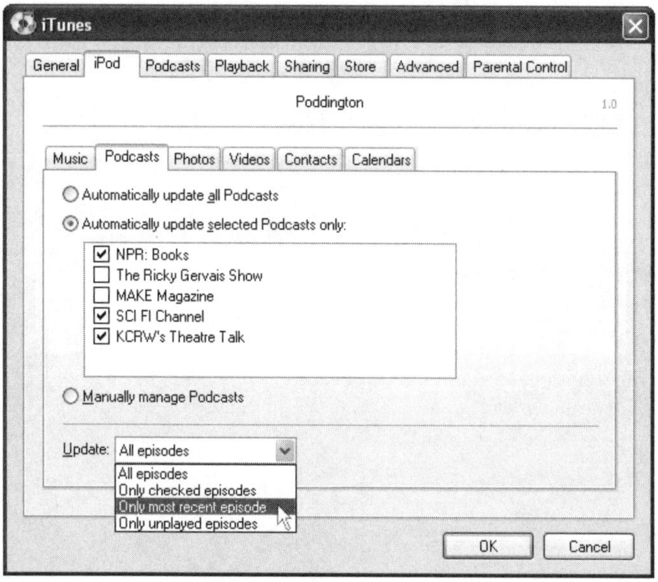

Figure 6-18:
In addition to telling iTunes how to manage your podcast subscriptions, you need to tell the iPod what you want and how much of it. If you don't want all your podcasts automatically copied to the iPod, you can pick and choose certain shows or go with manual control and drag them over to the iPod yourself. While you're in the iPod Preferences box, you can use the Contacts and Calendar tabs to add your social life to the mix, too. See Appendix B at www. missingmanuals.com for the details.

With photos, videos, audiobooks, and podcasts all nestled on your iPod alongside your music, you think the iPod would be out of tricks. But wait—there's more! In the pages ahead, Chapters 8 and 11 show you how to play videogames and read electronic books on your versatile little multimedia powerhouse, and Appendix B tells you how to get your contacts and calendar onto your iPod.

The iTunes Music Store

The recent explosion in Internet song swapping presented the recording industry with a paradoxical challenge: to stop music lovers from freely trading files over the Internet, while trying to make money themselves by selling copy-protected music online. The early attempts, backed by the major record companies, featured a monthly fee, a puny song catalog, and no ability to burn the purchased music to CDs or save it onto music players. What a deal!

Needless to say, people stayed away in droves. The free (and free-form) world of Napster, Grokster, KaZaA, LimeWire, and similar file-trading services were much more attractive, at least until they started getting sued off the planet by the recording industry.

Then Apple took a whack at it. In April 2003, the company unveiled its iTunes Music Store, an online component of iTunes 4 that scored the hat trick that other companies had yet to achieve: digital audio downloads that were easy, cheap, and—drum roll, please—legal. And it's not just for music lovers in the United States any more, as the store has since opened its doors in France, Germany, the United Kingdom, Canada, Japan, and Australia. As of 2005, the Music Store sells much more than music, with videos, animated films, and television shows available—plus thousands of free podcasts to peruse. Here's a look inside the store, and how to shop it.

Welcome to the Music Store

The iTunes Music Store is a super-simple, multimedia, download service that has the backing (and the song catalogs) of several big music companies, and more than

1,000 independent labels. Its inventory in the U.S. contains over 2 million songs from major-label artists like Bob Dylan, U2, Missy Elliott, Jewel, Sting, and hundreds of other musicians in a range of popular styles like rock, pop, R&B, jazz, folk, rap, Latin, classical, and more—and the collection grows by thousands of songs a week. And the iTunes Music Store was the first to offer classic soundtracks from the Walt Disney vaults. You can also browse, sample, or buy any of 10,000 audio books from Audible.com and buy entire seasons (or just particular episodes) of selected television shows from networks including NBC, ABC, MTV, Nickelodeon, and the Sci-Fi Channel.

Tip: For links to all the various departments of the store, like TV Shows or Audiobooks, just click the links along the left side of the store's main page.

Further down the page, you can also see and hear what famous people are listening to in the store's Celebrity Playlist section. It never hurts to know what Stephen King and Margaret Cho are listening to these days.

In the store's music aisles, you can browse the virtual CD racks from the comfort of your own computer, listen to 30 sample seconds free from any track, and download desired songs for 99 cents each with a click of the mouse. There are no monthly fees, and your digitally protected downloads don't go *poof!* into the ether after 30 days. Nor do the songs come with such confusing usage rights that you need your own lawyer to figure out if you can burn a song to a CD or not. You can play the downloaded songs on up to five different iTunes-equipped Macs or PCs (in any combination), burn them onto CDs, and download them to the iPod. Thousands of people use the Music Store every day, in fact, without even realizing that the songs are copy protected. All your downloaded songs stay right in iTunes, where they're just a sync away from your iPod's traveling music collection.

Music videos, animated film shorts from Pixar (Steve Jobs's *other* CEO day job), and TV shows cost $1.99 a pop and can be played right in iTunes 6 or later or on a video-enabled iPod. You can play the videos on up to five computers and copy them to as many iPods as you want.

A single iPod can host purchased store items from up to five different user accounts, but won't accept any files from a sixth user account—a restriction designed to prevent a single iPod from filling up with copyrighted content purchased, say by members of the entire sophomore class.

The Store also hosts more than 20,000 free audio and video podcasts (page 174) ready to download to computer and iPod; these portable audio programs cover everything from book-chat on National Public Radio to sports-talk from ESPN, plus thousands of shows from people podcasting about the topics they love.

Apple's early success with the iTunes Music Store—half a billion songs sold by July 2005—caught its rivals' attention. These days, Apple's imitators in the dollar-a-song biz include BuyMusic, Napster 2.0, Sony, MusicMatch, and even Wal-Mart. Microsoft itself has even lumbered into the digital download biz, with its MSN

Music store. (And speaking of Microsoft, remember that music from these other services come in Microsoft's Windows Media Audio format, which won't work on the iPod and can't be converted because of the copy protection.)

Note: The video and TV sections of iTunes Music Store are a feature of iTunes 6 and later. On the Mac, the basic music and podcast functions of iTunes 6 require Mac OS X 10.2.8 or later, a 500-megahertz G3 processor or better, and at least 256 megabytes of RAM. (You also need QuickTime—Apple's multimedia software—version 6.5.2 or later, to use any purchased music with iLife projects. You can download QuickTime from the iTunes download page.) To use the video parts of the Store, you need Mac OS 10.3.9, a 500-megahertz G4 processor, QuickTime 7.0.3, and 16 megabytes of video RAM in your Mac.

On the PC, you need Windows 2000 or XP, a 500-megahertz Pentium-class processor or faster, QuickTime 7.0.3, and 256 megabytes of memory for smooth performance. Watching video excerpts right from the store requires a 1.5-gigahertz Pentium-level processor and 32 megabytes of video memory on the computer's graphics card.

A Store Tour

With iTunes running, click the Music Store icon in the iTunes Source list on the left pane of the program's window (Figure 7-1). If you use a dial-up modem, fire it up as you would to check email or surf the Web. If you have a cable modem or DSL, a message about connecting to the store appears in the status display at the top of the iTunes window.

Figure 7-1:
The Browse button and Search box in the upper-right corner of the iTunes window locate songs on the store's inventory. Each genre of music in the Choose Genre pop-up menu has its own set of pages. Below it, you can see many of the store's latest additions: streaming movie trailers, music videos, and TV shows, to name a few.

Note: As you can imagine, the whole Music Store business—especially when buying videos—works *much* better over high-speed Internet connections.

Setting Up an Account

After you click the Music Store icon in the iTunes Source list and connect to the store, you land on the home page, which works like a Web page. If you're in the mood to buy, you might as well take care of setting up your Apple Account now. To do so, click the "Account: Sign In" button on the upper-right side of the iTunes window. A box like the one in Figure 7-2 appears.

If you've ever bought or registered an Apple product on the company's Web site, signed up for the AppleCare tech-support plan, have a .Mac membership, or used another Apple service, you probably have an Apple ID already. All you have to do is remember your user name (usually your email address) and password.

If you've never had an Apple ID, click Create Account. The iTunes Music Store Welcome screen lists the three steps you need to follow to set up your Apple account:

1. Agree to the terms for using the store and buying music.

2. Create an Apple Account.

3. Supply a credit card or PayPal account number and billing address.

Figure 7-2:
If you already have an Apple Account, you can sign in here. If not, just click the Create New Account button to get started. If you're an America Online member, you can skip the Apple Account and sign into the store using your AOL screen name and password.

As your first step to creating an Apple Account, you must read and agree to the long scrolling legal agreement on the first screen. The 23-part statement informs you of your rights and responsibilities as an iTunes Music Store customer. (It boils down to this: *Thou shalt not download an album, burn it to CD, and then sell bootleg copies of it down at your local convenience store.*)

Accounting for Your ID

Technically, an Apple ID and an Apple Account are two different things. Your Apple ID is the user name for your Apple Account. Another element of the Apple Account is your password, which, if you didn't already have one, you chose when you first set up your iPod.

Most Windows fans probably never had an Apple ID before they wandered into iTunes. But Macintosh mavens who buy and register Apple computers and software have had

them for years. You may have created your ID and password when you set up a .Mac account, signed up for Apple-Care, or bought something from the online Apple Store.

If you do have an existing Apple ID, you can use the same name and password to set up your Apple Account and shop the iTunes Music Store. You just need to add the final ingredient necessary for an Apple Account—a valid credit card number.

Click the Agree button to move on to step 2. On the next screen, you're asked to create a user name, password, and secret question and answer. If you later have to click the "Forgot Password?" button in the Music Store sign-in box because you've blanked on your password—hey, it could happen—this is the question you'll have to answer to prove that you're you. Apple also requests that you type in your birthday to help verify your identity.

On the third and final screen, provide a valid credit card number with a billing address. Instead of a credit card, you can also use a PayPal account for iTunes purchases. After you click Done, you see a screen congratulating you on your account-setup prowess.

Click Done. The account creation process is complete. From now on, you can log into the Music Store by clicking the "Account: Sign In" button in the upper-right corner of the iTunes window.

Changing the Information in Your Apple Account

I moved and need to change my billing address for the iTunes Music Store. How do I do that?

You can change your billing address, switch the credit card you have on file for your music purchases, or edit other information in your Apple Account without calling Apple. Just start up iTunes, click the Music Store icon on the Source list, and sign in to your account by clicking the Sign In button (next to where it says Account in the upper-right corner of the screen).

Once you've signed in, you'll see your account name (email address). Click it. In the box that pops up, type in your password again and click View Account, then click the Edit Credit

Card button. You're ready to change your billing address or credit card information. In the main account area, you can also set up an allowance (page 178) or buy iTunes Music Store gift certificates (page 177).

If you want to change your user name, password, or secret identity-proving question, click the Edit Account Info button. (Click Done when you're finished.)

Note, by the way, that any changes you make to your Apple Account through iTunes affect other programs or services you might also use with your account, like ordering picture prints with iPhoto.

The Shopping Cart

Thanks to Apple's 1-Click option, iTunes can instantly download a selected track as soon as you click the Buy Song button. That's a quick and painless experience for people with high-speed Internet connections.

If you have a dial-up modem, though, you may not want to sit there and wait for each song to download. Each song may take several minutes, which can severely impede your shopping rhythm.

To solve this problem, iTunes offers a Shopping Cart option. When you use it, all the songs you buy pile up until the end of the session; then iTunes downloads them all at once when you click on the Shopping Cart icon in your iTunes Source list (and then click Buy Now). This way, you can go off and do something productive (or unproductive) while the stack of tracks takes its time squeezing through the dial-up connection.

If this idea appeals to you, choose iTunes → Preferences on the Mac, or Edit → Preferences if you're of the PC persuasion. In the Preferences dialog box, click the Store icon, and proceed as shown in Figure 7-3.

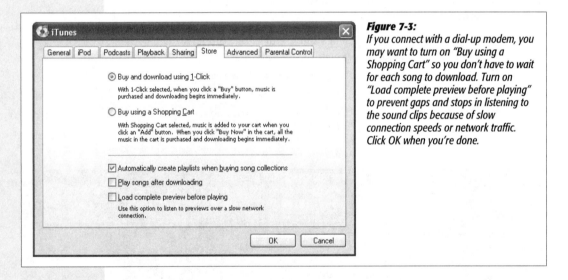

Figure 7-3:
If you connect with a dial-up modem, you may want to turn on "Buy using a Shopping Cart" so you don't have to wait for each song to download. Turn on "Load complete preview before playing" to prevent gaps and stops in listening to the sound clips because of slow connection speeds or network traffic. Click OK when you're done.

Searching and Shopping

You don't have to log in to browse the store—only when you want to buy music or audiobooks.

And music is everywhere you turn in the iTunes Music Store. Click any album cover or text link to zoom right to it. The upper-left corner area of the Music Store home page offers a pop-up menu to jump straight to the genres you want to explore. Links to the store's collection of podcasts, audiobooks, music videos, television shows, and other digital entertainment are also along the left side of the main page.

You can also use the Power Search tool, shown at top in Figure 7-4, to zero in on a specific song, artist, album, genre, or composer—or just peruse the text-based lists, as shown in Figure 7-4, bottom.

Figure 7-4:
Top: Click the Power Search link on the Music Store's home page to get to this search box in iTunes, where you can do some serious sleuthing for specific songs.

Bottom: Click the Browse icon (in the upper-right corner), pick a genre, and then click an artist on the next list to see the albums available by that musician or group.

When you find a performer you're interested in, click the name to see a list of songs or albums on hand for purchase. If you click an album name, all of the songs available from it appear below in the Details window. Double-click a track to hear a 30-second snippet to see how it suits you, or to make sure that's really the song you were thinking of, before buying it. Short previews of items in the store's video collection are also available.

You navigate the iTunes Music Store aisles just like a Web browser. Most song and artist names are hyperlinked—that is, you can click their names, or album cover images, to see what tracks are included.

Click the Back button in the Store window to go back to the page you were just on, or click the button with the small house on it to return to the Music Store home page.

Tip: When browsing the store, you may see a small, gray, circular icon bearing a white arrow in some columns of the Details window. That's the "More Info this way!" button, just like all the gray arrows all over your own library (assuming you've got the "Show links to the Music Store" checkbox turned on in the iTunes Preferences box). In the Store, click the white arrow to jump to a page bearing details about the subject, like a discography page next to a singer's name in the Artist column, or to the main page of artists for the genre listed.

The main iTunes Music Store page also displays links to new releases, free weekly song downloads, exclusive songs that can be purchased only from the Music Store, Apple staff favorites, songs scheduled to become available in the near future, sneak peeks at unreleased tunes, and the Billboard Top 100 charts going back to 1946 (see the box "Charting History"). And in case you don't have enough to overload your senses, there are also links to radio charts from around the country, and movie trailers that you can watch right in the iTunes window.

GEM IN THE ROUGH

Charting History

Quick! What was the Number One song during your senior year in high school? What tunes were topping the music charts during your college years? If you've ever paid attention to any sort of a Top 10 list, odds are you were looking at a Billboard chart.

Billboard, something of an industry bible among music professionals, is a weekly magazine that's been tabulating and reporting lists of the popular songs and albums for over 50 years. These days, the company now uses high-tech methods to chart the hits in several music categories. SoundScan, for example, is a computerized system that tracks retail music sales. The tabulators also keep a close ear on what songs are spilling out of radio stations around the country. All these numbers get crunched together into a formula that's part of the Billboard chart recipe.

In addition to all the other ways to find and buy your favorite songs, the iTunes Music Store lets you riffle through the Billboard Top 100 charts going all the way back to 1946.

(Missing entries in the song list—like the top three songs for 1968—reflect songs that iTunes doesn't have for sale, usually because the record companies or the bands haven't given permission for online sale yet.)

To see the charts, click the Billboard Charts link at the left side of the main page. Glancing at an old Billboard chart can serve as a sonic snapshot of a particular musical era: you see the songs listed, and you're instantly transformed back to the time when you heard them first (if, that is, you were even *alive* then).

Check out charts from the early 1960s, and you learn just how hip the girl-group sound was. Go back a few years further, and you discover the hip-shaking Reign of Elvis. Jump forward several decades, and you see hip hop transforming the cultural airwaves. Figure 7-5 below shows you some of the hit songs in 1984.

Tip: Ever wonder how something would play in Peoria? Now you can see for yourself *what's* playing in Peoria, thanks to the Radio Charts feature of the iTunes Music Store. On the Store's main page, just click the Radio Charts link to see what's at the top of the pops on 1,000 stations around the country.

Figure 7-5:
*Take a stroll down
memory lane: Select your
favorite year in the
Billboard Hot 100 list.
R&B and Country music
fans get to pick from their
own genre-specific
collections. Happy
wandering.*

Adjusting the Columns

Just as you can modify the look and information displayed for your own music
library in iTunes, you can customize your columns in the iTunes Music Store. See
Figure 7-6 for an example of how to modify which columns of detail information
to display.

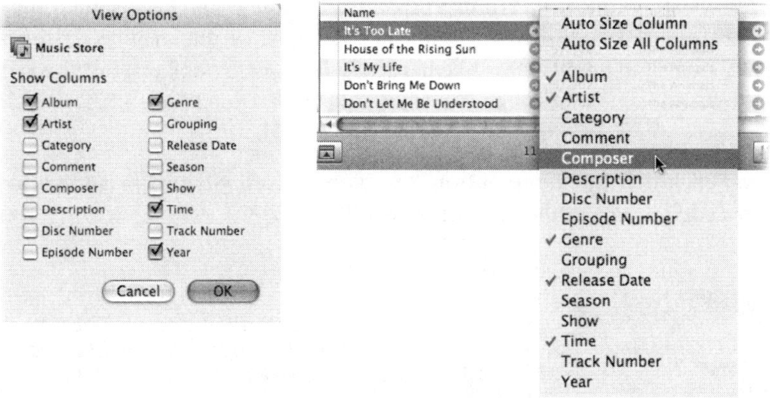

Figure 7-6:
*Left: After selecting the
Music Store in the Source
list, choose Edit → View
Options to specify which
columns of information
appear.*

*Right: Or just right-click
(Control-click) any
column heading to
produce this secret pop-
up menu of available
columns.*

Remember, too, that you can drag column headings (like Time, Artist, or Price)
horizontally to rearrange them, or drag the divider lines between them to adjust
the column widths.

Buying a Song or Album or Video

Making a purchase is as easy as clicking the Buy Song or Buy Video button next to a song or video (Figure 7-7).

Figure 7-7:
To purchase any tune, click the Buy Song button in the Price column. When you download an album, or even just one song, you get music files in the AAC format (page 79). A color picture of the album cover is attached to the song file, which you can display in the artwork pane of the iTunes program window when you're playing that song or on the color screen of your iPod.

The songs for sale in the iTunes Music Store cost 99¢ each; most video purchases are $1.99. Most albums cost $10 to $14, which is quite a bit cheaper than the $17 or so you'd pay to buy the same album on CD. Some people may prefer the high fidelity of a CD and enjoy extras like hardcopy jewel-case booklets, but the iTunes Music Store does make spontaneous shopping trips a lot faster. Plus, you don't have to worry about finding a parking space at the mall.

Once you click that Buy Song button, the iTunes Music Store comes to your service. Now you see an alert box like the one in Figure 7-8.

Figure 7-8:
The iTunes Music Store checks with you via an alert box to make sure you really want to buy the song you just clicked. In the iTunes Music Store, all sales are final. (Besides, it's awfully hard to return a download.)

Click the glowing Buy button to confirm your purchase decision, or Cancel if you suddenly remember that your credit card is a bit close to the edge this month.

(You can also turn on "Don't warn me about buying songs again" if you feel that there's quite enough nagging in your life already. You'll never see the box in Figure 7-8 again.)

Some albums now include bonus videos and digital booklets as part of the download package, as shown in Figure 7-7. You need iTunes 4.8 or later to play the videos, and the booklets—usually liner notes and other artist info—come in the PDF format that just about any modern computer can open and print.

Tip: Don't see a song or album in the iTunes Music Store that you really want to buy? Click the Requests & Feedback link on the Music Store's home page and send your plea to Apple. There's no guarantee they'll add it, but it can't hurt to make your wishes known.

Buying Videos

Apple quietly began to sell music videos as part of certain album packages in the spring of 2005. These videos were typically just a bonus track attached to a full album released by major artists like Coldplay and the Dave Matthews Band and, at the time, you could only play them in iTunes, as the iPods of the era weren't yet video-capable.

With the arrival of the fifth-generation rootin'-tootin', video-playin' iPod in the fall of 2005, though, things changed. Apple rounded up 3,000 music videos, television shows, and short animated flicks and put them up for sale in the store. Now, for less than $2 a pop, you could download that episode of *Desperate Housewives* you missed the other night or finally have your own copy of Madonna's "Vogue" video. Although the picture quality wasn't that spectacular when watched at full-screen size on a computer, the iTunes Store videos look simply smashing when viewed on an iPod. And as a cherry on the icing on the Cake of Joy: No commercials!

To buy video content, just click the link on the Store's main page for the type you want—a music video, a Pixar cartoon, or a TV show (Figure 7-9). Apple is still building its video library, but dozens of old and new TV classics are already available, including episodes from *Lost, The Tonight Show, Alfred Hitchcock Presents, Battlestar Galactica, The Office*, and *Law & Order*. You can buy single episodes or entire seasons of shows at once.

You buy a video just like you buy a song: Browse, preview a sample, and click the Buy button for the title if you want it. Keep in mind that video files are much heftier than music files (one 45-minute episode of *Battlestar Galactica*, for instance, is close to 200 megabytes), so make sure you have enough time and hard-drive space to accommodate your video shopping spree.

Once you purchase and download the files from the iTunes Store, they land in your Library and on your Purchased list just like songs do. If you have a computer with the ultra-zippy USB 2.0 connection, copying videos over to the iPod usually takes a fraction of the time it takes to get them from the store, but the transfer time over a USB 1.1 connection can be even more tedious. You might even have to go watch TV in the living room while your shows make the journey from computer to iPod.

Figure 7-9:
You can buy just one episode of a television show or click a button to download an entire season's worth of drama. Short descriptions give you an idea of that episode's events, and you can double-click the title for a short preview of the show.

Downloading Podcasts

As of iTunes 4.9 in mid-2005, the iTunes Music Store is host to thousands upon thousands of podcasts, those free audio (and video!) programs put out by everyone from big television networks to a guy in his basement with a microphone. Podcasts didn't start with iTunes, but iTunes makes it easy to find, download, and play the shows on your computer or iPod.

If you want to see what podcasts are out there, click the Podcasts link on the store's main page. You're then whisked into the Podcasts section (Figure 7-10), where you can browse shows by category, search for podcast names by keyword, or click around until you find something that sounds good. Just about every topic is covered—from sports to politics to books to music to news.

Many podcasters produce regular installments of their shows, releasing new episodes onto the Internet when they're ready. You can have iTunes keep a look out for fresh editions of your favorite podcasts and automatically download them for you. All you have to do is *subscribe* to the podcast, which takes a couple of clicks in the Store.

Figure 7-10:
Podcasts are just as neatly organized as the other content in the iTunes Music Store, making it easy to browse the offerings by category or keyword. Unlike the rest of the Music Store's merchandise, though, podcasts tend to be free.

If you want to try out a podcast, click the Get Episode link near its title to download just that one show. If you like it (or know that you're going to like it before you even download the first episode), there's also a Subscribe button at the top of the page that will sign you up to receive all future episodes. Some attention-needy podcast producers don't give you the single-episode download option; in those cases, you'll see a Subscribe Only link near the podcast title.

Note: Keeping the podcasts from piling up as iTunes goes out and grabs them can keep you busy. Flip back to Chapter 6 for information on managing your podcasts in both iTunes and on the iPod.

Publishing Your Own Playlists (iMixes)

An *iMix* is a playlist that you publish on the Music Store, so everyone on earth can see your masterwork. You can name it, write your own liner notes explaining your mixing inspiration, and put it out there for everyone to see (Figure 7-11).

Start by signing into your Music Store account. Then, in the iTunes Source list, select the playlist you want to publish. (If it contains any songs that Apple doesn't sell, they'll get knocked off the list—which may ruin your carefully constructed mix.)

Figure 7-11:
Here's a typical iMix in the iTunes Music Store, posted by a Latin-music aficionado. If you like someone's mixing skills, you can give the collection a 5-star rating, tell your friends about it, or even buy all the songs on the list.

When you click the playlist, a blue arrow appears next to its title. Click the arrow to begin the publishing process (or choose File → Publish Playlist to Music Store).

In the warning box that appears, click Publish (and turn on "Do not show this message again" if you've had your fill of neurotic dialog boxes popping up at you). On the next screen, name your iMix and add your thoughts on making it. Finally, in the iMix window, click Publish. Now other people can see your playlist, rate it, be inspired by it, or—and let's face it, here's the main thing—buy the songs for themselves.

To tell all your pals about your brand new iMix, click the "Tell a friend" button on your new iMix page. iTunes sends a virtual birth announcement by email, complete with album-cover art.

Tip: Want to email a friend a direct link to your brand new iMix or to anybody else's? Control-click or right-click the playlist's icon on the iMix page and, from the shortcut menu, choose Copy iTunes Music Store URL. Next, create a new message in your email program and paste in the link you just copied.

Apple will send you an email message congratulating you on your successful iMixing along with a link for your iMix. The Store keeps iMixes on its site for a year.

Gift Certificates

Gift certificates make perfect presents for People Who Have Everything, especially when purchased by People Who Are Lousy Shoppers. These redeemable email coupons are also an excellent way to save face in potentially unpleasant situations ("Honey, you may think I forgot our anniversary again, but…check your email!").

With iTunes Music Store gift certificates, available both from the iTunes store or from Apple's Web site, you can send your friends and family $10 to $200 worth of credit to go hog-wild in Apple's music emporium.

Buying

To buy one, click Gift Certificates on the main page of the iTunes Music Store. After you choose delivery by either email or U.S. Mail, the process is like buying anything on the Web: you fill in your address, gift amount, personalized message, and so on.

If you already have an Apple ID (page 166), you can log in and request to have your credit card billed; if not, sign up for one. Once you complete all the pixel paperwork, your gift certificate will be on its way.

Tip: Before sending off a gift certificate, discreetly check whether your recipient's computer meets the iTunes requirements. People on Windows 98, Windows Me, and older operating systems may be in for an even bigger pang of disappointment than if you gave them a box of tube socks.

Spending

Whether they come in the mailbox by the front door or the one on the computer, iTunes Music Store gift certificates are meant to be spent. Here's how they work:

- If you're lucky enough to be the recipient of an iTunes email gift certificate (Figure 7-12), redemption is just a click away. The Redeem Now button at the bottom of the message takes you straight to the Music Store, where the certificate's confirmation number pops up automatically. Click Redeem in the Music Store window to credit your account and start shopping.

- If the gift arrived by postal mail, start up iTunes and click Music Store in the Source list. On the main Music Store page, click the link for Gift Certificates. On the next screen, click Redeem Now. Type in the confirmation number printed on the lower edge of the gift certificate and click Redeem.

Tip: The brightly colored iTunes Music Store prepaid card is another fun spin on the gift certificate concept. Available in $15, $25, $30, and $50 amounts, givers can find the cards at places like Amazon.com, Target, and Apple's own stores. Recipients can spend it all in one place—the iTunes Music Store—by clicking the link for iTunes Music Cards on the main page.

Figure 7-12:
Receiving and redeeming an iTunes Music Store gift certificate is as easy as opening your email and clicking Redeem Now to add the gift credits to your account. You can also send paper gift certificates through the U.S. mail.

If you already have an iTunes Music Store account, log in and start shopping. If you've never set your mouse pointer inside the store before, you'll need to create an Apple Account. You have to provide your name and address, but you don't have to surrender a credit card number. If you choose None, you can use your gift certificate as the sole payment method—and end your shopping experience once you've burned through it.

Tip: In a daring feat of bending a noun into a verb, the iTunes store also lets you "gift" selections of music and videos to intended recipients, giving them the ability to download your thoughtful picks right from the Store onto their own computers. You can send songs, albums, and playlists to any pal with an e-mail address, as well as audiobooks, music videos, and TV shows. Just look for the "Gift This…" link on the item's page in the store.

iTunes Allowance Accounts

Allowance accounts are a lot like iTunes store gift certificates. You, the parent (or other financial authority), decide how many dollars' worth of music or audiobooks you want to give to a family member or friend (from $10 to $200, in increments of $10). Unlike gift certificates, however, allowance accounts automatically replenish themselves on the first day of each month—an excellent way to keep your music-loving kids out of your wallet while teaching the little nippers how to budget their money throughout the month.

Both you and the recipient need to have Apple IDs. To set up a monthly allowance, click the Allowance link on the main page of the iTunes Music Store and fill out the form on the next screen. After you select the amount of credit you want to deposit each month, fill in your recipient's Apple ID and password. (There's also an option to create a new account for the monthly allowance.)

Once the giftee logs into the designated Apple Account, the spending can begin—no credit card required. Once the allowance amount has been spent, that's it for music until the following month. (Of course, if the recipient *does* have a credit card on file, he can always put the difference on the card.) If you need to cancel an allowance account, go to your Account Info page (see the box on page 167) to take care of the matter.

Tip: Can't remember how much money you have left on your gift certificate or in your allowance account? Look at your iTunes window the next time you're logged into the store. Your balance appears right next to your account name.

Wish Lists

With no paper money flying about to remind you of reality, it's possible to go hog-wild in the Music Store and click yourself into a hefty credit card charge. But if you're on a spree because you're afraid you'll forget to get a song or album later, you can make an iTunes *wish list* to help you remember.

Making an iTunes wish list is basically just like making any ol' playlist, except you populate it with 30-second song previews from the iTunes Music Store—complete with their Buy Song buttons that take you right back to the store once you're ready to shop again.

Creating your iTunes wish list

1. **Make a new playlist in iTunes.**

   See page 122 if you don't know how. Give the playlist a name so you'll know what it is: "Wish List," "Songs to Buy," "Gimme Gimme Gimme," or "My Next Paycheck" all work fine.

2. **In the iTunes Source list, click the Music Store icon.**

   The Music Store, via your Internet connection, appears on screen.

3. **Shop around the store and drag store songs into the new playlist.**

   You can drag the tracks you want to buy right onto your own playlist, complete with their 30-second song previews. If you decided that, in retrospect, you really don't *need* the 12-inch remix of the Village People's "Macho Man," just click the undesired track and press Delete.

Once your Wish List is up there, sit back and see if your friends will send you the music as a gift through the iTunes store, or perhaps give you a prepaid card or gift certificate so you can go shopping yourself.

The Interrupted Download

If your computer crashes or you get knocked offline while you're downloading your song purchases, iTunes is designed to pick up where it left off after you restart the program and reconnect to the Internet. If, for some reason, it doesn't go back to downloading, choose Advanced → Check for Purchased Music to log back into the Music Store to resume your downloading business.

Signing Out

If other people have access to your computer when you're not around, consider wrapping up your shopping session by clicking your name (next to the Account button on the Music Store window) and then Sign Out. Unless you're one of those exceedingly benevolent types, you probably don't want anyone else to come along and charge up your credit card with a music-buying marathon.

Locating Your New Tracks

You can find your new tracks by clicking Purchased Music in the iTunes Source list (Figure 7-13). As the dialog box says, you can work with the Purchased Music playlist as though it were any other playlist. That is, even if you delete a track from it, the song itself still remains in the iTunes music library. And behind the scenes, the corresponding music file stays in your Home → Music → iTunes → iTunes Music folder (Mac) or My Music → iTunes → iTunes Music (Windows).

Figure 7-13:
When you click the Purchased Music playlist after buying music, iTunes offers an explanation of how the playlist works and fills out your list with the newly bought songs and videos. From here, you can play the songs, drag them into other playlists, transfer them to your iPod, or burn them to a CD to play on the stereo.

Note: The iPod isn't the only Apple-approved portable device for playing iTunes tracks. Apple and Motorola have banded together to bring a pocket version of iTunes to the mobile Motorola ROKR phone; details are at *www.apple.com/itunes/mobile*. By linking phone to computer with a Bluetooth wireless or USB cable connection, music lovers will be able to copy songs and other items from the iTunes library over to the Motorola handset.

Thinking of Linking?

Web logs—also known as *blogs*—are online journals. You post your blog on the Web so that anybody passing by can read your deepest thoughts on everything from politics to Saturday morning cartoons. You don't even have to be a Webmaster to create your own blog because the software usually handles most of the formatting and uploading for you. Movable Type (*www.sixapart.com/movabletype*) and Live Journal (*www.livejournal.com*) are two of the many companies that sell blogware, and even America Online offers a journal feature to its members.

Like blogs, music is often best when shared. If you've found a hot new band or singer that you just have to share with the world via your blog, Apple gives you an easy way to point your pals directly to the artist's song, album, or page in the iTunes Music Store. You're spared the hassle of figuring out the correct URL to type into your blogware.

Just point your Web browser to the iTunes Link Maker page (*www.apple.com/itunes/linkmaker*). Type the artist, album, or song name into the Link Maker form as shown in Figure 7-14; it will then crunch out and present you with a complicated chunk of HTML code containing the Internet address that will take your visitors directly to the appropriate page in the iTunes Music Store.

All you have to do is paste that entire blob of text into your blog program, so with just a click, everyone can see the band you're raving about. The code is already in the language of Web pages and blogs. You can even paste it into an email message.

If you know how to turn a graphic image into a link (using a Web-design program), you can also use the Link Maker-generated code as the link for a graphic button—the better to get your readers hooked and spread the joy of iTunes across the land.

Figure 7-14:
Apple's Link Maker Web page (www.apple.com/itunes/linkmaker) generates the HTML code you need to point to a specific song in the Music Store. Enter info into one or more of the three boxes (song, album, or artist name), click Search, and Link Maker rewards you with a Web link that you can add to a Web page or send in an email.

What to Do with Purchased Content

As you know, the iTunes Music Store gives you a lot more freedom to use your downloaded songs than other online services. There are a *few* restrictions, though.

Play It on Five Computers

You can play Music Store–bought songs only on an *authorized* computer. Authorization is Apple's copy-protection scheme.

Between work, home, and the family network, not everyone spends time on just one computer these days. So Apple lets you play your Music Store purchases on up to five computers at once: Macs, PCs, or any combination. You just need to type in your Apple user name and password on each computer to authorize it to play any songs, videos, or audiobooks purchased with that account. Each computer must make an Internet connection to relay the information back to Music Store headquarters. (And don't worry—you don't have to authorize each and every song because you authorize the computer to play *all* the songs purchased from an account.)

Authorizing computers

You authorized your first machine when you signed up for an Apple Account for the iTunes store.

To authorize a song—for example, to play on another computer—follow these steps:

1. **Find the song you want to transfer.**

   This step, of course, involves *finding* the song on your hard drive.

   — **Method 1:** On the Mac, open your Home → Music → iTunes → iTunes Music folder; in Windows, open My Documents → My Music → iTunes → iTunes Music. Music Store files are easily recognizable by their .m4p or .m4v file extensions.

   — **Method 2:** Just drag the song you want out of the iTunes window and onto your desktop.

2. **Copy the song to the second computer.**

   Copy the song file onto a CD or USB flash drive, email it to yourself, transfer it across the network, or use whatever method you prefer for schlepping files from machine to machine.

   Deposit the songs in the iTunes Music folder on the second computer. (See Method 1 for the location of this folder.)

3. **Bring the copied song into iTunes on the second computer.**

   To do that, you can either choose File → Add to Library (and then select and open them), or just drag their icons right into the iTunes window.

4. **In your iTunes list, select a transferred song and click the Play button.**

   iTunes asks for your Apple Account user name and password.

5. **Type your Apple ID and password, and click OK.**

This second computer is now authorized to play that song—and any other songs you bought using the same Apple Account.

Copy Protection and You

Apple's AAC music files are copy protected, but not all AAC files are. Some, which you may have collected from other Web sites, are freely copyable. Likewise, the store's video products use a protected version of the MPEG-4 video format.

How can you tell the difference?

In iTunes, click the questionable track in the music library and then press ⌘-I (Mac) or Ctrl+I (Windows). The Summary tab of the song shows the album cover, technical information about its encoding, who bought it, and where

it lives on the computer. If the Kind says "Protected AAC audio file" (as shown in Figure 7-15) or "Protected MPEG-4 video file," well, you've got your answer.

Incidentally, the suffix on a protected AAC file (as viewed on your desktop, for example) is .m4p, while protected MPEG-4 video carries the .m4v suffix. iTunes can play files that were ripped in iTunes, and it can play protected files downloaded from the iTunes Music Store.

But beware: You may have problems playing non-iTunes AAC tracks from another online music service or Web site.

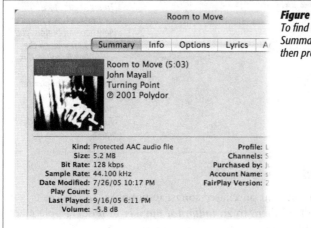

Figure 7-15:
To find out whether a song's copy protected, check out its Summary tab by clicking the song's name in iTunes and then pressing ⌘-I (Mac) or Ctrl+I (Windows).

Note: Although you may feel like AAC stands for Always Authorizing Computers, remember that this whole authorizing business is necessary only to play songs you've *bought.* To play songs you've ripped into AAC format from CDs, for example, or to play everyday MP3 files, you don't have to authorize anything.

Deauthorizing computers

You won't be able to play the purchased music on a sixth computer if you try to authorize it. When you connect to the authorization system over the Internet, it will see five other computers already on its list and deny your request.

That's a drag, but copy protection is copy protection—and it's much better than rival music services, which permit you to play downloaded music only on *three* machines (just like iTunes did before 2004).

In any case, you have to deauthorize one of the other computers if you want to play the music on Number 6. To deauthorize a computer, choose Advance → Deauthorize Computer, and then type in your Apple Account user name and password. The updated information zips back to Apple over the Internet.

Tip: Thinking of putting that older computer up for sale? Before you wipe the drive clean and send it on its way, be sure to deauthorize it, so your new machine will be able to play your songs from the iTunes Music Store. Erasing a hard drive, by itself, does not deauthorize a computer.

If you do forget to deauthorize a machine before you get rid of it, you can still knock it off your List of Five, but you have to reauthorize every machine in your iTunes arsenal all over again. To make it so, log into the Music Store by clicking your account name in the upper-right corner. Type in your password and click the View Account button. On the Apple Account Information page, there's a button (Figure 7-16) to click that deauthorizes *all* your computers that are allowed to play content purchased with this account,

---

Country: USA	(Change Country)
Computer Authorizations: 5 machines are authorized to play music purchased with this account.	(Deauthorize All)
Most Recent Purchase: December 13, 2005	(Purchase History)

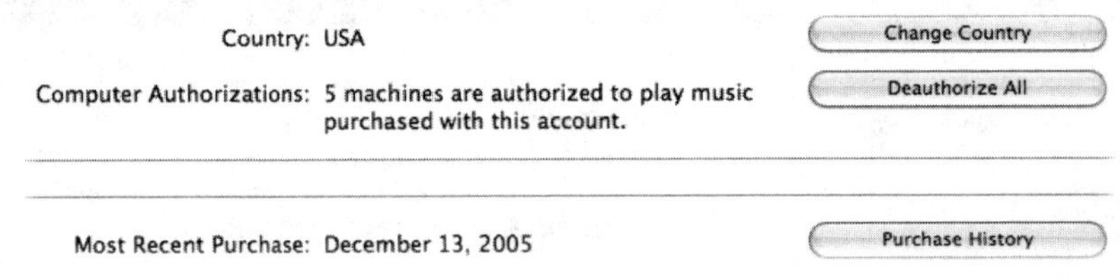

Figure 7-16:
Once you log onto your iTunes Music Store account and click the View account button, you can deauthorize all the computers linked to this account at once. You have to go through and reauthorize your machines to play your iTunes purchases all over again.

Copy It to Your iPod

Not only can you download your purchased songs, audiobooks, and videos to your iPod, but you can download them to an *unlimited number* of iPods. Apple placed no copy restrictions on iPod joy.

When you buy an item, it lands in the iTunes playlist called Purchased. But you can easily drag it into other playlists you've concocted within iTunes. The songs, artists, and albums appear just like any other tracks in iTunes.

Burn It to a CD

You can also burn purchased tracks to blank CDs, so you can listen to them in the car or on the big component rack in the living room. Here, Apple has put in only one tiny, almost irrelevant form of copy protection: If you've made store-bought songs part of a certain playlist, you can't burn more than seven CD copies of it in a row without making at least one change to the song list.

And if you find *that* limitation restrictive, you must be so dedicated a music pirate that you wear an eye patch and a parrot on your shoulder.

Note: You can burn your purchased *video* content to a CD or DVD as a file backup, but you can't make playable DVDs that let you watch the shows on the living room DVD player.

Share It Across the Network

You can also share purchased music tracks with other people on your same home or office network after you've authorized their computers—by playing them live, not by copying the actual files. Details are on page 129.

Back It Up

If your hard drive croaks and takes your entire digital library with it, you have three alternatives: (a) buy all of your Music Store booty all over again, which even Apple doesn't want you to have to do, judging by Figure 7-17; (b) copy the files *from* the iPod to your hard drive (page 49); or (c) calmly reach for the backup CD or DVD you had the foresight to make before disaster struck.

Figure 7-17:
Hard drives don't last forever and Apple strongly suggests that you back up your purchases from the iTunes Music Store to avoid the anger and heartbreak that can occur after a major hardware failure.

Thank you for purchasing from the iTunes Music Store. Your music is valuable - please back it up in case your computer fails.

☐ Do not show this message again

OK

Backing up your music library

To back up your entire music collection, you want to copy the *iTunes* folder.

- **Macintosh.** This folder is in your Home → Music folder.

- **Windows.** The iTunes folder is in your My Music folder.

Backing up this folder, huge though it may be, backs up not just your songs and videos, but all the other work you've done in iTunes (creating and naming your playlists, organizing your columns, and so on). If you've changed where your computer stores your iTunes folder, or you've opted to have your music files scattered around your system, you'll need to track down that maverick music to back it up.

You can use any standard backup method for this:

- Copy the folder to another computer via network cable.

- Burn it onto a blank CD (if the folder fits) or a DVD (if you have a DVD-burning computer).

• Use a program like Dantz Retrospect to back it up onto Zip disks, multiple CDs, or whatever you've got.

When your hard drive croaks, restore your backed-up iTunes folder by dragging it back into your Music folder (Mac) or My Music folder (Windows). You're saved.

Backing up playlists

iTunes also has a built-in backup feature. Note, however, that it can back up only one playlist at a time.

This backup procedure isn't the same thing as burning an *audio* CD. Here, you're burning a *data* disc. That's important if you want to preserve the original file formats in your iTunes music library and avoid turning your high-quality AIFF files, for example, into squished-down MP3 files. To make this important change to your Burning desires, see Figure 7-18.

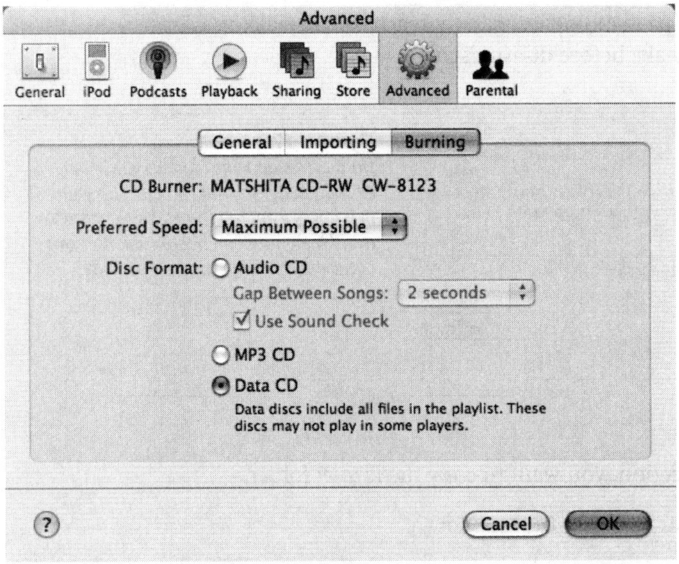

Figure 7-18:
Choose iTunes → Preferences → Advanced → Burning (Mac) or Edit → Preferences → Advanced → Burning (Windows), and click the button for Data CD or DVD. Selecting the Data format for your disc will copy your files in their original MP3, ACC, or Audible formats without converting them to standard audio CD files.

After you've chosen the Data format for your backup disc, make a playlist that includes all the files you want to copy to the CD or DVD. Keep an eye on the total size at the bottom of the window to be sure it will fit on one disc: about 650 megabytes for a CD, 4.7 gigabytes for a single-sided DVD. (If not, iTunes will prompt you with a message box, letting you know you'll need multiple CDs or DVDs.)

Burn it to disc by clicking the Burn Disc button on the iTunes window. Insert a blank disc when the machine asks for one, and then click the Burn Disc button again to start copying.

If your hard drive ever dies, copy this data disc's files back onto the computer and reimport them into iTunes to rebuild your library from the backup disc.

Backing up non-music data

If you've got a .Mac account (Apple's $100-a-year suite of online services), you can use the handy Backup program to save copies of your personal files to a remote Web site, recordable disc, or external hard drive—including your Purchased playlist. (See Figure 7-19 for details.)

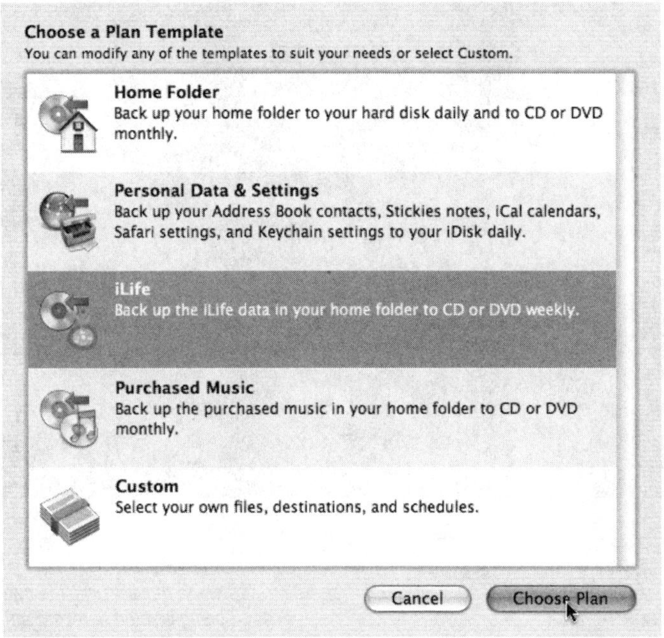

Figure 7-19:
The free Backup program that comes with a .Mac account has some built-in options for backing up your Mac's valuable contents, including your iLife files and all the music you've purchased from iTunes. In Backup 3, you just need to pick what you want to back up, and the program handles the heavy lifting.

Music Store Billing

The iTunes Music store keeps track of what you buy and when you buy it. If you think your credit card was wrongly charged for something, or if you suspect that one of the kids knows your password and is sneaking in some forbidden downloads before you get home from work, you can contact the store or check your account's purchase history page to see what's been downloaded in your name.

The Customer Service Page

If you have general questions about using the iTunes Music Store, have a problem with your bill, or want to submit a specific query or comment, the online Customer Service center awaits. To get there, connect to the Internet and then choose Help → Music Store Customer Service.

Click the link that best describes what you want to learn or complain about. For billing or credit card issues, click Purchase Information.

Note: The iTunes Music Store sends out invoices by email, but they don't come right after you buy a song. You usually get an invoice that groups together all the songs you purchased within a 12-hour period, or for every $20 worth of tunes that you buy.

GEM IN THE ROUGH

Back Up Only What Needs Backing Up

They say that backing up is hard to do—but mainly, it's hard to remember what you've already backed up and what still needs attention.

Here, however, is a sneaky trick that makes iTunes help you make backups of all the songs you've bought or ripped since the last time you backed up your iTunes Music folder. This means you won't have to burn the whole darn library to a stack of CDs or DVDs each time, and can just fill a disc with the new stuff you've added.

After you've backed up your music files to disc for the first or latest time, open iTunes and choose File → New Smart Playlist.

In the Smart Playlist set-up box that appears (see Figure 7-20), change the pop-up menus to say "Date Added–is after–[today's date]." Make sure Live Updating is turned on, and that there's no limit set for the amount of songs on the playlist. When you click OK, give your new playlist a name, like Smart Backup.

The next time you're ready to burn a data backup disc, back up only your Smart Backup playlist to get the latest library additions.

Then, once you've burned it to CD, choose File → Edit Smart Playlist, and change the Date Added to today's date so that iTunes starts keeping track of the new stuff for your next backup.

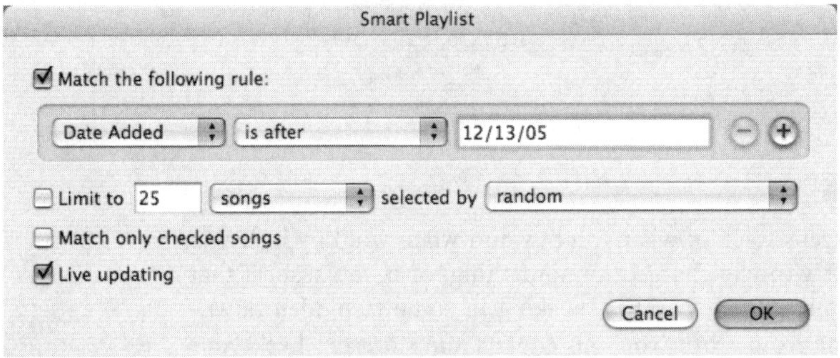

Figure 7-20:
Smart Playlists, like the one being created here, are an easy way to automate your iTunes music backup chores. See the box on page 187 for details on how to use this setup box to create a foolproof backup system.

Your Purchase History

To have a look at just how addicted you've grown to buying songs, open iTunes, click the Music Store icon in the Source List, and sign into the store. When you see your user name appear next to the Account button in the iTunes Music Store window, click it. In the box that pops up, click the View Account button.

When you get to the Account Information screen, click Purchase History. In the list that comes up, you see all of the songs you've bought (Figure 7-21).

Purchase History
Latest Purchase

🔒 Secure Connection

Date: 12/15/05 12:49 PM
Order: M124360875

Item	Artist	Type	Downloaded	Price
The Chronicles of Narnia: The Lion, the Witc...	Harry Gregson-Wi...	Playlist		$9.99
The Blitz, 1940	Harry Gregson-Wi...	Song	12/15/05 12:50 PM	
Evacuating London	Harry Gregson-Wi...	Song	12/15/05 12:51 PM	
The Wardrobe	Harry Gregson-Wi...	Song	12/15/05 12:52 PM	
Lucy Meets Mr. Tumnus	Harry Gregson-Wi...	Song	12/15/05 12:53 PM	
A Narnia Lullaby	Harry Gregson-Wi...	Song	12/15/05 12:54 PM	
The White Witch	Harry Gregson-Wi...	Song	12/15/05 12:55 PM	
From Western Woods to Beaversdam	Harry Gregson-Wi...	Song	12/15/05 12:56 PM	
Father Christmas	Harry Gregson-Wi...	Song	12/15/05 12:57 PM	
The Aslan's Camp	Harry Gregson-Wi...	Song	12/15/05 12:58 PM	
Knighting Peter	Harry Gregson-Wi...	Song	12/15/05 12:59 PM	
The Stone Table	Harry Gregson-Wi...	Song	12/15/05 01:01 PM	
The Battle	Harry Gregson-Wi...	Song	12/15/05 01:03 PM	
Only the Beginning of the Adventure	Harry Gregson-Wi...	Song	12/15/05 01:04 PM	
Can't Take It In	Imogen Heap	Song	12/15/05 01:05 PM	
Wunderkind	Alanis Morissette	Song	12/15/05 01:08 PM	
Winter Light	Tim Finn	Song	12/15/05 01:09 PM	
Where	Lisbeth Scott	Song	12/15/05 01:09 PM	

Subtotal: $9.99
Tax: $0.00
Store Credit Total: $9.99

Previous Purchases

Order Date	Order	Titles included in order	Total Price
⊕ 12/13/05	M123855453	Bullet In a Bible, The Office: An American Workplace (Pilot), 33	$18.97
⊕ 12/02/05	M119629034	Let My Love Open the Door, Dueling Banjos, Minority (Live), Wake Me Up When S...	$9.94

Figure 7-21:
With the Purchase History list tucked away in your Apple account settings, you can see everything you ever bought (or didn't) from the iTunes Music Store in one list.

If you see songs on the list that you didn't buy, and you're sure that other people who use your computer didn't buy them, contact Apple. Because the account is linked to a credit card, you'll want to take care of the situation right away.

With iTunes music, television shows, podcasts, and videos all within reach of your mouse these days, that Purchase History list might be pretty long—but think of all the gas, stamps, blank videotape, and aggravation you've saved by shopping at home!

Part Three: Beyond the Music

3

iPod Games and Other Extras

The very first iPod model was all music, all the time—unless you knew the secret Easter egg: the classic breakout Brick computer game, hidden from everyone who didn't know the sequence of button presses that called it to the screen. Once the secret began to spread across the Internet, Apple's engineers admitted that the jig was up and brought the game out into the open—or at least into the Extras menu, under a command called Game.

The iPods of Now have come a long way, baby. The color-screen models, including the iPod Nano and the fifth-generation video iPod, have four different games on board, plus a stopwatch function, a world clock to keep you current in multiple time zones, and a screen-locking feature to keep snoops from prying into your Pod. The notes feature, first introduced with the iPods of 2003, is still around and looks even better on a crisp backlight color screen—you don't even need a flashlight to read eBooks in bed after lights-out.

Games

The iPod is a personal entertainment machine on many levels. All models have at least one game: Brick. The iPods in 2003 and beyond come with three others: Music Quiz, Parachute and—perhaps the most popular program ever in the history of the computer—Solitaire.

Brick

The Brick game (Figure 8-1) has wandered all over the iPod's system software. In the first version of the iPod software, you unearthed it by holding down the Select button for five seconds on the About menu. In version 1.1, Brick surfaced in the Legal copyright info area in the Settings menu. Ever since version 1.2 of the iPod software, Brick has lived in an Extras submenu called Games.

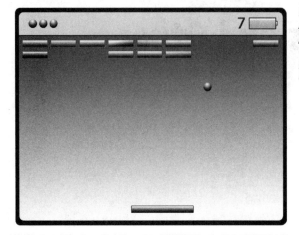

Figure 8-1:
Adventure games and flight simulation programs may come and go, but there'll always be Breakout. The iPod's Brick game, once playfully hidden, is now right up front on the Extras menu.

On the latest iPod models, choose Extras → Games → Brick. Wherever you find it on your iPod, Brick is instantly recognizable as a miniature version of the Atari arcade staple Breakout, which Apple co-founder Steve Wozniak created. Your mission, should you choose to accept it, is to use a ricocheting ball to break through rows of bricks at the top of the screen. Press the Select button to start the game: As the small ball rockets in from the side, use the scroll wheel to move the paddle (at the bottom) from side to side in an effort to deflect the ball into the bricks above.

You get one point for each brick you knock out. If you miss the ball, you lose it. Losing three balls ends the game. If you manage to knock out all the bricks at the top of the screen, you move up a level, and the game begins again. It continues until you use all your balls—or suffer a horrible thumb cramp.

Music Quiz

Fans of the old *Name That Tune* show will recognize the concept behind the latest game in the iPod's toy box. You need iPod Update 2.1 to play it (see page 269), or a new iPod purchased in 2004 or later.

Put on your headphones, and then navigate to Extras → Games → Music Quiz (see Figure 8-2). The game plays the first few seconds of a random song from your iPod's music library. You have 10 seconds to pick out the song's title from the 5 names listed on the iPod's screen. If you miss, you get a "Wrong" message onscreen and a deep sense of shame for not knowing your own music collection. Choosing the correct title adds to your running score and advances you to the next random song.

An iPod stuffed with thousands of songs makes this game all the more challenging. And if you've got an exam coming up in Music Appreciation, why not download all the works on the syllabus onto your iPod so you can quiz yourself? Let iPod be your personal tutor!

Parachute

Shooting at things has always been a popular theme for games, particularly computer games. (Originally, this may have been a tactic to help people manage their anger without taking a shotgun to the computer itself.)

The iPod's Parachute game lets you assume the controls of a ground-based antiaircraft gun. You're supposed to shoot at the helicopters that fly overhead and drop tiny little parachuting stick-people, as shown on the left in Figure 8-3.

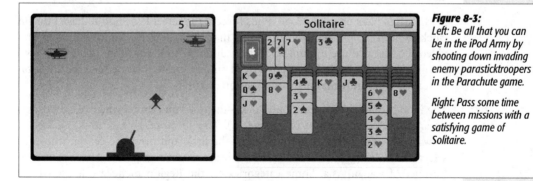

Figure 8-3:
Left: Be all that you can be in the iPod Army by shooting down invading enemy parasticktroopers in the Parachute game.

Right: Pass some time between missions with a satisfying game of Solitaire.

To play Parachute, choose Extras → Games → Parachute, and then press the Select button to start the game. The gun sits in the center bottom of the screen, but you can use the scroll wheel to pivot the barrel and direct your fire to the helicopters that buzz overhead. Press the Select button to fire at either the helicopters or the tiny parachutists. You get points for hitting a helicopter with one shot, but lose points if you miss.

Note: Once a paratrooper lands safely on the ground, he can lob grenades at you, so it's best to hit those guys while they're in the air. If one of the parachuting troops lands on your gun, you lose. Nobody said war is pretty.

Solitaire

This single-player card game has been entertaining the bored and lonely for centuries, and Solitaire's arrival on the iPod is sure to give many people something to do. Although it's not as large as the versions you can play on a desktop computer, iPod Solitaire (Figure 8-3, right) has its advantages. For instance, you can play it with one hand while riding the bus or waiting around for a friend to show up.

To begin play, go to Extras → Games → Solitaire and tap the Select button to deal out the first three cards. The game is standard Klondike: You get a row of seven card piles, on which you're supposed to alternate black and red cards in descending numerical order. Because you can't physically touch the cards, the iPod provides a helping hand cursor.

Use the scroll wheel to pass the hand over each stack of cards. When you get to the card you want, click the Select button to move the selected card to the bottom of the screen. Then scroll the disembodied hand to the pile where you want to place the card, and click the Select button again to make the play.

When you need to deal out another three cards, place the hand over the deck at the top of the screen and tap the Select button. After you go through the deck once, the remaining cards automatically restack so you can continue dealing.

Clock

As discussed back on page 27, all iPods (except the screenless Shuffle) have built-in clocks with a simple alarm feature. But that's *so* last week. The iPod Nano and video iPod let you use multiple clocks, in different time zones and with their own alarms. If you travel frequently, you can simply create a clock for each location instead of constantly fiddling with time zone settings.

The iPod should already have one clock—the one you created when you first set it up and selected your time zone (page 27). To add more, go to Extras → Clock → New Clock (it's always at the bottom of the list), and press the center button to select New Clock. On the next screen, select a world region, like North America, Europe, Africa, or Asia. Some categories on the Region menu are less obvious: Select Atlantic if you live in Iceland or the Azores; choose Pacific if you live in Hawaii, Guam, or Pago Pago.

After you select a region, the next screen takes you to a list of major cities and the current time in that part of the world. Scroll and select the town of your choice. Once you pick a city, the iPod creates a clock showing the local time and adds it to your Clock menu.

Note: The clock face appears white with black hands during the location's daytime hours, but changes to a black face with white hands at night.

Adjusting a clock's settings

Each clock you create has its own sublevel of settings you can change. Say you want to change the settings on your Indianapolis clock because those Hoosiers refuse to observe Daylight Savings Time. (When the rest of the Eastern time zone switches to Daylight Savings Time, Indy remains an hour behind.)

To get to the settings for your Indianapolis clock, choose Extra → Clock → Indianapolis and tap the center button once you get there. The next screen reveals a host of hidden settings, including:

- **Alarm Clock.** See page 28 for instructions on how to set your clock's alarm.

- **Change City.** Choose this option to return to the Region menu, where you can start all over again picking a country and city for this clock to represent.

- **Daylight Savings Time.** The center button is an on/off toggle for Daylight Savings Time (called Summer Time in some parts of the world). For example, you'd set it to Off in the summer to keep Indianapolis properly represented on your iPod.

- **Delete This Clock.** If you're tired of this town and its time, take it off the menu with this command.

- **Sleep Timer.** The iPod can lull you to sleep and shut itself off automatically. See page 29 for the details.

Stopwatch

The Stopwatch feature (iPod Nano and video iPod only) is just the ticket for runners and other obsessive people who want to know exactly how much time something takes. It not only clocks your time around the track, it also *keeps* track of your running sessions. It logs times for individual laps and displays your shortest, longest, and average lap times. To turn your iPod into a stopwatch, choose Extras → Stopwatch → Timer.

The Stopwatch screen displays separate sets of numbers stacked on top of each other, like this:

00:07:34.18
Lap 1 00:07:34.178

The top number is the total time of the session in hours, minutes, seconds, and hundredths of a second. The smaller number underneath is the time for the current lap in hours, minutes, seconds, and milliseconds. (The lap time is a subpart of the total session time.) On the video-playing iPods, the screen is large enough for you to see three laps listed at once, but the Nano doesn't quite have that much screen presence.

The buttons underneath the timer screen are the same controls you find on any stopwatch—Start and Clear. Use the click wheel to highlight the button you want to use and press the iPod's center Select button to click it. For example, spin around until the Start button on the left side of the screen is highlighted, then press the center Select button to start the timer. The stopwatch starts counting and changes the Start button to Pause.

To stop the timer, press the Select button to choose Pause. When you click Pause, the button's name changes yet again, to Resume. If you need to take a breather before going back for more exercise—but want to keep track of your total time spent exercising, click the Resume button when you're ready to start again, and the timer picks up where it left off. When you're truly done for the day and want to stop the timer for good, spin the click wheel to the Done button on the right side of the screen.

Here's a rundown of how the button names change as you start and stop the timer:

- When you press **Start**, the buttons change to Pause and Lap.

- When you click **Pause**, the timer stops counting and the buttons change to Resume and Done.

- When you click **Lap**, you reset the lap timer (the smaller clock underneath the main one).

- When you click **Resume**, the timer restarts and the buttons change back to Pause and Lap.

- When you click **Done**, the stopwatch slides over to the session log screen.

Note: Yes, you can still play music through the iPod's headphones and use the click wheel's music playback controls (Play/Pause, Next, Previous) while you're using the Stopwatch function. Apple wouldn't be so cruel as to cut off the energetic exercise tunes right when you need them the most.

If the Stopwatch screen still shows an old time listed in the counter, the next time you call it up, slide the click wheel around until the Clear button is highlighted and tap the center button to reset the clock back to 00:00:00.00.

The iPod won't go into Sleep mode if the Stopwatch is running, and the Stopwatch keeps running even if you *manually* put the iPod or Nano to sleep by pressing Play/Pause for a few seconds until the screen goes off. Things (besides you) that can stop the Stopwatch include connecting the iPod to the computer, and reaching 24 hours of total time on the counter.

Counting laps

If you're running laps around a track or timing yourself for different stretches of the Boston Marathon, you can also record separate lap times. After you pause the timer for the first time, the button on the right side of the iPod's screen changes to Lap. Each time you finish a lap around the track, tap the Lap button to record that lap's time and restart the lap counter to 00:00:00 so it can begin recording the next one.

If you need to take a breather between laps but aren't done with your exercise session, slide the click wheel around until the Pause button is highlighted and tap the center button. This stops all the timers until you get your wind back. When you're ready to run more laps, click the Resume button and then tap Lap again each time you finish a trip around the track.

The iPod keeps a log of your overall session time and the individual time for each lap, as described next.

Session logs

The iPod stores logs of your last five workout sessions, deleting older sessions as you record new ones. To review your progress, scroll to Extras → Stopwatch, where there's a list of your past exercise sessions listed by date and time of day recorded. Scroll to any session and tap the center button to call it up. As shown in Figure 8-4, each session has its own log of activity, which you can scroll to see specific information about your timing and performance.

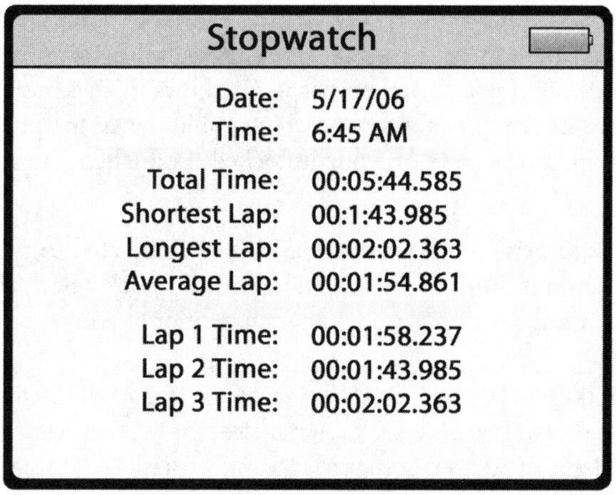

Stopwatch

Date:	5/17/06
Time:	6:45 AM
Total Time:	00:05:44.585
Shortest Lap:	00:1:43.985
Longest Lap:	00:02:02.363
Average Lap:	00:01:54.861
Lap 1 Time:	00:01:58.237
Lap 2 Time:	00:01:43.985
Lap 3 Time:	00:02:02.363

Figure 8-4:
Each session log can record up to 21 separate lap times. After that, the overall time and lap counters still work, but you can't see the individual lap times.

In addition to the date and time of the session, each log entry lists the amount of time the total session lasted, the shortest, longest, and average lap times (if you counted your laps separately), and a notation of each separate lap time. If you want to erase a particular session right there after you've looked at it and don't want the iPod to keep it around, tap the Select button while the session log is displayed to get a Delete option.

Screen Lock

It's no secret that the iPod can store contacts, calendars, notes, and other important information alongside your music and photos. (Check out Appendix B, online at *www.missingmanuals.com*, for details on getting your contacts and calendar onto your iPod.) But if you lose your iPod or leave it out where your roommates can find it, your private information may end up in the palm of someone else's hand. Considering the unfortunate rise of identity theft, it pays to be careful.

To help keep your personal information personal, the newest iPods come with a security feature—Screen Lock. It's much like assigning a password to your computer's screensaver—one that reveals the desktop only if you type the secret code. When you turn Screen Lock on, the iPod's screen displays a safe's door icon that stubbornly refuses to go away until you enter your combination.

To activate this protective layer, choose Extras → Screen Lock. On the next screen, you have two choices: Set Combination or Turn Screen Lock On. The first time, select Set Combination to create your secret code. On the next screen, you see the combination dial with four numbers above it. Using the iPod's click wheel, navigate to each box (outlined in red when you've scrolled to it). By spinning the wheel, you can pick a number from 0 to 9, and the animated safe dial on the screen even moves along as you move your thumb.

When the number you want appears in the box, press the center button to go to the next one, and repeat until you've filled in all four boxes. This four-digit number is the code to unlock your iPod, so remember it.

Now, when you want to lock your Pod, choose Extras → Screen Lock → Turn Screen Lock On → Lock. Like a concerned mother, the iPod flashes a screen displaying your lock code and warns you to remember it. (It shows this warning and code every time you turn on Screen Lock, though, which could defeat the purpose if your brother sneaks a peek at the code on your unlocked iPod when you're not around.)

The iPod displays the Lock screen—even when it's asleep or connected to a computer—until you dial in the right number combination with the click wheel. If you enter the wrong digits, the number boxes flash an angry red color at you.

Tip: If you plan to use Screen Lock all the time, you can add it to your iPod's main menu screen so you don't have to burrow around in the Extras menu every time you want a little security. To add it to the main screen, choose Settings → Main Menu → Screen Lock and press the iPod's center button to toggle the setting to On. Screen Lock then appears on your iPod's main screen along with Music, Extras, and all the usual items.

Unlocking the screen

Entering the correct number combination is the obvious way to unlock your iPod's vault, but you can also get into the iPod by connecting it to the very first computer you synched it to and starting up iTunes. When you eject the iPod from the computer through iTunes, its screen unlocks.

If you can't remember your code, can't get to the computer you first used with the iPod, and can't believe you turned on this dang Screen Lock thing in the first place, you can fix the situation by restoring the iPod's software back to its factory settings. This step also has the unfortunate side effect of erasing all your music and data. The steps for restoring an iPod's software start on page 273. (And no, you can't call Apple to find out what your secret code is. They don't know it either.)

Notes

The squint factor may be a little high, but the iPod can also lend its screen for displaying text files, which can come in handy if you want to review class notes while relaxing to a little Queen Latifah or skim your talking points before a presentation.

If you have an iPod 2003-or-later model, all of this comes to you courtesy of a text-reader program called Notes (Figure 8-5). Notes can hold about 1,000 plain text files and display one at a time onscreen.

Grocery List

Milk
Bread
Cap'n Crunch Crunchberries
Side of beef
Fresca
Pop-Tarts
Cool Ranch Doritos
Frozen waffles
Popsicles
Carrots

Figure 8-5:
If you can save it as a plain text file, you can read it on your iPod with its convenient Notes feature. With your iPod in tow, you'll never forget to bring home milk again.

You create iPod Notes from plain text files—those with a .txt extension. You can't use full-fledged word-processing documents from Microsoft Word or Apple-Works, unless you save them as plain text files. (As Chapter 9 makes clear, you can certainly use the iPod as a portable drive to ferry big files from one computer to another, but you can only *display* text files in Notes). Most word-processing programs, however, can export a file's contents into Text Only or Plain Text.

For example, if you have a Word or AppleWorks document that you want to read on the iPod, open it and choose File → Save As (or the equivalent command in whatever program you're using). Select plain text formatting for the newly saved copy. Fancy formatting, graphics, and other niceties don't show up in the .txt file, but on the bright side, the file size gets a lot smaller. The iPod Notes program can display files up to 4 KB in size, which is plenty of room for lists, itineraries, or brief chunks of text. The iPod truncates files bigger than 4 KB after they pass the size limit.

To use the Notes feature, attach the iPod as an external disk (page 203). When you've saved your text files as described above, drag the files into the Notes folder on the iPod. To do so, open the iPod by double-clicking its icon on the Mac desktop or in the My Computer window. The Notes folder, as seen in Figure 8-6, appears alongside the Contacts and Calendars folders. (For the story on what these folders do, see the online appendix, "iPod As Organizer," available on the "Missing CD" page at *www.missingmanuals.com.*)

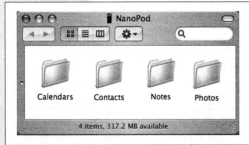

Figure 8-6:
Drag your text files into the Notes folder (right) to read them later on the iPod. To remove files, reconnect the iPod to the computer (page 204), and open the Notes folder on the desktop. Drag the unwanted files into the Trash or Recycle Bin and empty it.

After you've copied your text files, *unmount* the iPod (page 207). When you're ready to start reading, choose Extras → Notes. You'll see the names of your text files listed in the Notes menu. Scroll to the one you want and click the Select button to bring it onscreen.

Tip: Want to compose, format, and link your own Notes files together? A free six-page guide from Apple's Web site gives you the basics. You can download a copy from *http://developer.apple.com/ hardware/ipod/ipodnotereader.pdf.*

As you read, you can use the scroll wheel to page up and down through the file. Press the Menu button to close the file and return to the list of Notes files. If you can't find a document you're looking for in the Notes menu, open the Notes folder on the iPod and make sure it's indeed a .txt file.

Note: Want to use your iPod as an eBook reader or portable newsstand? Check out the online appendix, "Reading eBooks and More on Your iPod" (available on the "Missing CD" at *www.missingmanuals.com*).

The iPod as External Drive

There may come a time when the size of your files grows to exceed the size of a blank CD or 128-megabyte pocket flash drive. For many people, that time is *now*. Thanks to the boom in digital audio, photography, and video, our supersized files don't fit on such meager disks anymore, which makes it harder to cart them around from computer to computer.

That's where the iPod's most magnificent hidden feature comes into play. Remember that the iPod is essentially, at heart, a hard drive (which is why it can hold so many thousands of songs). Even the tiny Nano is big on the inside, with up to 4 gigabytes of flash memory at your disposal. With a single click in Preferences, in fact, the iPod can turn itself into an external hard drive—a real live icon-on-your-screen hard drive. Depending on the capacity of your iPod—and how much music you have on it—you could easily have a spare 2, 10, or 25 gigabytes of space available for backing up your Documents folder or transporting that 800 MB movie of your baby's first steps. Before Apple switched its iPod line to USB 2.0 connections in 2005, you could even boot up a Mac from a FireWire-based iPod—something owners of those slightly older models can still do.

The iPod's Hard Disk Format

The iPod's drive is formatted in such a way that it can communicate with a computer much like any other hard drive—depending on which model iPod and computer you're using.

The first iPods, released in 2001, functioned only as *Macintosh* hard disks. The 2002 iPods came in separate Macintosh or Windows versions. And 2003-and-later iPods, Minis, and Nanos are compatible with both Mac and Windows (you don't have to pick a format at purchase time; see page 4).

Tip: You can tell if an iPod was formatted for Macintosh or Windows in the About menu on the main iPod screen. If the last item in the list is the iPod's serial number, you've got a Macintosh-formatted iPod. If it says, "Format: Windows" underneath the serial number…well, you can figure it out from there.

A Windows PC won't recognize a Macintosh-formatted iPod. On the other hand, a Mac can recognize *both* PC-and-Mac-formatted iPods. Some people even go back and forth between a Mac and a PC with their Windows-formatted iPods, merrily and manually updating their music collection between iTunes for each platform. If you split your time between a PC at work and a Mac at home, and want to load music from both machines, a Windows-formatted iPod is the way to go.

You can reformat a Mac iPod for Windows, or a Windows iPod for Macintosh, but only by erasing it completely and reformatting it.

Note: Do not reformat or partition the iPod's hard drive with any utility software other than the iPod installer program that came with your player. These installers format the drive in HFS Plus (Mac) or FAT32 (Windows), which is what the iPod needs to play music. Formatting the drive with, say, the Unix or Mac OS Standard file systems spell the end of your iPod's career as a music player until you reformat it properly with the iPod installer.

The iPod as an External Hard Disk

To set up the iPod as an external hard disk, you don't have to jump through complicated technical hoops. The days of installing disk drivers, fiddling with jumper switches, SCSI-chain termination, and IRQ settings are long gone.

Tip: Even though they're tiny in comparison, the flash-memory iPod Shuffles can get into the external drive game, too. Flip back to page 71 for the details on turning your Shuffle into a USB flash drive.

In iTunes for both the Mac and Windows systems, just follow the steps in Figure 9-1 to turn that simple music player into a music player *and* a portable hard drive for all your ginormous file-toting needs. (The look of this Preferences box may vary slightly, depending on which version of iTunes you're using.)

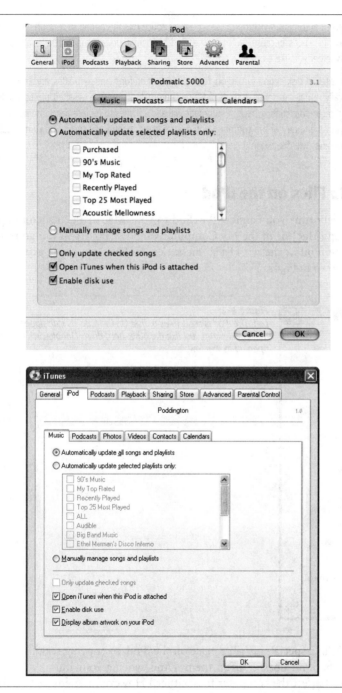

Figure 9-1:
Turning the iPod into an external hard drive is a matter of turning on a special checkbox in the iPod Preferences dialog box. Here's how you do it in iTunes for Windows and Macintosh: Attach the iPod, open iTunes, select the iPod in the Source list, and click the small iPod icon at the bottom of the iTunes window. You've just opened the iPod Preferences dialog box (shown here in Mac OS X, top, and Windows, bottom). Finally, click the Music tab, turn on the "Enable disk use" checkbox, and then click OK.

Note: If you've disabled automatic synchronization, you may notice that the option to turn on the external mode is dimmed out. That's because switching the iPod to manual-update mode *also* enables the external disk mode, whether you like it or not.

If you don't want the external disk option turned on, turn off the button for manual updates, and then turn on either "Automatically update all songs and playlists" or "Automatically update selected playlists only" instead. Be warned, though, that shifting back to automatic will allow iTunes to replace the contents of the iPod with whatever is in the library of the computer you're connected to, and any songs you've manually added from other machines will disappear.

Storing Data Files on the iPod

From now on, every time you connect the iPod to your Mac or PC, its icon pops up on the desktop (Mac) or in the My Computer window (PC). You can go right to town using the iPod as the world's shiniest, best-looking, and most expensive floppy disk, as shown in Figure 9-2.

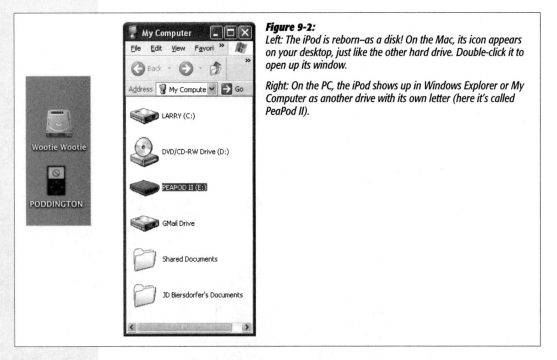

Figure 9-2:
Left: The iPod is reborn–as a disk! On the Mac, its icon appears on your desktop, just like the other hard drive. Double-click it to open up its window.

Right: On the PC, the iPod shows up in Windows Explorer or My Computer as another drive with its own letter (here it's called PeaPod II).

The music is kept in a special, invisible place on the iPod, so copying regular computer files onto the iPod doesn't affect them. (And syncing your music with the Mac or PC doesn't affect the computer files, either.) However, remember that the more you fill up your iPod with music, the less room you have to store data files—and vice versa.

Deleting Data Files

Deleting files from the iPod when it's impersonating a hard drive is just like erasing them from any other kind of disk: just drag them to the Trash or Recycle Bin—or use keyboard shortcuts, like the Delete key in Windows or ⌘-Delete on the Macintosh—and empty it.

Just remember that this isn't how you delete *songs.* You delete songs in iTunes.

Tip: Don't use a disk utility program like Drive Setup or Norton Utilities to erase the iPod's data files. You could damage its music-playing powers—and then be stuck having to reformat the drive with the iPod software installer and *then* copy all of your songs over again.

Unmounting the iPod Drive

You're not supposed to detach any kind of hard drive just by ripping its cord out of your computer. If it happens to be right in the middle of copying a file, or performing some automatic internal maintenance that you're not even aware of, you risk badly scrambling the data on that disk.

The same goes for the iPod. Yes, you can "eject" it as you would a CD—that, after all, is its whole delicious advantage—but only after first *unmounting* it (that is, removing its icon from the screen).

One method that works on both Mac and Windows systems is to go to the iTunes Source list, select the iPod and then click the Eject iPod button at the bottom of the window (see Figure 9-3). In iTunes 4.5 and later, there's also a conveniently located Eject button *right next to the iPod* in the Source list that saves you some mousing around.

Figure 9-3:
Here in iTunes, click the first button to get to the iPod Preferences box, or the fourth button to safely eject the iPod from the Mac.

Tip: In all cases, don't disconnect the iPod until you see the iPod's main menu screen or an "OK to Disconnect" message—which may take as long as 15 seconds.

At this point, if you have iTunes open, the iPod disappears from the Source list and from your desktop. Depending on your iPod model and software, either the main menu or the "OK to Disconnect" message appears on the iPod's screen. Each computer platform also has its own disk-ditching methods:

- **Mac.** You can use any of the usual disk-ejection methods: drag the iPod icon on the desktop to the Trash, Control-click the iPod icon and choose Eject from the shortcut menu, click the Eject icon next to the iPod's icon in the Sidebar (Mac OS X 10.3 or later), and so on.

- **Windows.** In the notification area, click the Safely Remove Hardware icon, which looks like a small green arrow floating above a gray box (Figure 9-4). Choose whatever variation of the Stop IEEE 1394 Disk Drive option you see. When the Safely Remove Hardware message appears, click OK.

Figure 9-4:
Here's another way to release the iPod: the Safely Remove Hardware icon that lives in the Windows notification area.

Tip: Apple advises that you *not* eject the iPod by right-clicking its icon in the My Computer window and using the Eject option from the shortcut menu.

CHAPTER 10

Connecting the iPod

You've labored over ripping CDs and composing playlists for months now, and you just want to share your music with the world—or at least with the people at your party. But how? By playing Pass the iPod? And what about all those songs that are perfect for cranking up in the car? Are they locked away in your iPod forever, never to provide the music for impromptu sessions of Stoplight Shimmy?

Absolutely not. If you can load it onto your iPod, you can channel it through most any stereo system or blast it through your car's speakers. This chapter explains the simple procedures for playing your iPod songs through the woofers and tweeters in your life.

Note: The prices, Web sites, and model numbers in this chapter are intended to get your geek saliva flowing—not to serve as an up-to-date catalog. One spec or another has almost certainly changed since this book went to press, or even since you started reading this paragraph. Even so, you'll certainly learn one thing from this chapter: there's a lot of neat stuff out there.

Connecting the iPod to a Stereo System

CD players that can play discs of MP3s cost less than $100. But if you have an iPod, you already have a state-of-the-art MP3 player that you can connect to your existing system for under $20.

When connected to a stereo system, the iPod's wide frequency-response range and 60-milliwatt amplifier give it the audio oomph to fill a room. To link the iPod to your stereo, you need the right kind of cable (page 211) and a set of input jacks on the back of your receiver. Most audio systems come with at least one extra set of

---

inputs (after accounting for the CD player, cassette deck, and other common components). Look for an empty AUX jack, like the one shown in Figure 10-1.

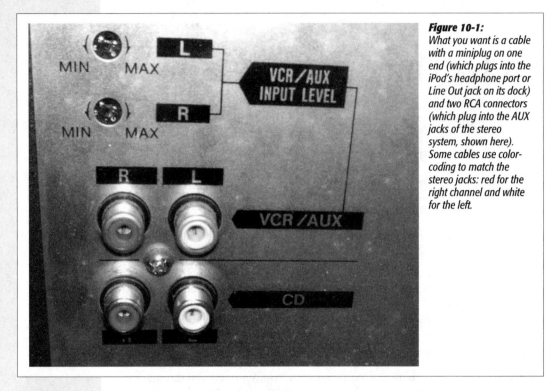

Figure 10-1:
What you want is a cable with a miniplug on one end (which plugs into the iPod's headphone port or Line Out jack on its dock) and two RCA connectors (which plug into the AUX jacks of the stereo system, shown here). Some cables use color-coding to match the stereo jacks: red for the right channel and white for the left.

The cable you need is a Y-shaped cord with a 3.5 mm (1/8") stereo miniplug on one end and two bigger RCA plugs at the other end. The stereo miniplug is the standard connector for Walkman-style headphones (and for speakers and microphones); RCA plugs are standard connectors for linking stereo components together.

You plug the smaller end into the iPod's headphones jack, and the RCA plugs into the left and right channel jacks on the back of your stereo.

Over the years, Apple has sold several models of the iPod charging dock, including the ones that used to come free with the third-generation iPod (Figure 10-2, left) and the AV dock that came with the original iPod Photo in 2004. The company now sells docks and the cables that go with them as separate accessories, including the Universal Dock, which fits most iPod models. All of these docks feature a line-out jack that you can connect with the mini-plug end of your stereo cable, thus bringing booming sound from your upright iPod to your stereo system.

The Universal Dock sells for $40 at *http://store.apple.com* and even works with Apple's own miniature white remote control (available for another $30) to command your iPod from across the room. The U-Dock comes with plastic adapters that serve as little iPod booster seats so the Nano and the Mini can sit just as securely as a full-sized iPod.

Companies like Kensington and DLO also sell docks to connect the iPod to a stereo system. DLO's HomeDock, shown on the right side of Figure 10-2, comes with its own remote control and can pipe your iPod's music, photos, and videos through your home entertainment altar.

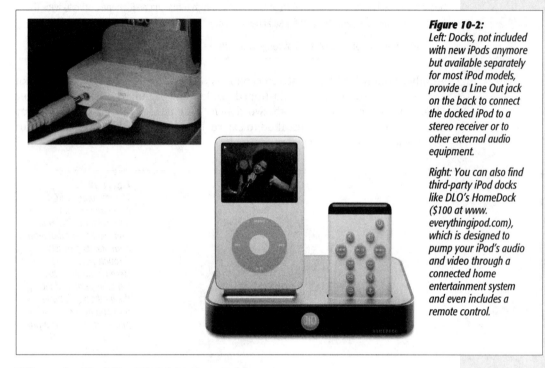

Figure 10-2:
Left: Docks, not included with new iPods anymore but available separately for most iPod models, provide a Line Out jack on the back to connect the docked iPod to a stereo receiver or to other external audio equipment.

Right: You can also find third-party iPod docks like DLO's HomeDock ($100 at www. everythingipod.com), which is designed to pump your iPod's audio and video through a connected home entertainment system and even includes a remote control.

Where to Find the Right Stereo Cable

At your friendly neighborhood Radio Shack, ask for a Y-adapter audio cable, which costs about $7. You can also visit Radio Shack's Web site at *www.radioshack.com*.

Note: When shopping for audio cables, you may see or hear reference to "male" and "female" plugs. In this case, technology mimics nature: Male plugs are the kind with prongs and female connectors are hollowed out at the end. (No wisecracks, please.) The jacks on both the iPod and the back of the stereo receiver are female, so you want a male-to-male cable.

For a little more glamor, you can buy the Xwire Gold RCA audio cable from XtremeMac. It's sheathed-in-white Apple-chic plastic with gleaming gold connector plugs on the end. (Gold-tipped cables are supposed to provide better audio quality.) The 7-foot cable costs about $13.

If you need more distance than seven feet, XtremeMac also sells a female-to-male extension cable that you can plug into the RCA cable to double its length. There's a wide selection of audio cables designed to plug the iPod into several different audio sources at *www.xtrememac.com.*

Tip: If you and your significant other are dreading the Hollywood C-picture that's sure to be the in-flight movie on your upcoming trip together, why not zone out and share the iPod instead? You just need an adapter like the iShare Earbud Splitter from XtremeMac, which turns one headphone port into two. The Y-shaped white and gold adapter sells for $8 at *www.xtrememac.com.*

Just make sure to create a playlist full of songs you *both* like.

Another option for iPod-to-stereo cabling is the iPod Home Connect Kit. The kit comes with two different gold-tipped cables: the standard RCA audio cable (Figure 10-3) and a model with two *female* RCA plugs, which comes in handy when you want to connect the iPod to external computer speakers. The kit sells for $15 at *www.griffintechnology.com.*

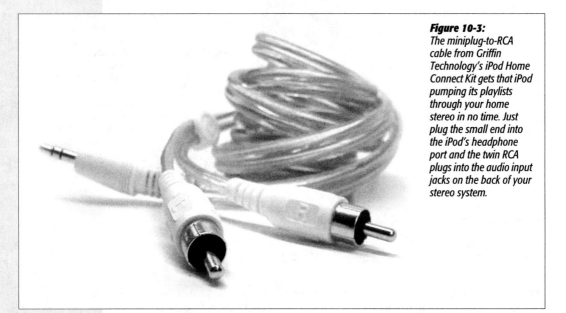

Figure 10-3:
The miniplug-to-RCA cable from Griffin Technology's iPod Home Connect Kit gets that iPod pumping its playlists through your home stereo in no time. Just plug the small end into the iPod's headphone port and the twin RCA plugs into the audio input jacks on the back of your stereo system.

Tip: When playing your iPod through another audio system, don't spin its scroll wheel up to the highest volume. You risk distorting the sound by overamplification. Instead, take the volume level on the iPod to about half the maximum and, if you still need more volume, use the controls on the *receiver.* This technique gives you the best audio quality.

Monster Cable, the venerable cordmeisters favored by AV fanatics, has even jumped into the iPod accessory game. Its gold-tipped, 7-foot Monster iCable for iPod goes for about $30. The company's Web site has more information and a link to stores that carry Monster cables at *www.monstercable.com.*

Note: Want to hook up a pair of external speakers to your iPod? Check out the online appendix "iStuff," available on the "Missing CD" page at *www.missingmanuals.com*, for a quick introduction to some of your best options.

Using iTunes with AirPort Express

Two very exciting possibilities arrived with the release of Apple's $129 AirPort Express mobile wireless base station in mid-2004. The first was that you could now have a portable base station so that you could make your own super-fast 802.11g wireless network wherever you found a broadband connection—whether it be in a hotel room, a board room, or a play room.

The second great thing, and way more exciting because this is *iPod & iTunes: The Missing Manual,* is that the AirPort Express also makes it possible to call up a playlist on your computer upstairs and have the music come out downstairs through your stereo's speakers. This is because the AirPort Express has a stereo cable jack in addition to its Ethernet cable jack (Figure 10-4). The AirTunes software, included with the AirPort Express, makes it happen, but you also need to be running iTunes 4.6 or later.

The Airport Express comes with software that guides you through setting up your network and connecting it to iTunes. You can also find more details on the AirPort Express installation online at the "Missing CD" page at *www.missingmanuals.com*.

Note: Only one computer at a time can play iTunes music with a particular AirPort Express, so if you've got only one Express and a house full of music lovers all jockeying to be the AirTunes disc jockey, you may want to set up a programming schedule so everyone gets a turn.

Connecting the iPod to a Car Stereo

Since the glorious days of crackly AM radio, music and driving have gone hand in hand. These days, a stereo system with AM/FM radio and a cassette deck is the bare minimum for most cars, and late-model vehicles now cruise around with all sorts of high-end equipment tucked inside, from MP3-compatible CD players to satellite radio. (Whether the music you can play on them has improved over the years is the subject of debate.)

If having your playlists with you is your idea of paradise by the dashboard light, there are several inexpensive ways to get your iPod nestled right in with your car's stereo system.

You have to consider two factors when taking the iPod along to play in the car:

• **How to wire it to your existing auto audio system.** You have your pick of using either a cable or wireless connection.

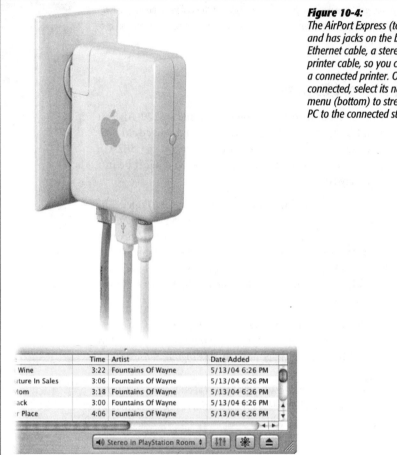

Figure 10-4:
The AirPort Express (top) plugs into a wall outlet and has jacks on the bottom to connect an Ethernet cable, a stereo cable, and even a USB printer cable, so you can beam your documents to a connected printer. Once the AirPort Express is connected, select its name in the iTunes pop-up menu (bottom) to stream music from your Mac or PC to the connected stereo or speakers.

	Time	Artist	Date Added
Wine	3:22	Fountains Of Wayne	5/13/04 6:26 PM
...ture In Sales	3:06	Fountains Of Wayne	5/13/04 6:26 PM
...om	3:18	Fountains Of Wayne	5/13/04 6:26 PM
...ack	3:00	Fountains Of Wayne	5/13/04 6:26 PM
...r Place	4:06	Fountains Of Wayne	5/13/04 6:26 PM

Stereo in PlayStation Room

- **How to power it.** Of course, your iPod can run fine on its battery for short trips. If you're retracing historic Route 66 or barreling down I-95 from Maine to Miami, however, you'll probably want to invest in an adapter that can power your iPod from the car's electrical system.

The Wireless Way

Gadgets that transmit a personal signal over an existing FM frequency have been around for decades. Today, you can hook up an FM transmitter that connects to an MP3 player's headphone port and broadcasts its sound through an unoccupied FM channel on the car radio—and out through the speakers.

This method offers several advantages. For one thing, you don't have to deal with cables or cords snaking around the dashboard. Also, most FM transmitters are inexpensive, often costing less than $30, and many are designed to just pop right into the headphone jack with a standard stereo miniplug, making them compatible with iPods of all shapes and sizes, including the iPod Shuffle.

But there are disadvantages, too. The sound quality isn't so great—it depends on the strength of the signal—and radio is frustratingly prone to interference (static). Furthermore, you'll need to keep the iPod physically close to the radio. Some FM transmitters offer a few preset frequencies down on the lower half of the FM band to use for broadcasting your own music, but you might have trouble finding an unused frequency if you live in an area with lots of radio stations at the lower end of the dial.

Still, if you think an FM transmitter is your ticket to ride, you have several choices:

- **iTrip or RoadTrip.** Griffin technology makes several eye-catching gadgets designed to pump your music through the dashboard (Figure 10-5). The iTrip comes in two models that plug into the iPod either through the headphone jack or dock-connector port to transmit the FM signal. The iTrip can use any FM frequency, and it uses the iPod's battery for its juice. If you play the iPod a lot while you drive, you may want to consider Griffin's RoadTrip device, which is a combination FM transmitter/charger that plugs right into your car's 12-volt power outlet. As a special bonus, the transmitter unit is detachable so you can take it into the house, plug it into your computer's USB port, and play music over an FM channel from the desktop. You can order iTrips for any iPod model for about $30 or the RoadTrip (which works with dock-connecting iPods, Minis, and Nanos) for $90 at *www.griffintechnology.com*.

Figure 10-5:
Griffin Technology has a variety of automotive-themed iPod attachments, including the dock-connecting iTrip (left), the standard iTrip (middle), and the RoadTrip (right), which plugs into the car's charger for power and uses a digital FM transmitter to borrow a radio frequency for dashboard iPodding.

- **The DLO TransPod.** This transmitter with a digital tuner also serves as a secure dashboard mount for the iPod (Figure 10-6). For power, it plugs into the car's cigarette lighter, so you don't have to worry about your batteries. For these reasons, this $100 unit may be your best bet if you frequently use your iPod while driving. The TransPod, which works with all recent click wheel–sporting iPods, including the Nano and the video-playing iPod, is available at *www. everythingipod.com*, along with other versions of the TransPod that work with older iPods. The company also makes the $40 Transcast FM transmitter that works with all iPods.

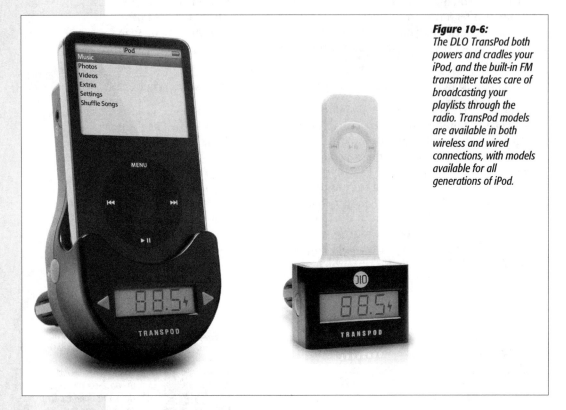

Figure 10-6:
The DLO TransPod both powers and cradles your iPod, and the built-in FM transmitter takes care of broadcasting your playlists through the radio. TransPod models are available in both wireless and wired connections, with models available for all generations of iPod.

- **TuneCast Mobile FM Transmitter.** Here's a gadget on a budget: Belkin sells it for under $40. This small white accessory plugs into the iPod's headphone jack and plays through one of four frequencies on the low end of the FM dial. You can find it at *www.belkin.com*. The company also makes the Belkin Digital FM Transmitter, which can transmit on any frequency from 88.1 to 107.9. It sells for $40 in the iPod accessories area at *http://store.apple.com*.

- **Kensington Digital FM Transmitter/Auto Charger.** This variation on the FM transmitter from Kensington comes with an integrated auto-charger plug that snaps right into the car's 12-volt outlet while the cable connects to the iPod's dock connector port. The device sells for $80 at *www.kensington.com*.

- **Monster iCarPlay Wireless.** Designed to charge the iPod through the car's power outlet while its digital tuner borrows an available radio frequency for your playlists, Monster Cable's own FM transmitter for iPod keeps the hits coming without battery fear as you head down the highway. It's available in two versions at *www.monstercable.com*: the $70 iCarPlay Wireless and the $80 iCarPlay Wireless Plus model, which adds in an LED screen and programmable presets to use for your favorite empty frequencies.

Tip: Not going anywhere but still want to play your iPod through a nearby FM radio? The PodFreq from Sonnet Technologies (Figure 10-7) combines an upright desk stand to prop up the Pod and a digital FM tuner with a telescoping antenna. The PodFreq draws its power from the iPod itself, so there's no need to load up on the AAs, and it can tap into any radio frequency on the FM dial. It works with most dock-connecting iPods except the Nano, comes with a car charger, and sells for $100 online at *www.podfreq.com*.

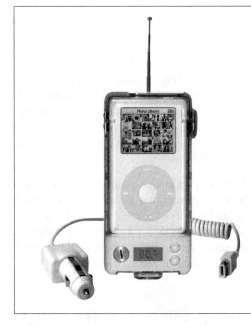

Figure 10-7:
The PodFreq FM transmitter turns your desk into a DJ booth. The iPod snaps into the stand and the telescoping antenna increases the broadcasting range. It also works with its own car charger. The PodFreq works with full-size iPods with the dock-connector port, and there's a model for Minis as well.

The Wired Way

You may prefer to stick with cables, either because the sound quality is better or because you can't get a consistently clear signal in your part of FM Land.

One solution is an adapter that resembles an audiocassette. An attached cable and stereo miniplug link the iPod to the car's stereo—if your stereo is equipped with a cassette player, that is. You just plug the cable into the iPod, slip the cassette end into the dashboard, and press Play.

Some examples:

- **The Sony CPA-9C Car Connecting Cassette.** The Sony unit is designed for connecting Sony's own portable Discman and MiniDisc players to the car's stereo, but it also works with the iPod and costs less than $20 at *www.sonystyle.com*.

- **XtremeMac iPod Cassette Adapter.** This white cassette adapter matches the iPod and comes with a gold-tipped miniplug (see Figure 10-8). It's about $20 from *www.xtrememac.com*.

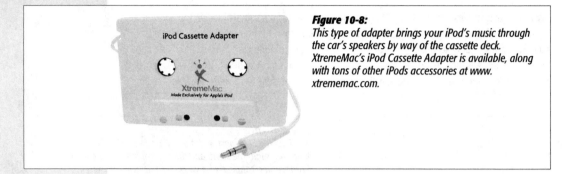

iPod Cassette Adapter

XtremeMac
Made Exclusively for Apple's iPod

Figure 10-8:
*This type of adapter brings your iPod's music through
the car's speakers by way of the cassette deck.
XtremeMac's iPod Cassette Adapter is available, along
with tons of other iPods accessories at www.
xtrememac.com.*

- **Griffin Technology SmartDeck.** Not only does this $30 adapter bring your iPod and cassette deck together to make music though the iPod's dock connector, it also lets you use the forward and reverse buttons on the stereo to advance or retreat through the tracks on your iPod's playlists. The SmartDeck, available at *www.griffintechnology.com/products*, also enhances the audio quality through the stereo by selecting the optimal volume on the iPod.

Incidentally, if your car's stereo console has a 3.5 mm jack on the front as an auxiliary input, you can use a simple male-to-male miniplug audio cable to connect your iPod (under $10 at Radio Shack or audio stores). Some stereo units have the auxiliary jack on the back of the unit, so if you're installing a new stereo in the car, it might be worth remembering to hook up a cable to the auxiliary jack and run it through the dash so it's there for easy RoadPodding, if you ever need it.

The Custom Installation Way

Automobile manufacturers and car audio specialists have also fallen under the spell of the iPod's sweet siren song and are even making modifications to accommodate it. Apple has a list of car makers that support iPod connections at *www. apple.com/ipod/ipodyourcar*, where there's also a link to after-market solutions to retrofit your car's sound system for an iPod connection.

BMW

BMW, the maker of powerful German driving machines that are not Mercedes-Benzes, recognized in 2004 that the iPod makes a great travel companion and introduced a special iPod adapter that works with several of its models. The adapter, which runs about $150 plus labor costs, takes less than an hour to install.

Once the adapter is in place, you plug your iPod into a familiar-looking flat connector cable inside the car's glove compartment, tuck your Pod in the box, and then navigate through your iPod's playlists and library tracks with buttons on the steering wheel. No more fiddling with the scroll wheel while trying to find Exit 12 on the interstate or trying to turn up the volume when you need to be paying attention to the road—volume controls are also built into the steering wheel. There's more information on the BMW system at *www.ipodyourbmw.com*.

Granted, this is a pretty expensive option, buying a whole BMW just to spin your iPod playlists, but if you can't afford a BMW, don't worry—Volvo, Mercedes-Benz, Nissan, Ferrari, and Alfa Romeo are now members in good standing of the iPod Connectivity Club.

Alpine iPod Interface KCA-420i

Alpine Electronics has also developed an iPod adapter to work with some of its in-car stereo systems. The Alpine iPod Interface KCA-420i costs around $100 and works with any of the company's 2004 Ai-NET head units—that's the industry name for the dashboard stereo—which start at about $200. The Alpine iPod Interface is compatible with most dock-connecting iPods and can be installed by an Alpine-authorized car audio dealer. Check out *www.alpine-usa.com* for more information. Alpine also has some iPod-ready head units available as well.

Monster iCruze for iPod

Monster Cable comes to the rescue of those without a BMW or Alpine Stereo with its $200 iCruze interface box (Figure 10-9) that connects the iPod to a factory-installed or aftermarket car stereo. The iCruze plugs into the car's satellite radio port or CD changer, and songs and playlists on the connected iPod can be called up through the CD player controls either on the dashboard or, in some cars, built into the steering wheel. The iCruze and an optional LCD display for it are at *www. monstercable.com/icruze*.

Figure 10-9:
The iCruze from Monster Cable bridges the gap between your iPod and the CD changer or satellite radio port on many car stereos to bring the power of the playlist right into your ride.

Dension iceLink for iPod

The Dension iceLink is another connection system that brings iPod and car stereo together for high-fidelity fun. Once your Pod is strapped in and wired up, you can control your playlist navigation through the dashboard and see song information from the iPod on your stereo's display. Not only does the iceLink (*www.densionusa.com*) work with a number of existing stereo units in cars from Ford, Chrysler, Honda, Toyota, Subaru, and other manufacturers, it has compatible hardware to cradle all versions of the iPod and the iPod Mini. Prices range from about $200 to $400, depending on your equipment.

Chargers

Your car's cigarette lighter can provide a far healthier use than its original intention because it can accommodate an iPod battery charger. You'll live a long, healthy life without ever having to worry about the iPod conking out in the middle of your favorite song. Several companies make these car chargers, including three well-known iPod accessory mavens:

- **PowerJolt.** Sporting a two-tone color scheme, this $25 doodad from Griffin Technology powers Pods on the road (Figure 10-10). It comes with a four-foot USB cable to string between the PowerJolt and the iPod. It works with most modern dock-connecting iPods, including the Nano (and also the tiny Shuffle) and can be had for $25 at *www.griffintechnolgy.com*.

- **DLO AutoPod AutoCharger.** If you're the proud owner of an iPod Mini or a late-model iPod with the connector on the bottom, this appliance powers your player and recharges it through the car's cigarette lighter as you travel. The $30 charger comes in either black or white and has a coiled cord that can stretch out to about 3 feet. You can get them at *www.everythingipod.com*.

- **Xtreme Mac iPod Car Charger.** Like its rivals, this charging cable connects the cigarette lighter socket to the iPod's dock connector. It sells for $20, comes in black or white, and features a replaceable fuse and an LED power indicator that lets you keep tabs on your charging situation. A version for the iPod Shuffle is $25; all are at *www.xtrememac.com*.

- **Belkin Auto Kit.** Designed for dock-connecting models, the Belkin Auto Kit includes a cable for charging your iPod from the car's power port, plus an audio-out jack and adjustable amplifier that works with Belkin's Tunecast or cassette adapter (neither of which is included) for blasting iPod tunes through the car radio. The kit sells for $40 in the iPod accessories area at *http://store.apple.com*.

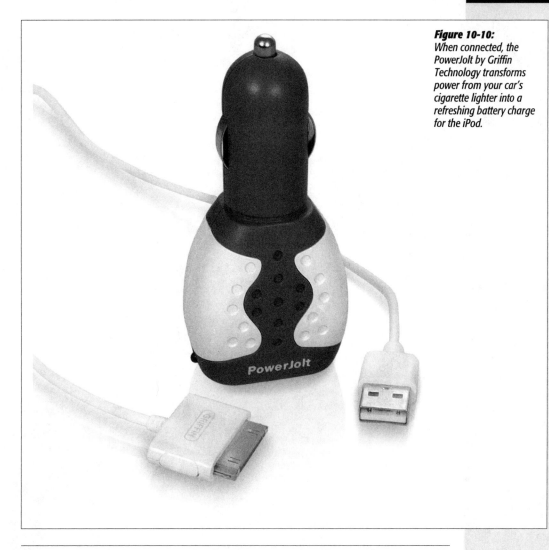

Figure 10-10:
When connected, the PowerJolt by Griffin Technology transforms power from your car's cigarette lighter into a refreshing battery charge for the iPod.

Note: A guided tour of even more iPod-friendly gadgets awaits in the online appendix "iStuff," available on the "Missing CD" at *www.missingmanuals.com*.

Part Four:
Extreme iPodding

4

Hot Hacks and Cool Tools

If you've read this book from the beginning, you know that you can do a lot more with your iPod than just play music on it. You can use it as an alarm clock, stopwatch, or portable game player. You can make it do double-duty as a music player *and* a portable hard drive, as well as wire it up to be your portable jukebox for the car and home stereo.

But did you know that most iPods of recent vintage can serve up recipes, display your email, and even tell you how to get to Albuquerque? Or that you can turn your computer into a recording studio to whip up your own podcasts to play on your (and anybody's) iPod? And you can make your iPod even more useful with dozens of AppleScripts designed to automate and augment certain iPod-related tasks. This chapter takes your iPod skills—and your iPod—to the next level.

The AppleScripted iPod

AppleScript is a simple programming language that lets Mac fans write mini programs to perform certain tasks. For instance, you could rig AppleScript to make iTunes play "We Will Rock You" at 8:03 every morning. Or you could use an AppleScript to send an email every three hours to your co-workers telling them how many shopping days are left until Christmas.

There are plenty of frivolous uses for AppleScript, too.

Installing the Script Menu

Mac OS X comes with a handful of ready-made AppleScript programs (called *scripts*), including one that checks the current temperature in your Zip code and one that lets you count messages in all your mailboxes.

Most Mac fans never even know they exist, because these scripts are buried in the Applications → AppleScript → Example Scripts folder. Fortunately, they're also listed in something called the *Script menu,* an icon on your menu bar that puts the scripts at your fingertips. To install the Script menu in Mac OS X 10.4, open your Applications → AppleScript folder, double-click the AppleScript Utility, and turn on the checkboxes next to "Show Script menu in menu bar" to make the Apple-Script icon do just that. If you want to see all the scripts in the Mac's Library folder (many of which can be seen in Figure 11-1), put a check in the box next to "Show Library scripts" as well before you click OK and close the AppleScript Utility.

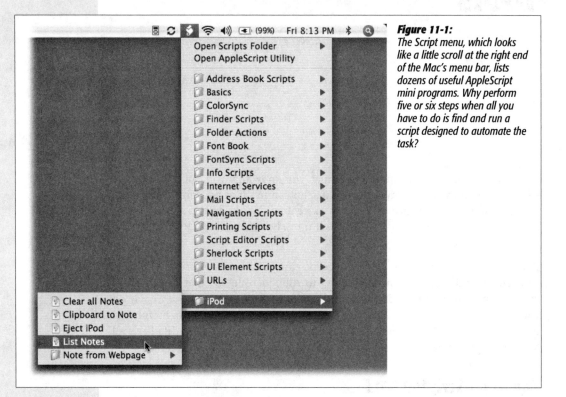

Figure 11-1:
The Script menu, which looks like a little scroll at the right end of the Mac's menu bar, lists dozens of useful AppleScript mini programs. Why perform five or six steps when all you have to do is find and run a script designed to automate the task?

Apple's iPod Scripts

If you want to maximize the potential of the Notes feature (page 201), Apple has a collection of scripts just for you. You can download the collection at *www.apple.com/ applescript/ipod.* (These scripts work with Mac OS X 10.2 and later.)

Install them by dragging the downloaded folder (called iPod) into your Home → Library → Scripts folder. Magically, they now appear in your Script menu, as shown in Figure 11-1.

Note: Want to be a full-fledged AppleScript writer? Check out *AppleScript: The Missing Manual* (O'Reilly) for plenty more details on how to use this powerful, yet (sort of) easy-to-use language.

Here are the names of the iPod scripts in the collection and the actions they perform:

- **Clear All Notes.** If you've read all the notes on your iPod and want to dump them all at once, use this command to delete all the files in the iPod's Notes folder. You have the option to trash any subfolders within the Notes folder as well.

- **Clipboard to Note.** Whenever your work brings you to a scrap of information you think would be handy to have on your iPod—driving directions, a recipe, a news story, a detailed email message—highlight it, copy it to the Mac's clipboard by pressing ⌘-C, and then choose iPod → Clipboard to Note from your Script menu. In one fell swoop, the script creates a note on the iPod.

Note: If the text is longer than about 4,000 characters, the script chops it up into multiple linked files on the iPod.

- **Eject iPod.** Run the Eject iPod script to safely unmount the iPod (page 207). It's just an alternative to dragging the iPod icon to the Trash.

- **List Notes.** This script shows you a list of all the Notes files currently stored on the connected iPod. If you want to revise a note, select it from the list that appears and open it for editing.

- **Note from Web page.** Web pages often contain interesting articles that you want to read later or save for future reference. As long as you're using Apple's own Safari browser, you can grab the text from an open Web page and turn it into an iPod Note just by using this script.

To copy the article or text to your iPod, visit the "printer friendly" version of the page (which ditches all the ads, blinking banners, Flash files, and other ornaments), if one is offered. Then, from the Script menu, choose iPod → Note from Webpage → Printer Friendly. Another script in the same folder, called MacCentral, does the same thing with an article you're viewing on the MacCentral.com Web site.

Tip: If you've sampled the iPod collection and found you have a taste for AppleScripts, Apple also has a set devoted to iTunes that you can download for free at *www.apple.com/applescript/itunes*. The iTunes collection has more than 20 scripts that can do everything from create a summary of what's in your music library to set all the songs in a particular genre to a specified EQ setting.

Doug's AppleScripts

Doug's AppleScripts for iTunes has a Wal-Mart–sized inventory of AppleScripts for Mac music adventures—including a section devoted to iPod-related scripts. New scripts appear here frequently, so it's a good site to look in on every so often.

Many of the scripts automate the transfer or deletion of songs between iPod and Mac. For example, the collection called Four iPod Scripts X (which actually contains *five* scripts and seems to be designed for people who have far too much music to fit on their iPods) contains AppleScripts like these:

- **Random Albums to iPod, Random Artist to iPod, and Random iPod** deletes the iPod's songs and playlists, then randomly adds albums, artist repertoires, or tracks from the iTunes Library to the iPod until it's full.

- **Clean iPod** deletes all songs and playlists on the iPod.

Other scripts can automatically add or remove artwork from your iTunes songs, find lyrics with Google, and even search the Web for the guitar chords to the current song playing, You'll find a link to the iPod scripts at *www.missingmanuals. com*. They're worth a look by anybody who loves making the Mac do stuff on its own. (The same author has created a vast library of more than 350 iTunes-related AppleScripts, including the popular iTunes Library Manager, a script that lets you swap in and swap out multiple music libraries within iTunes; see www.dougscripts. com/itunes.)

Tip: There's also a bunch of AppleScripts for iPod and iTunes functions that are available to download at the MacScripter site: *http://scriptbuilders.net*. Just type in "iPod" or "iTunes" in the Search box.

More Mac Shareware

AppleScript isn't the only way code warriors have crafted helpful utility programs for the iPod. Here's an assortment of standalone software programs that do wacky and useful things for Mac iPods:

- **PodQuest.** If you're already planning on taking your iPod along on your next driving trip, make that little white jukebox do double-duty as a navigator. The $10 PodQuest program from Mibasoft, shown in Figure 11-2, downloads driving directions for destinations in North America and Europe from Google Maps, MapQuest, Yahoo Maps, and MapBlast to the iPod's Notes or Contacts folder. This program works with Mac OS X 10.2.8 or later, Safari 1.0.3 or later, and all versions of the iPod except the Shuffle.

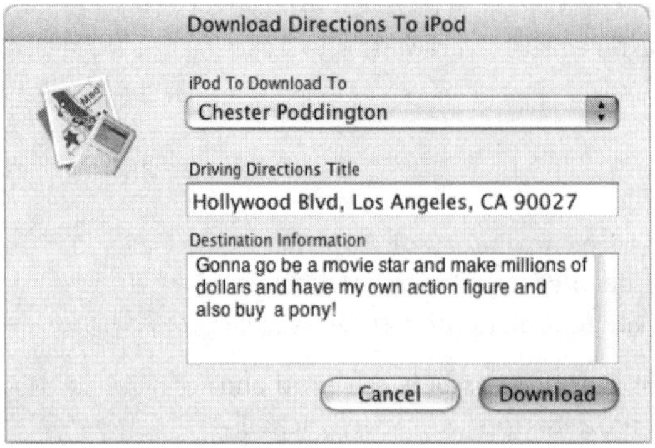

Figure 11-2:
With PodQuest, your iPod not only rides shotgun as a music machine, but also can display driving directions downloaded from trusted travel sites like Google Maps and MapQuest.

- **iPod Launcher.** This starts up a whole batch of programs and scripts automatically whenever you connect the iPod to your Mac OS X system. You might use it to trigger auto-backups of the data files on the iPod, for example. Or, if you use it in tandem with iPod It, you can synchronize your Entourage data as well as download news, headlines, and weather reports without having to think about any of it. iPod Launcher works with Mac OS X 10.2 and later and sells for $5.

- **VoodooPad.** This is a versatile notepad with delusions of grandeur, as you can see in Figure 11-3. VoodooPad ($25) works with Mac OS X 10.3.9 and later.

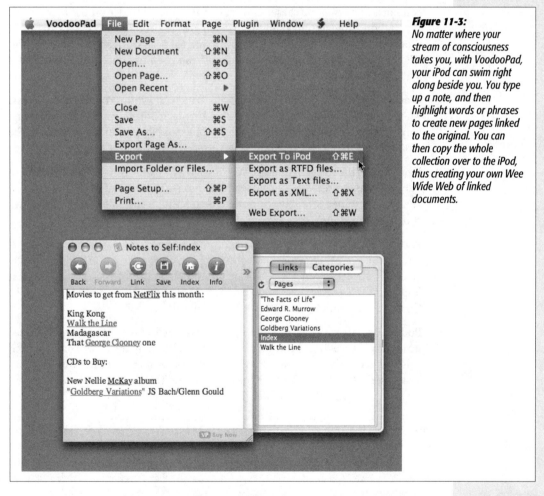

Figure 11-3:
No matter where your stream of consciousness takes you, with VoodooPad, your iPod can swim right along beside you. You type up a note, and then highlight words or phrases to create new pages linked to the original. You can then copy the whole collection over to the iPod, thus creating your own Wee Wide Web of linked documents.

- **iPodVolume Booster.** Due to stricter regulations overseas, iPods sold in Europe have a volume restriction that won't let them play as loudly as their American counterparts. The iPodVolume Booster, like its Windows counterpart mentioned on page 231, gets around that restriction but comes with a sober warning that the program may cause hearing damage if used too loudly.

Note: You can find links to all of these programs on the "Missing CD" page at *www.missingmanuals.com*.

Software for Mac and Windows

Like Apple itself, many software developers saw the wisdom in making products that would work for both Macintosh and Windows systems. Here are a few Pod-centric programs that cross that great platform divide.

- **iPod Access.** This industrious program can provide a backup copy of the iPod's contents, including purchased music, to a designated folder on the Mac or PC. If you didn't find an iPod song-transferring utility you liked back in Chapter 2, iPod Access does that, too. This $10 program for Mac OS X and Windows 2000/XP copies the songs in a tidy fashion and can even organize them into album and artist folders.

- **iRocker.** This $30 program from Talking Panda lets your iPod *teach* you music when it's not playing your music. With a Virtual Chordbook that plays and displays 200 guitar chords, a built-in metronome, and lessons in musical scales, the iPod is likely to be the least cranky music teacher you've ever had.

- **iPodiWay.** This traveler-friendly Web site (*www.ipodiway.com*) downloads free Yahoo driving directions and maps from your chosen Point A to Point Z and gives you a folder of picture files to sync up with your color-screen iPod and chosen photo album program.

- **PodGourmet.** Kitchen neophytes, fear not! Cooking can be as simple as just following the recipe, and the PodGourmet program gives you 260 dishes in the palm of your hand. The 14 food categories include Beef, Vegetables, and, most importantly, *Desserts*. PodGourmet costs $7.50—much less than tuition at Le Cordon Bleu—and works with 2003-and-later iPods.

- **PodTender.** If you want to whip up a cocktail before dinner and have no idea what to make, call up the PodTender. The program, by the same computerized culinary artistes who created PodGourmet, comes to the rescue with 900 suggestions right in your iPod's Notes folder. PodTender, a $10 shareware program, works with 2003-and-later iPods.

Note: Although PodGourmet and PodTender appear to be Mac OS X programs, their creator's Web site (*www.enriquequinterodesign.com*) lists instructions for Windows owners to download and install the files. A visit to the site also reveals two other Pod programs: PodGourmet Vegan Edition and Apple Store Locations for iPod (so you'll always know where to go when you have the compelling urge to buy shiny white computer products).

- **PodSecret.** In these days of scams, frauds, identity theft, and other grim realities of life online, data security is a hot topic. You can move all your private data off your computer and safely store it on your iPod with PodSecret, a $30 program. PodSecret, shown in Figure 11-4, encrypts things like bank account numbers, passwords, and other top-secret personal data on the iPod itself, demanding a password to view the files and locking itself up after a few minutes. You keep your secrets with you on your iPod's hard drive and not on your computer where someone can find them. PodSecret's free trial version works for seven days—don't forget your password!

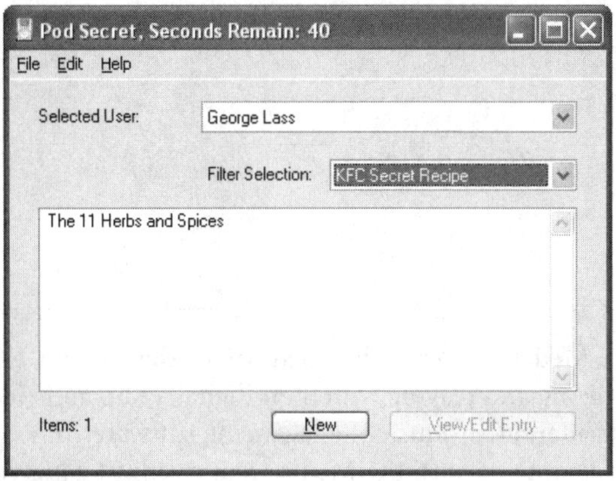

Figure 11-4:
Copy the PodSecret program onto your iPod and turn it into a pocket data vault where you must type a password to view the encrypted files.

Tip: Digital daredevils with a taste for the Hacking Arts will find plenty of intriguing iPod-modification projects over at *www.endgadget.com*. The site has distinguished itself by providing fully illustrated how-to guides for such adventurous tinkering as burrowing into the iPod's firmware, changing its onscreen graphics, and setting up rudimentary movies on the iPod Photo.

More Windows Shareware

The Mac people may have gotten a head start on handcrafted iPod shareware, but the Windows crew is beginning to develop programs of their own to extend the iPod's abilities. Like the Mac software described earlier, all of these programs are available on the "Missing CD" page at *www.missingmanuals.com*.

- **euPod Pro.** It's not your imagination: European iPods *can't* play as loudly as American ones. Not because Americans are any wilder, but because of government-mandated volume restrictions on European music players.

  Hackers to the rescue! euPod Pro, formerly known as euPodVolume Boost, lets everyone around the world melt their ears off at higher volumes. The software tinkers with a setting in the iPod's database to alter the sound output.

- **K-Pod.** Keeping up with email is a full-time job for some people, but K-Pod (Figure 11-5) lets you download copies of your incoming messages directly to the Notes folder of your iPod for reading on the run. The program works with POP and IMAP email accounts and, with a little bit of tweaking, can also handle Gmail mail.

Figure 11-5:
No matter which email program you use, from Outlook Express to Eudora, you just need to know your account's settings–like user name, password, and mail server name–to set up K-Pod for mobile mail. The program copies only the messages, so you'll still have them waiting for you the next time you check mail on your PC.

- **J. River Media Center.** The Media Center is designed for media mavens who spend hour after hour organizing and playing with their digital audio and video files. For those looking for alternative music-management software, this $40 program can sync the iPod's contents with the Media Center, adjust song volumes, and bookmark Audible files. (A free 30-day trial version is also available.)

Tip: Want to learn basic French before that vacation in Paris or brush up your German before that business trip to Berlin? The iPod is right there with you in six different languages with the Talking Panda iLingo software. Available in French, German, Italian, Russian, Portuguese, and Spanish, iLingo comes with 400 travel-wise words and phrases recorded by native speakers to help you get around town without mangling the local tongue.

The program, available for Mac OS X 10.2 and Windows 2000 and later, works with 2003-and-later iPods. It sells for $50 for all six European languages at *www.talkingpanda.com*. The company also sells a $40 Asian language pack that includes Japanese, Korean, and both Mandarin and Cantonese Chinese.

Recording Your Own Podcasts

In addition to songs downloaded from the iTunes Music Store (Chapter 7) or ripped from CDs (Chapter 5), the iPod can play digital audio files that you've recorded yourself. This sort of thing can come in handy in situations where, say, you have a recital or music lesson coming up and want to record yourself for analysis later. Or perhaps you have to give a speech and want to record a sample of yourself practicing to weed out the "ums" and "you knows."

You can take either of two approaches. First, you can record on the iPod and transfer the finished recordings to the computer. (You need one of the snap-on iPod microphones like Griffin Technology's iTalk or Belkin's Voice Recorder. Although these particular mics are designed for iPod models released in 2003 and 2004 and are on their way to extinction, new microphones designed for the current iPods should be along any day now.)

GEM IN THE ROUGH

Making the iPod Play with the Xbox 360

Want a little background music while you creep through dark places blasting aliens or speed through the streets in your virtual sports car? Just hitch your iPod up to the Xbox 360, Microsoft's newest version of its thumb-rattling videogame console, to play your own music as you fight the good fight.

Start by plugging the iPod's USB cable into one of the controller ports on the Xbox 360. Next, use the Xbox controller to navigate to the Xbox Dashboard area, select Media, and pick or make a playlist of tunes on your iPod.

The Xbox 360 can play MP3 files without help, but you need to download a *codec* (a file that lets you play a certain audio format) to play AAC files through the Xbox system. And once you install the codec, you can only play *unprotected* AAC files that you ripped yourself, not songs from the iTunes Music Store.

To get the AAC codec for the Xbox 360, go back to the Xbox Dashboard and, in the Xbox Live area, choose Xbox Live Marketplace → Game Downloads. Needless to say, your Xbox needs to be connected to the Internet for this part.

Next, choose All Games → Alphabetical List of Games → Optional iPod Support. You have to choose this iPod Support option twice—once from the Xbox Live Marketplace and also from the Xbox Guide area. After that, select Confirm Download.

When the download is finished, choose Done. When you go back to the Xbox Dashboard (press the B key or BACK three times to retrace your steps), your game console can now play the MP3 *and* the unprotected AAC files on your iPod, and you can get back to shooting scary monsters in sonic style.

Second, you can record on the computer and transfer the recording to the iPod. In this case, your Mac or PC needs a microphone, as described in the next sections.

Tip: Got a microphone but no sound port? If you don't have a sound-in port on your computer, you can do it the USB way with the iMic from Griffin Technology. The iMic works with both Windows and Macs through the USB port, as described in Appendix C, available on the "Missing CD" page at *www. missingmanuals.com*. If you don't have the microphone either, consider the $40 MicFlex from MacMice (*www.macmice.com*), a flexible microphone that plugs right into the USB port.

Windows

Most new desktop systems these days include a small external microphone, and many laptops have built-in microphones. Check your manual.

You can record WAV files using the Sound Recorder program that comes with Windows, of course (choose Start → Programs → Accessories → Entertainment → Sound Recorder). But the shareware archives on the Web are bursting with more flexible and robust programs for recording your own WAV and MP3 files.

If you want to transfer old LPs or tapes to your hard drive, connecting a stereo receiver, cassette deck, or turntable and preamplifier to the PC requires audio patch cables. You'll most likely need a Y-shaped cable with two RCA connector plugs on one end (for the stereo) and a single 3.5 mm stereo miniplug on the other end for the PC's mic jack.

Professional programs can cost several hundred dollars, but there are cheaper shareware options to tinker around with if you're just dipping a toe into the audio waters. Try *www.hitsquad.com*, *www.download.com*, or *www.tucows.com* for starters, and you'll find plenty of audio-recording programs to sample.

Among the offerings is FASoft's N-Track Studio, a versatile recording and mixing program that you can sample for free at *www.fasoft.com* and buy for about $50. As shown in Figure 11-6, once you record yourself with the program, there are several options for saving and exporting it, including as a WAV file and as an MP3.

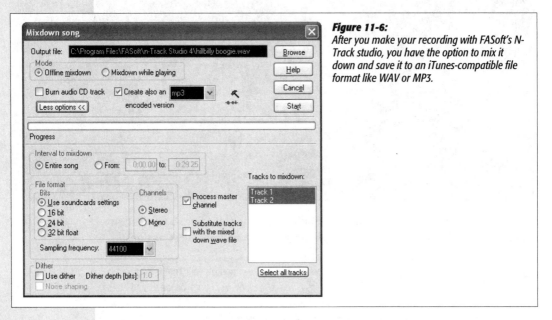

Figure 11-6:
After you make your recording with FASoft's N-Track studio, you have the option to mix it down and save it to an iTunes-compatible file format like WAV or MP3.

As you know from earlier chapters of this book, you can import WAV and MP3 files right into iTunes in a variety of ways (including File → Add to Library). And once you get a song into iTunes, the rest of the way to the iPod is as easy as plugging in a FireWire or USB cable.

Macintosh

Many recent Macintosh models, including the iMac, eMac, white iBook, and titanium PowerBook, have microphones built into the screens. Older Macs from the Beige Days usually came with an external PlainTalk microphone, and later Power Macs take in sounds with USB microphones from other companies. If you don't have a built-in microphone or even a sound-in port on your Mac, the iMic (page 327) can pull in stereo sound input through the USB port.

Connecting the Mac to a stereo receiver, cassette deck, or turntable and preamplifier requires audio patch cables. In most cases, you'll need a Y-shaped cable with two RCA connector plugs on one end—for the stereo—and a single 3.5 mm stereo miniplug on the other end—for the Mac's sound-in jack or an iMic. (If you're recording from a portable cassette or MiniDisc player, you'll probably need a stereo miniplug-to-miniplug cable.)

When you've connected the cables, direct your Mac's Sound preferences to the correct jack (microphone, line in, or whatever). In Mac OS X, open System Preferences and click the Sound icon, then click the Input tab.

Once you have the hardware, rustle up some recording software (iTunes doesn't offer recording capability). Plenty of inexpensive Macintosh shareware programs for audio recording await on the Web; visit, for example, *www.osxaudio.com* or *www.hitsquad.com/smm/mac/RECORDING*. Two popular shareware programs for audio recording for Mac OS X are Amadeus II ($30) and Audiocorder ($20), shown in Figure 11-7. (Both are available on the "Missing CD" page at *www. missingmanuals.com*.)

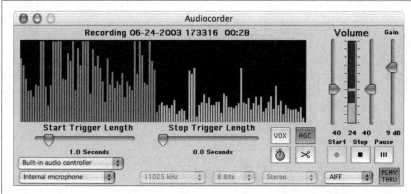

Figure 11-7:
If you have a Mac, a mike, and a copy of Audiocorder, you can record yourself practicing that difficult harmonica solo, or hook up your stereo and digitize your old vinyl and copy the files onto the iPod. You'll never have to buy the White Album again.

Follow the instructions provided with whatever sound-recording program you decide to use. Once you've recorded your sound files, named them, and saved them, you can add them into the iTunes library by dragging them onto the iTunes window or choosing File → Add to Library. Now you can edit their track tags, add them to playlists, and copy them onto your iPod, just like any other audio file.

Some audio-recording programs may save the sound files in the AIFF format, and if you don't have the option to convert the files to MP3 or AAC there, you can always use the iTunes command Advanced → Convert Selection to MP3 (or whatever format you want).

Podcast software

Recording audio for personal use on your computer is fairly easy, but there's an extra step you have to take if you want to turn that home-recorded soliloquy or radio-style rant into a podcast that can be heard around the world: You have to *publish* it on the Web—that is, upload a copy of the file onto a publicly accessible file server so that anybody looking for your podcast can find it.

Additionally, if you plan to do this sort of podcasting thing regularly and want your listeners to be alerted to your new episodes and have the files automatically download in iTunes or their preferred podcast-grabbing programs, you need to create and upload a special RSS (Really Simple Syndication) file in XML (Extensible Markup Language) that points to your podcast on the server.

If the alphabetical mumbo-jumbo paragraph above made your eyes blur, cross, or roll—you're not alone. Fortunately, there are several programs around to help ease and automate podcast creation and publication. Here are a couple of them:

- **ePodcast Creator.** This $90 program from Industrial Audio Software works with Windows 2000 and XP and helps you record and edit multiple audio tracks for your podcast. Once the podcast is complete, the program creates the RSS feed and uploads the new podcast to your server. There's a free trial version and free podcasting tutorials at *www.industrialaudiosoftware.com*; a professional version called ePodcast producer with more audio-editing features is also available for $250.

- **Podcast Factory.** M-Audio's Podcast Factory gives you everything you need to get rolling, all in one box: desktop microphone, an audio interface box for connecting the mic, headphones, or musical instruments to the computer's USB port, and audio-mixing software that also supplies RSS feeds and publishes your podcasts. The Podcast Factory kit (shown in Figure 11-8) works with Windows XP and Mac OS X and sells for about $180; there's more info at *www.m-audio.com*.

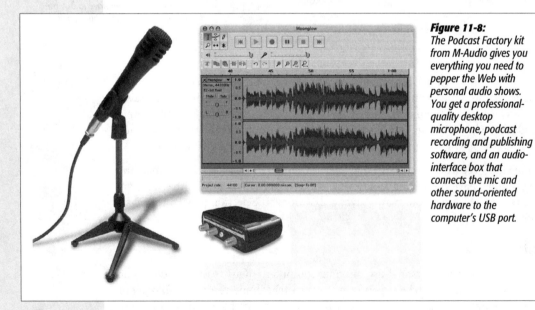

Figure 11-8:
The Podcast Factory kit from M-Audio gives you everything you need to pepper the Web with personal audio shows. You get a professional-quality desktop microphone, podcast recording and publishing software, and an audio-interface box that connects the mic and other sound-oriented hardware to the computer's USB port.

Tip: The Podcasting News site has a lengthy list of podcast-publishing programs and services for both Windows and Mac pod-jockeys. If you're in search of software to make the whole getting-my-voice-heard-on-the-Web part of the podcast process easier, check out *www.podcastingnews.com/topics/Podcasting_ Software.html*.

Creating podcasts in GarageBand

GarageBand is the music studio on your Mac that's also part of Apple's iLife suite of programs. GarageBand's enormous library of musical instrument sound clips and loops make it easy to compose your own instrumental work—and you can even plug your own guitar or keyboard into your Mac and add yourself to the mix. *And* you can use it to make your own podcasts. In fact, GarageBand 3, part of iLife '06, *encourages* you to make your own podcasts by including a whole suite of tools that lets you easily add artwork, Web site links, sound effects, and background music.

If you've noodled around enough in GarageBand to have made up a few songs with the built-in instruments, but aren't quite sure how to record a talk show, here's a quick guide to get you up and recording your very first podcast:

1. **Attach your preferred audio interface device and a microphone to your Mac.**

   Audio-interface boxes like Griffin Technology's iMic (*www.griffintechnology. com*) or M-Audio's Fast Track USB (*www.m-audio.com*) connect to your computer's USB port and give you ports to plug in a microphone and headphones for use while recording. You can also just use your Mac's built-in microphone, but the quality may not be as good.

2. **Open GarageBand and chose New → New Podcast Episode.**

   As shown in Figure 11-9, GarageBand offers a ready made podcast playpen with basic vocal tracks and sound effects ready to go. (If you have an older version of GarageBand, choose New Track → Real Instrument → Vocals, which gives you several presets you can pick from to alter your vocalizing. Turning on the checkboxes for Gate and Compressor can help cut down on background noise and smooth out the sound of your voice.)

3. **Check the recording levels.**

   "Testing 1...2...3." Experiment with your microphone's sound levels and adjust the volume settings in GarageBand and on your audio-interface box so you sound as clear and sonically undistorted as possible.

Tip: If you're having trouble getting a USB-microphone working, make sure you've selected it as your audio input device. To do so, go to GarageBand → Preferences, click the Audio/MIDI tab, and then select your microphone from the Audio Input pop-up menu.

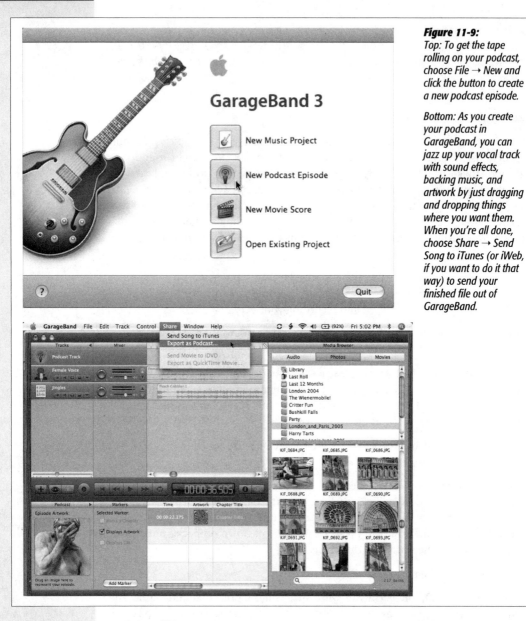

Figure 11-9:
Top: To get the tape rolling on your podcast, choose File → New and click the button to create a new podcast episode.

Bottom: As you create your podcast in GarageBand, you can jazz up your vocal track with sound effects, backing music, and artwork by just dragging and dropping things where you want them. When you're all done, choose Share → Send Song to iTunes (or iWeb, if you want to do it that way) to send your finished file out of GarageBand.

4. **Start talking.**

Keep your mouth close to the microphone for consistent sound, and don't worry if you flub a word here and there. GarageBand is a wondrous program where you can not only add musical loops and background music to your podcast, you can also re-record the parts you messed up and edit them into the final version.

1. **Edit and Save.**

   You can enhance your podcast with artwork that displays itself in the iTunes artwork window as your show plays. To do so in GarageBand 3, choose Control → Media Browser to open the Media Browser window. The Media Browser is your window into all the photos, movies, and, audio files you can add to your GarageBand projects, including songs from iTunes. Drag the photos you want to use to the Episode Artwork well in the GarageBand window, as shown in Figure 11-9, bottom.

2. **Export your show.**

   Once you've added your sound effects, fixed your slip-ups, and perfected your podcast, save your finished file. Now you're ready to take your podcast out of GarageBand and release it into the wilds of the Web. If you have iLife '06 with the iWeb feature and a .Mac account, all you need to do is choose Share → Send Podcast to iWeb, and your show is beamed up to the Internet for the world to hear.

   If you don't have iWeb or a .Mac account, you can export your podcast and put it up on the Web site of your choosing. To do so, choose GarageBand → Preferences and click Export. In the Export pane (under Publish Podcast), click the "Save to Disk" button. Now, when you choose Share → Export as Podcast, your podcast lands on your desktop, where you can take it from there.

   You can also export it into iTunes, as explained in the next section.

Tip: Apple has a whole Web page of tips and suggestions on making podcasts with GarageBand, and there's also a link to a free Chapter Tool, which lets you insert Web links, pictures, and chapter markers into your files. It's at *www.apple.com/support/garageband/podcasts*.

Exporting your GarageBand songs or podcasts to iTunes

One great thing about the iLife suite is that the programs communicate amongst themselves quite well, even better than some human siblings talk to each other. Using a song in your iTunes library as the soundtrack for an iPhoto slide show is quite easy to do, for example. And as you can imagine, getting those pithy podcasts and great booming musical masterpieces you composed yourself into iTunes is pretty easy, too.

Once you've saved your audio masterpiece in GarageBand, go to Share → Send Song to iTunes (Figure 11-10), and the program mixes the song and exports it as an AIFF file into a special playlist in iTunes. By default, the playlist will be named after whoever is logged on to the Mac, but you can change it in the GarageBand preferences. Choose GarageBand → Preferences → General (Figure 11-11) to personalize your "Composer" and "Album" names and bestow a proper title for the iTunes playlist where your songs will land.

Figure 11-10:
*Once you get your
magnum opus so perfect
that you want to take it
with you on your iPod,
start by sending it from
GarageBand to iTunes
from the Share menu.
Once the song lands in
iTunes, the iPod is only a
sync away.*

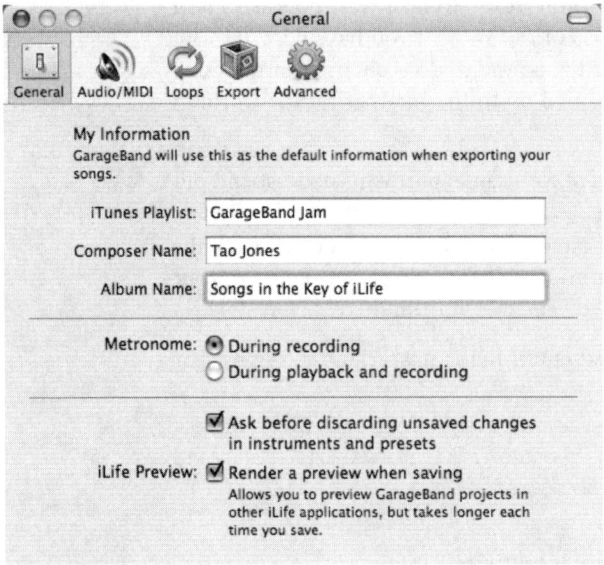

Figure 11-11:
*If you don't like GarageBand's standard
settings, you can rename your GarageBand
playlist name and other labels for your
composition's journey into iTunes. Choose
GarageBand → Preferences → General to have
your say.*

Note: AIFF files, as you know from Chapter 4, are huge, but you can convert them to AAC, MP3, or the
format of your choice once in iTunes. Just make sure your desired format is selected in iTunes → Preferences → Importing, then go to the iTunes menu bar and choose Advanced → Convert Selection to AAC
(or MP3 or whatever you picked).

CHAPTER 12

Troubleshooting

The iPod is a fairly uncomplicated device, at least compared to towering desktop machines with printers and scanners attached, or even one of your more sophisticated microwave ovens. But a number of things can temporarily trip up your iPod—hard-drive glitches, wonky cables, or a wrong turn at the crossroads where hardware meets software.

At least five hardware generations of iPods, two Mini-Mes, a Nano, and a Shuffle now stalk the earth. Some problems may apply only to certain models, but many of the hardware-oriented issues are universal. You can remedy some problems by simply pressing a couple of buttons, but others require a little more time and effort.

This chapter covers all of the above, and includes a section devoted to troubleshooting the iTunes Music Store. And if you don't find the answer, turn to the last section, which lists iPod troubleshooting and repair resources.

Apple's Alphabet: The 5 R's of iPod Repair

After years of misbehaving iPods to contend with—not to mention misbehaving, irate iPod owners heating up its phone lines and message boards—Apple's tech support team has come up with a memorable formula designed to fix most iPod/ iTunes problems. As posted in the iPod support section of its Web site (page 275), Apple recommends "The 5 R's" to try in your troubleshooting journey: Reset, Retry, Restart, Remove, and Restore.

Here's what each R stands for, with more detail:

- **Reset** your iPod (see below).

- **Retry** the connection by plugging the iPod in to a different USB or FireWire port on the computer.

- **Restart** your computer and check for any new software updates you may need to download and install.

- **Remove** your current iPod and iTunes software and reinstall fresh versions downloaded from *www.apple.com* (page 259).

- **Restore** the iPod's software (page 273).

The following sections cover these five steps and more, so that you can avoid that sixth, painful R: *Ram* your head into the wall because this stupid iPod won't work.

The iPod's Self-Help Modes

If you've used a computer for any length of time, you know they can sometimes crash, lock up, or have days when they're just not feeling well. Fortunately, just like your computer, you can reboot your iPod; all you have to do is push the right sets of buttons.

Note: Starting with the iPod Mini in early 2004, Apple fundamentally changed the iPod's hardware controls by placing the buttons directly on the scroll wheel and turning it into a *click wheel.* Pretty much every new iPod model made after that used the click wheel, including the iPod Photo, the iPod from HP, the U2 Special Edition iPod, the iPod Nano, and the video iPod. If you see button-pushing instructions that refer to a *click wheel iPod,* they're referring to any and all of the aforementioned models.

How to Reset an iPod

If your iPod seems frozen, locked up, confused, or otherwise unresponsive, you can *reset* it without losing your music and data files. Some customized settings may get wiped, and things like Bookmarks in long files, the backlight timer preferences, and On-The-Go Playlists may only be saved from the last time the iPod's hard drive turned on.

Here's the iPod's reset sequence:

1. **Slide the Hold switch on and off again.**

2. **On click wheel iPods—which include most models released in 2004 or later— press and hold down the Menu and center Select buttons. On non-click wheel iPods, press the Menu and Play/Pause buttons on the front of the iPod simultaneously.**

   Hold the buttons down until you see the Apple logo appear on the screen. This could take several seconds (but less than 10) to kick in, and you may have to do it twice, but keep pressing until you see the Apple logo.

If you're trying to reset a click wheel iPod and are having a hard time getting Menu and Select properly pressed, try putting the iPod down on a flat surface before pressing the buttons.

If the technology gods are smiling, the iPod goes through its little boot sequence and then returns you to the main menu. If your battery is low and you're not getting any Apple-logo action, try connecting the iPod to the computer or its AC adapter to juice it up before trying the reset sequence.

How to Reset an iPod Shuffle

A stalled or befuddled iPod Shuffle may also need a good firm reset from time to time, but like the Shuffle itself, resetting it is a bit simpler than wrestling with a regular iPod.

1. **If it's plugged into the computer, disconnect the Shuffle.**

2. **On the back of the Shuffle, slide the switch to the Off position so that the green stripe is hidden.**

3. **Wait five seconds or so.**

4. **Slide the switch on the back to either Shuffle or the Play In Order setting.**

The iPod Shuffle is now reset.

Force the iPod into Disk Mode

It's usually easy to put your iPod into Disk Mode through iTunes, as described on page 204. However, if your computer seems to have amnesia and doesn't recognize your iPod when you try to connect it, you can usually goose it into Disk Mode by pressing a couple of buttons.

For click-wheel iPods, it goes like this:

1. **Make sure the iPod has some battery power left; charge it up if it doesn't.**

   If you have an AC adapter for your iPod, just plug it in between wall and iPod to get some power going. You can put the iPod into Disk Mode when it's charging from the AC adapter. If you don't have an AC adapter, use your iPod cable and plug it into the computer so it can draw some power, even if iTunes is ignoring the iPod.

2. **Flip the Hold switch on and off.**

3. **Reset the iPod.**

   Use one of the methods described on page 242.

4. **Wait until the Apple logo appears and then press the Select and Play/Pause buttons until the Disk Mode screen appears.**

   On older iPods that don't have a click wheel (usually those born before 2003), press down the Previous and Next buttons after you reset the iPod to force it into Disk Mode. You can tell you're in Disk Mode when that phrase appears at the top of the iPod's screen.

5. **Plug the iPod into the computer.**

When you plug it into the computer, you see the Do Not Disconnect message on the screen.

Now the computer should get the message from the iPod and recognize it as a beloved friend and hard drive. The iPod shows up as a disk on your desktop or in the My Computer window shortly thereafter, making it possible to do such things like restore the iPod's software (page 273) when it's acting up and having a real identity crisis.

Note: To get the iPod out of Disk Mode, perform the reset sequence again.

---

iPod Hardware Problems

If your iPod syncs up fine to the computer and seems only to misbehave when you're out trying to listen to your Rockabilly Workout playlist at the gym, the problems could lie within the iPod itself.

The iPod Keeps Freezing Up

Inside the iPod spins a busy hard drive, just like the one inside a desktop computer, (unless, of course, you have a Nano or a Shuffle tooting along on its quiet chip of flash memory). Still, software can trip over itself, and hard drives have been known to freeze, crash, and lock up when you least expect it—and the iPod's is no different.

Rebooting (resetting) usually thaws a freeze, so grab the iPod and reset it as described on page 242. But if a simple reset doesn't solve the problem, read on.

Restoring the iPod Software

If the iPod still freezes up again after you reset it, restoring its software may help smooth things out; see page 273.

The iPod Won't Turn On or Wake Up from Sleep

Some days you just don't want to get out of bed. In its own way, the iPod has days like that, too. If you're pushing its buttons and nothing's happening, run through this troubleshooting checklist:

• **Make sure the HOLD switch isn't on.** Yes, this is obvious, but it's surprisingly easy to overlook in a panic. If it's on, slide it so that the orange band doesn't show, and then try to turn on the iPod again.

- **Check your battery charge.** Even if you're sure you recently charged it up, your iPod could have gotten bumped inside a backpack or purse and run itself down. The iPod can't turn on if the battery doesn't have enough juice. You may even see a flash of the Low Battery icon, or a message. Plug the iPod into the computer or AC adapter to get some power flowing, wait a few minutes, and then try to turn it on while it's recharging.

- **Reset the iPod.** See page 242.

The iPod Won't Reset

If the iPod doesn't respond to any amount of poking and prodding, and you can't even reset it, you may have to take more drastic measures.

First, unplug it from power and put it away for at least 24 hours to let the battery's power drain. Once the iPod has had its little time-out, reconnect it to the AC adapter (or your computer) so it can draw power, and then try to reset it again.

Also, make sure the iPod is actually getting power when you plug it in. The AC adapter that came with the iPod could be plugged into a dead power outlet, or a turned-off power strip could be at fault. Look for the charging-battery icon to confirm that your iPod's power cell is getting filled up.

Note: The iPod's battery won't charge when connected to a computer in Sleep mode. Make sure the computer is up and running.

If you charge the iPod via its cable, note that a bent or damaged iPod cable may fail to deliver power to the iPod. Make sure you're using the cable that came with the iPod, too, because a different cord may not work properly. Finally, try plugging the iPod's USB or FireWire cable into a different port (most modern Macs and add-in cards have two).

Tip: Check the dock port on the iPod to make sure it's free from anything that might block some of the connector pins.

If you've managed to revive the iPod with any of the above steps, updating or restoring its software may help prevent this situation from happening again. See page 273 for the restore instructions.

Alas, if none of these methods revive the iPod, your next step should be having Apple or a qualified iPod service company look at it (see page 275).

Tip: If you're having problems getting any of your iPod or other FireWire devices to show up on the Mac, a little time out may help matters. Unplug all the FireWire devices and then shut down the Mac. Unplug the power cord from the wall for a few minutes. Then plug it back in, start it back up, and after it boots up all the way, try plugging in the iPod again.

Weird Icons When iPod Boots Up

If you turn on the iPod one day and see odd icons instead of the familiar menus, the iPod may be trying to tell you something. Here are explanations for some icons you may see, pictured in Figure 12-1.

Figure 12-1:
The Folder with Exclamation Mark (left) means something's wrong with your iPod's hardware or software. Sad Mac (middle) appears when an older iPod flunks its internal hard drive diagnostics. If the Apple logo (right) remains, you probably need to force the iPod into Disk Mode and then restore its software.

Folder icon with exclamation point

Longtime Mac fans may remember the dreaded Disk Icon With Flashing Question Mark, which indicates a corrupted System Folder or a hard drive problem. This icon on an iPod could have similar meanings. Among the possible causes:

- **You have the wrong version of iPod software.** If you inadvertently installed a version of the iPod software that's earlier than the software it came with, download and install the latest version (page 269).

- **The battery is too low.** Plug your iPod into its AC adapter or a powered FireWire cable to see if juicing it up makes the icon go away.

- **The iPod's hard drive was formatted incorrectly.** If you were just tinkering and decided to wipe the iPod's drive and reformat it with your favorite Mac or Windows disk utility instead of the iPod Software Updater, the iPod might have a hissy fit. Download and use the Restore option to install the latest version of the iPod Update software on your iPod.

If none of the above seems to mirror your situation, try resetting the iPod to see if the folder icon goes away. If not, it may be time to contact Apple or the holder of your extended warranty about repairs.

Note: If you see a hard disk icon with a magnifying glass looking at it, the iPod suspects trouble with its own hard drive. This icon doesn't appear on newer iPods with color screens, but is still a staple on older iPods. If the iPod flunks its own test, you could see the dreaded Sad Mac (Figure 12-1, center) and need professional help—for your iPod, at least.

Apple logo won't go away

If you turn on your 'Pod and see only the Apple logo (Figure 12-1, right), and it seems like your poor device is stuck in a continuous loop of restarts, try one of the following steps:

- Plug the iPod into your computer's powered FireWire port, if your iPod is a model that can use FireWire. (If it's a click wheel model, you can plug it into your computer's USB 2.0 port instead.) Then reset the iPod, as described on page 242.

- Go into forced Disk Mode, as described on page 243, which should let you see the iPod on the computer's desktop.

- Download and use the Restore option to install the latest version of the iPod Update software on your iPod. Remember, doing a restore wipes the iPod's drive; you'll have to copy all of your songs, contacts, and other data back to it.

- If your iPod is so trashed that it never even displays the Do Not Disconnect message, try the first two steps above again to see if you can get to the point where you can restore the iPod software.

If nothing works, contact Apple (page 275) to inquire about repair options.

Battery Life Issues

Since the iPod's introduction, the subject of battery life has consistently lit up online forums and message boards around the Internet. For one, the proud recipients of new iPods were jumping for joy at the estimated 12-hour lifespan of *their* batteries back in 2004, but the tiny Nano of 2005 clocks in with 14 hours of music play per charge. And the 60-gigabyte video iPod has its own set of battery estimates: 20 hours of music playback, 4 hours of musical slideshows, or 3 solid hours of *Desperate Housewives* episodes or other video playback.

Charging the battery

Remember how you were taught that certain kinds of batteries (in laptops and camcorders, say) worked better if you occasionally fully drained and then recharged them? Forget it. You want to keep the iPod's lithium-ion battery charged *always,* or else you'll lose your clock, date, and other settings.

Many dedicated iPod People prefer to charge the player only when the AC adapter is connected. That's because connecting the player to a computer makes its hard drive spin, which uses up the battery juice faster.

If you see a dull gray charging icon on your video iPod or iPod Nano's screen, this means the iPod's battery was run all the way down and the poor thing doesn't even have the energy to show its animated battery-charging color icon and needs about half an hour of power to get back to its regular screen graphic. When the battery gets this depleted, you may also have to charge it up for awhile to even get the iPod to show up in iTunes and on the computer.

Battery life

Apple has posted various recommendations on its Web site for treating the iPod battery to help ensure a long life, including the items described in the list that follows.

- Don't expose the iPod to extreme hot or cold temperature ranges. (In other words, don't leave it in a hot, parked car, and don't expect it to operate on Mt. Everest.)

- Take the iPod out of any heat-trapping cases or covers when you charge it.

- Put the iPod to sleep to conserve battery power. (Press the Play/Pause button until the iPod display goes blank and the iPod settles into slumber.)

- Even when you're not using the iPod, charge the battery every 14 to 28 days to keep it powered even while it's sleeping. (It still needs power in sleep mode.)

- When you see the Low Battery icon or message, plug the iPod into the computer or an electrical outlet with the AC adapter. The iPod battery indicator shows roughly how much charge is left in the battery.

Note: The Battery Indicator icon in the upper-right corner of the iPod screen is an approximation of the battery's charge, not the ultimate authority.

Replacing the battery

The iPod uses a rechargeable lithium-ion battery. It's rated to last for 500 full-up chargings. If you use and charge your iPod weekly, you'll get two or three years out of it; but constant recharging could negatively affect the battery's lifespan. Since the iPod has only been around since 2001, however, there are no definitive long-term case studies, and some batteries give out sooner than others.

That wasn't good enough for Van and Casey Neistat, two brothers who, following a less-than-satisfying adventure in Apple tech support in the fall of 2003, spray-painted a stenciled slogan, "iPod's unreplaceable battery lasts only 18 months" across iPod posters all over Manhattan, and then released a Web movie documenting their revenge.

It wasn't exactly accurate—you'd have to be a serious 10-hour-a-day iPodaholic to burn out the battery in 18 months, and many original 2001 iPod batteries are still going strong. However, the incident caused panic among prospective and current iPod owners. At just about the same time, Apple introduced the $59 battery-replacement program described on page 275. (Coincidence? You decide.)

If your iPod battery clearly isn't retaining its charge, and you've taken all of the other steps described here, and it's out of warranty, you can find replacement batteries for sale on the Web. Shop around at *www.ipodbattery,com*, *www.pdasmart. com*, *www.smalldog.com*, or *www.ipodresq.com* for parts and service. Some companies will install it for you for a small fee.

Owners of the early iPods (those that Apple released in 2001, 2002, and 2003) might want to consider the high-capacity replacement battery (Figure 12-2) from Newer Technology—for $30 or less, you get a replacement with 70 percent more life between charges than Apple's original power cell. The long-life batteries, as well as regular replacement cells, are at *www.eshop.macsales.com/shop/ipod/batteryreplacement.*

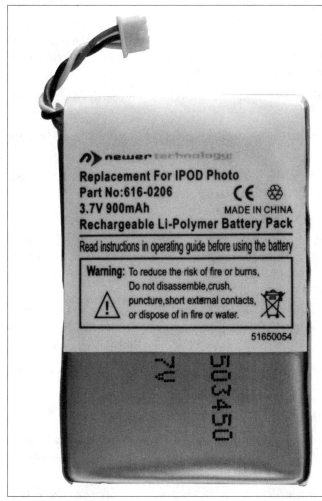

Figure 12-2:
Just because your battery dies doesn't mean your iPod does, too. With replacement power cells from Newer Technology, you not only get life back in the ol' Pod, you can also get longer times between charges, thanks to the company's line of higher capacity batteries.

Of course, installing them voids the warranty (if indeed your iPod is still under warranty at all). If it's still covered, or if the thought of opening your iPod gives you the wiggins, let Apple's repair crew take care of it instead.

Tip: The iPod's battery has become such a hot topic that a helpful fan created a Web site (*www.ipodbatteryfaq.com*) specifically to collect all the latest news and technical documentation on the little power cell.

Some Idiot Set the iPod Menus to Korean

Changing the iPod's operating system language to an unfamiliar alphabet is an obvious trick used by jealous co-workers and older brothers. Fortunately, you have a couple ways to get the iPod back to English:

One quick way is to click the Menu button until you get back to the iPod's main menu screen. You'll see "iPod" in English at the top, and five lines of text in whatever language your wisenheimer pal picked out for you.

1. **Scroll down to the fifth line on your video iPod—or the fourth line if you have a Nano.**

   If you can't read Korean, you've actually highlighted what would have been the Settings menu.

2. **Select this item. Scroll to the end of the list to the words, "Reset All Settings," which are conveniently in English.**

   Here, you can make a decision:

   — **Option 1:** The *third* menu item from the bottom of the list (two up from Reset All Settings) is the Language setting. Click there to get to the list of languages, and then scroll all the way to the top to get back to English (or whatever language you were using before this incident).

   — **Option 2:** If you're tired of your iPod settings anyway, you can wipe them out and start over. Press the Select button on Reset All Settings. You now come to a screen that gives you a choice: Cancel or Reset.

3. **Scroll to and choose Reset (also in English) to get back to the Language menu, where you can select "English" for the iPod.**

Broken Screen Glass

A smashed and broken iPod is a sad sight indeed. Wrap it up gently and contact Apple to inquire about the repair procedure. A list of resources appears at the end of this chapter.

PDASmart, an iPod-repair firm in Texas, also repairs and replaces damaged LCD screens for most iPod models by mail. Prices range from $85 to $150 at *www.pdasmart.com/ipodpartscenter.htm*. iPodRésQ (*www.ipodresq.com*) offers similar screen-repair services as well.

Troubleshooting the iPod Shuffle

Even without a screen or hard drive, the iPod Shuffle may encounter a few glitches along the way. Here are a few of the more common problems.

The Buttons on My iPod Shuffle Don't Respond

The iPod Shuffle doesn't have a Hold switch like the big Pods, but you can lock up its buttons to prevent the accidental pressing that really runs a battery down. If your Shuffle is ignoring you, odds are it got put into a holding pattern—which happens when the Play/Pause button is held down for about three seconds. (The LED will flash orange three times to announce that the Shuffle's buttons are locked, but if you didn't notice the Play/Pause button being pressed down, you probably missed the orange light show, too.)

Try pressing down the Play/Pause button for three seconds to release the hold. The Shuffle's LED should flash green three times so you can once again navigate through your songs, crank up the volume, and do all your typical button-driven tasks.

Resetting the iPod Shuffle (page 243) may also fix the problem.

It's also possible that your Shuffle's battery has run out of juice. Press the battery status button on the back of the Shuffle—if you have a red light or no light at all, you need to plug that baby in and fill 'er up with power.

If none of the above works, try restoring the Shuffle's software (page 273).

My Mac Says It Can't Copy Certain Files to My Shuffle

Although the bad old days of total Mac and PC incompatibility are largely behind us, a few quirks linger, including the fact that Macs can deal with certain typographical characters (asterisks, slashes, semicolons, and brackets, to name a few) that just freak out Windows systems. None of this should really matter, but since the iPod Shuffle comes with the same FAT32 formatting that's used by Windows systems, using these Mac-only characters in file names may stymie your Shuffle when you try to copy over data from your Mac.

In addition to the Mac griping about file errors, you may find that any Windows-unfriendly file names on the Mac have been changed by the time they arrive on the Shuffle. One way to get around this is to just rename the file and ditch the offending characters, but folks running Mac OS X 10.3 or later can just Control-click the file they want to copy, choose Create Archive, and zip up the file into a compressed archive before shuffling it off to the Shuffle—which usually saves some space anyway.

Windows Takes Forever to Start Up with iPod Shuffle

Some Windows systems can boot up from devices other than the computer's main hard disk, including CDs and external hard drives. If you've got your Shuffle plugged in and Windows is just dawdling every time you boot up or restart, the silly computer is probably trying to boot from your Shuffle. Just remember to properly unplug your iPod Shuffle from your PC's USB port before cranking up Windows, and things should proceed much faster.

Windows Says I Have a Corrupt iTunes File

If Windows has a problem reading one of the files you stored on your Shuffle, it may pop up a message from its System Tray area announcing "iTunes.exe – Corrupt File" and suggest that you run the Windows Chkdsk utility (the modern Windows version of the old ScanDisk program) to fix things.

Apple recommends using its own iPod updater program (available at *www.apple. com/ipod/download*) to restore the Shuffle's software to its pristine condition and defragment the drive—something Chkdsk can't do for you anyway. You'll have to reload all your music back on the Shuffle, but if you're a big fan of Autofill, this won't take long after you reformat the player. (See page 269 for more on updating and reinstalling the iPod Shuffle's software.)

Headphone and Remote Problems

If you're having sound-quality issues with your headphones, check to make sure that they're firmly plugged in. Some headphone cords are notoriously fragile, and the wires encased in the plastic sheathing can break if the headphone cord is bent, twisted, yanked out roughly, slammed in a car door, or chomped on by a pet rabbit (Figure 12-3).

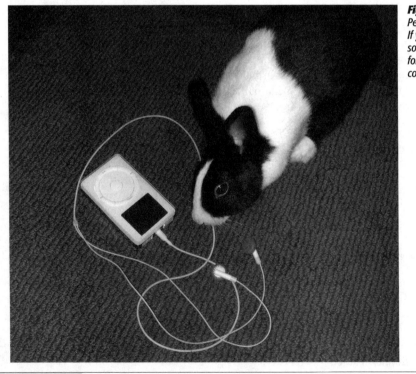

Figure 12-3:
Pets and iPods don't mix! If your headphones don't sound very good, check for teeth marks along the cord.

If you are getting patchy, scratchy sound from your iPod headphones, try using them with another portable player or stereo to confirm that it's the headphones having the problem and not the iPod's headphones port. If the headphones sound fine on other players, you might have a loose headphone jack that requires professional help.

Some iPod models can use a small wired remote control to command the iPod's playback functions. If the remote isn't controlling much of anything, make sure it's firmly pushed into the iPod's top jack. Late-model iPods like the Nano and the video-player Pod can't use the remote controls designed for earlier iPods because they lack that extra oval jack next to the headphones port.

Problems with Song Quality

The sound quality of your digital audio files is affected by a number of things. If you find that your MP3 files sound thin and tinny no matter what you play them on, check the bit rate you used to rip them from the original CDs (page 93). Bit rates below 128 kilobits per second generally don't have CD-quality sound. If you've downloaded songs from Web sites, you're usually at the mercy of whoever encoded the songs in the first place.

Some Songs Skip

If the same songs always skip, the song files themselves may be damaged. Maybe a hiccup or power fluctuation while you were ripping the tune from a CD dinged up the file, or maybe you had several memory-hogging programs open and running while you were recording songs. Try deleting the song files from iTunes and then reripping and reimporting fresh copies.

Shaking or banging the iPod while it's playing can cause its hard drive to skip while playing a song. (Shaking and banging are two things you want to avoid with *any* hard drive.)

True, the iPod comes with a memory stash designed to prevent skipping for at least 20 minutes. But as noted on page 82, enormous song files—either hugely long pieces of music or files encoded in uncompressed formats like AIFF—could be maxing out the iPod's RAM buffer. Here are your options:

- **Rerip AIFF or WAV files into the smaller, compressed MP3 format.** They may not sound as pure, but they're less likely to skip.

- **Break down larger files into smaller ones.** If you've used the Join Tracks feature of iTunes (page 119) to create a sonic tapestry or simulate that live concert feeling, try re-encoding the songs in smaller chunks.

- **Reset the iPod.** Performing a reset (page 242) or, as a last-ditch effort, running a restore with the latest version of the iPod Software Updater (page 270) may also help stop the skipping.

iTunes Blues

The iPod and iTunes were designed to work hand-in-hand to manage your music, but occasionally, certain things may come between them. Here are a few of the common issues and problems that may interfere with that good old syncing feeling.

I Just Bought This iPod and It's Already Giving Me Grief

You've just taken your iPod out of its box, charged it up, and connected it to your Windows computer for the first time. But then, when you try to use the iPod, you see the disheartening Folder-With-An-Exclamation-Mark icon (page 246). If this is happening, you probably skipped the setup step in which you install the software that came on the iPod CD. Even if you already have iTunes installed on your computer, you need to run the program on the iPod CD to get all of the necessary iPod files on there as well.

Install the iPod software on the CD before connecting the iPod. If it's too late for that and you can't find your CD, download the latest version of the iPod updater from Apple's Web site (*www.apple.com/ipod/download/*) and follow the instructions for installing it on page 270.

If your software is up to date, make sure the iPod's battery is charged up before connecting it to the computer.

I Can't Get the Software to Install on Windows

The trio of iTunes, QuickTime, and the iPod's software can send some Windows PCs into a tizzy when you try to install the programs to use with your new iPod. There are a vast number of reasons why this could be happening and at least 15 separate error messages relating to why exactly Windows couldn't get the software installed and the iPod up and running.

To troubleshoot this sort of thing, you should first start with the basics: make sure you have administrator access on the PC and not an account with lesser installation privileges. Also make sure that your Windows system is up to date and meets all the software's requirements. Uninstalling previous versions of QuickTime and iTunes may also help you install the new ones.

Little things, like storing the iTunes installer software inside a folder with non-alphanumeric characters in its name or having an overstuffed Windows temp file directory can also trip up the iTunes installer. (To fix either of these, move the iTunes installer to a different location or rename the folder you stashed it in and delete the files in the Windows Temp directory before you restart the PC.) Overaggressive anti-virus software may also hinder iTunes.

To help corral solutions to all the aforementioned problems, as well as attempting to fix the larger collection of individual error messages, Apple has compiled a Web page in the support area of its site just for beleaguered Windows folks. It's Knowledge Base Article No. 93976, and you can find it by typing 93976 into the Search box at *www.apple.com/support* or by going directly to *http://docs.info.apple.com/ article.html?artnum=93976.*

The iPod Doesn't Show Up

Communication is a vital part of any relationship, and the partnership between the iPod and iTunes is no different. If the iPod doesn't show up as a disk on your computer (or in iTunes) when it's connected, ask yourself:

- Are you plugging the iPod's cable firmly into a built-in FireWire or Windows USB 2.0 port? If you added the FireWire or USB 2.0 card yourself, is it an Apple-approved expansion card, or some cheap third-party card that hasn't been certified to work with Windows or the Macintosh operating system?

- Does your computer meet the system requirements (page 3)?

- Is the computer (especially a Windows laptop) set to turn off power to the USB ports when set to conserve power?

Other reasons the iPod may be shy and not showing up:

- **A bad cable or connector (FireWire or USB 2.0) on either the computer or iPod.** Try a different port on the computer and make sure the iPod's FireWire or USB 2.0 port is unobstructed. If your cable is bent or crimped, it may not be working properly, and you may need to replace it.

- **Other hardware plugged into the FireWire chain may be butting in.** Try unplugging the other FireWire devices and plug the iPod directly into a FireWire port on the back of the computer.

Tip: One way to test the cable is to plug it into the iPod on one end and the AC adapter on the other, and then plug the AC adapter into an electrical outlet. If your iPod begins to charge, you know signals are getting through.

- **The iPod is frozen and needs resetting.** See page 242.

- **The iPod's hard drive is damaged and unable to communicate.** If you recently reformatted it with software other than Apple's iPod Software Updater, the iPod might not be able to recognize its best friend iTunes. Performing the software restore procedure described on page 273 might help. If the iPod doesn't respond to a reset, you may have to try the "forced disk mode" procedure described on page 243.

Songs Don't Automatically Update

Make sure the iPod is connected to the computer, select it from the iTunes Source list, then click the iPod Preferences button in the lower-right corner of the iTunes window. Make sure the "Automatically update all songs and playlists" option is turned on. If the iPod's preferences are set to "Manually manage songs and playlists," as shown in Figure 12-4, then the iPod is waiting for you to make the first move. (Details on page 47.)

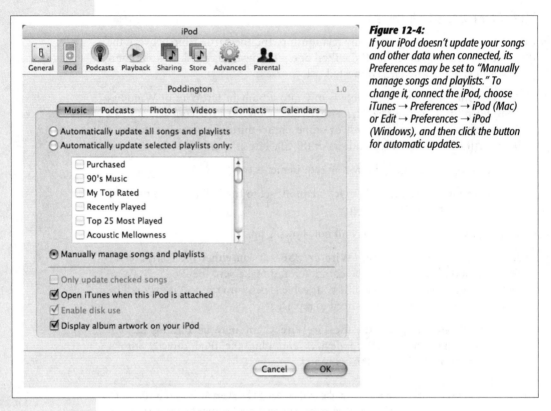

Figure 12-4:
If your iPod doesn't update your songs and other data when connected, its Preferences may be set to "Manually manage songs and playlists." To change it, connect the iPod, choose iTunes → Preferences → iPod (Mac) or Edit → Preferences → iPod (Windows), and then click the button for automatic updates.

Some of My Videos Won't Sync to the iPod

If you get a warning box sternly informing you that "some of the videos in your library could not be copied because they won't play on this iPod," iTunes is telling you that certain clips in your collection are in formats the iPod can't handle. The videos could be in the .mpg or .avi format—neither of which are iPod-friendly.

To get the video to copy to the iPod, you have to convert it into one of the formats the iPod can play: .mov, .mp4, or .m4v. First, try right-clicking the video file name in iTunes; if you see an option to "Convert Selection for iPod," pick that and you're all set. Another option is to use the full version of QuickTime 7 Pro, which can easily convert many clips for the iPod, and you can get it for $30 at *www.apple. com/quicktime*. A number of other programs floating around the Web (and mentioned on page 139) can also make those files iPod Cinema–ready for you.

iTunes Doesn't Open When I Plug in the iPod

Click the iPod button in the iTunes window and turn on the "Open iTunes when this iPod is attached" box, shown in Figure 12-4.

I Filled Up My Hard Drive and Need to Move My Music

If you're adding an extra hard drive to hold your gigabytes of accumulated data, you can relocate your iTunes library without having to rerip all those CDs. You just need to drag your iTunes Music folder over to the new drive and then tell iTunes where you put it. To do that, choose iTunes → Preferences → Advanced → General on the Mac or Edit → Preferences → Advanced → General in Windows. In the iTunes Music folder location area, click the Change button and navigate to the place where you just dragged your folder.

Once you have confirmed that all the songs are there and seem to be playing properly, you can delete the Music folder from its old location and get all that hard drive space back.

If you're moving to a new computer, just figure out how you want to transfer the song files—burn them as data files to a CD or DVD, network the two computers together and copy them over, load them on a temporary external hard drive to transfer them, or whatever. Export your playlists as well to take along.

Once you have iTunes installed on your new computer, choose iTunes → Preferences → Advanced → General on the Mac or Edit → Preferences → Advanced → General in Windows, and make sure the "Copy files to iTunes Music folder when adding to library" option is turned on. Then, with the File → Add to Library menu command, import your songs and playlists from your discs or drive.

As an alternate method of moving songs and playlists simultaneously, some people have even copied the entire iTunes folder from their home directories and replaced the new, unused iTunes folder in the home directories of their new computers.

Tip: It may take some time, but burning all your songs to discs in order to move them from one computer to another does leave you with all your songs on a set of discs—and the happy side effect of having a backup of your collection after you copy them over to the new machine. Just be sure to burn *data* discs, not music CDs.

iTunes Doesn't Open

If you try to open iTunes, but get only an error message ("Not a Valid Library File" or "Error -208 Cannot Open iTunes Music Library"), you might experience a mighty stomach lurch as you imagine your entire digital audio library disappearing in a puff of bytes. Fortunately, it refers only to the database file that iTunes uses to keep track of the *library entries and playlists,* not the actual music files.

In most cases, you can get iTunes to start up again by opening your iTunes folder and dragging the problematic iTunes Music Library.xml file to the desktop. (On the Mac, the iTunes folder is in your Home → Music folder; in Windows, it's in your My Documents → My Music folder. If the iTunes Music Library file isn't where it's supposed to be, search your computer for "iTunes Music Library.")

When you restart iTunes, the program creates a fresh, untarnished Music Library file. It's so untarnished, in fact, that it probably shows a completely empty music library, or one that is way out of date. The following Apple-recommended quick fix should get iTunes up and running, but alas, it involves having to recreate playlists.

To save yourself some of this grief, back up your playlists and Music Library file every once in a while. Some of the iPod utilities mentioned in Chapters 2 and 11 can also back up playlists or retrieve them from the iPod for you, but you can also do it the old-fashioned way.

To back up your playlists manually:

1. **In iTunes, select a playlist you wish to back up. Choose File → Export Song List.**

   In the Export Song List box, there are a few file format options to choose from.

2. **Pick the XML format. Save the playlist to a folder on your computer or on an external hard drive so that you can easily find it if something ever goes kablooey with iTunes.**

   XML is the language of the iTunes Library.

3. **Repeat steps 1 to 3 until you've exported all your playlists.**

   It may take awhile if you have a ton of playlists. (You can skip the playlists called 60's Music, My Top Rated, Recently Played, and Top 25 Most Played; those are Smart Playlists that iTunes generates on its own.)

Now your playlists are safely backed up for safekeeping. Cut to the unhappy day that you start up your computer and iTunes is either spewing library-related error messages at you or just crashing. If that happens, you'll need to recreate your Library file and import your saved playlists.

Here's the routine for recreating the iTunes Library file:

1. **Quit iTunes, if it's open. Find your iTunes folder.**

   By default, the iTunes folder lives in your Home → Music folder (Macintosh) or the My Documents → My Music folder (Windows).

2. **Open the iTunes folder. Find the files called iTunes Library (Mac) and iTunes Library.itl (Windows). Drag them to the Trash or Recycle Bin.**

   These are the messed-up versions of the files that are causing iTunes its internal grief. When you start iTunes again, though, the program automatically generates fresh new, empty copies of the files. These new files have nothing to do with what's in your library—*yet.*

3. **Open iTunes. Choose File → Import.**

   Now, it's time to get that massive collection back in the library's listings.

4. Navigate to the iTunes Music Library.xml file you pulled out to the desktop earlier and click Choose.

All the items that used to be listed in your iTunes library window should be there again, just like they were before that horrible moment when you discovered that they weren't.

New library file—*check*. Songs reappearing in the iTunes Library—*check*. Now, you just need to get those backed-up playlists back into the program, and then all will be as it was before this little incident. (If you *didn't* back up your playlists, you need to recreate them by hand at this point, which can be a colossal pain if you had one for every possible occasion.)

Here's how you reimport your playlists:

1. **In iTunes, choose File → Import.**

   The Import dialog box appears.

2. **Navigate to the location where you safely exported your playlists. Double-click the first one to bring it back into iTunes.**

   You've just restored the first playlist.

3. **Repeat for each playlist you need to restore.**

   This process can be tedious, but it's not nearly as tedious as having to recreate them all from scratch if you *didn't* back them up.

If you have a Mac.com account and have recently taken advantage of the service's Backup program for easy iTunes library file backups, log onto the service and use the program's Restore function to place the saved copy back on your Mac.

What's This "Please Reinstall iTunes" Message on My Windows PC?

Windows 2000 and XP have a lot going on behind the scenes, and sometimes these service functions can interfere with the iPod and iTunes. You may see a message that says something like "Software communicating with the iPod is installed incorrectly. Please reinstall iTunes," and you won't see the iPod listed in the iTunes Source list. Don't worry, *you* didn't do anything wrong; it's due to a software rumble within iTunes.

Note: The "iPod Service Error" when you try to update your iPod is another symptom of this fistfight backstage at Windows World.

One situation that may cause this problem is if you (or another user on the machine) forget to properly log out of the first user account in Windows before switching to another account. If you think this is the case, go back and make sure the first user has been logged out all the way before logging back in and starting up iTunes.

If that didn't solve your problem, you need to take more serious steps.

Reinstall iTunes

1. **Remove your copy of iTunes.**

   This is time-consuming, but often works. Choose Start → Control Panel → Add/ Remove Programs and select iTunes from the list of installed programs. Click Remove and restart the computer after Windows removes the program. Then go to Apple's Web site and download the latest version of iTunes at *www.apple.com/ itunes*. Install the new version.

2. **Update the iPod.**

   See page 269 for steps on updating the iPod.

3. **Connect the freshly updated iPod to the freshly updated iTunes and see if it works.**

   If you are still getting the error messages, it's time to go under the hood in Windows and turn off any services (programs running in the background as you work on the computer) that are interfering with the iPod.

Disable Startup Items and System Services

1. **Choose Start → Run and type "msconfig" in the box.**

2. **Click the General tab.**

   On the General tab, click Selective Startup and turn off the Load Startup Items checkbox (Figure 12-5).

3. **Click the Startup tab (Figure 12-5).**

   Select the iTunesHelper and "qttask" items on the list.

4. **Click the Services tab.**

   Turn on the checkbox next to Hide All Microsoft Services.

   Click "Disable all" to turn off all options and then select iPodService in the list.

5. **Click Apply and then Close.**

   The System Configuration message suggests a reboot. Restart Windows and see if the iPod and iTunes are any happier.

If all of that still fails to solve your problem, go back and turn off the iPod Service item in step 4 as well, then download the latest version of iTunes and install it again.

Note: The System Configuration Utility just described is only in Windows XP.

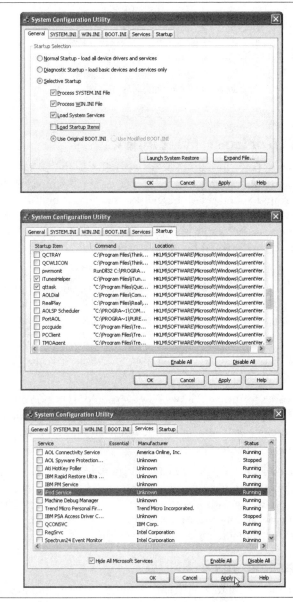

Figure 12-5:
The iPod Service Error or repeated requests from your PC to reinstall iTunes may lead you into the Windows XP System Configuration utility. Once in the box, turn off Load Startup Items (top), make sure only iTunesHelper and qttask programs are running (middle), and turn off everything but iPod Service (bottom) as part of Apple's troubleshooting steps.

"Another User" Error Message

Windows XP and Mac OS X have a feature called Fast User Switching that lets people who all use the same computer quickly log into their own accounts without making other people log off first. If you have iTunes open in your account and someone else—possibly your little sister who wants to start yakking on AOL Instant Messenger—logs onto her account with Fast User Switching, iTunes gets locked up in *your* account. If Sis wants to listen to tunes while she talks, she gets an error message that says, "You cannot open the application 'iTunes' because another user has it open. Ask the other user to quit the application, then try again." To fix the problem, switch back into your account and quit the program. Now your sister can switch back into her account and start iTunes from there.

Note: If you've got Mac OS X 10.4 or later running—congratulations! You're immune from this one-iTunes-per-one-Mac problem.

---

iTunes Won't Play a CD or Import Music from It

Newfangled compact discs in fancy formats like Super Audio CD and DVD-Audio are designed to excite audiophiles who live to hear every pick-scrape on Bob Dylan's guitar in 5.1 Surround Sound. Alas, these discs usually have built-in copyright protection that prevents you from ripping them to digital audio files on your computer. Some computers, in fact, can't read these discs at all. So, if you've got yourself one of these new formats, you'd better stick to playing it on your expensive stereo system.

Worse, these days, even some non-SACD and DVD-A discs include copy protection that prevents a computer from ripping or even reading the songs on the CD. To confirm that this is the problem, try playing the troublesome disc on another computer, to rule out the possibility that something is funky with your own drive.

If you're having trouble with a regular old CD that you've played successfully before on your computer, proceed as shown in Figure 12-6.

There's also a CD Diagnostics feature in the Windows version of iTunes. To use it, choose Help → Run CD Diagnostics and insert a CD into the drive you want to check out. After iTunes runs its tests, it displays the results in a window and may offer more troubleshooting steps to try.

If you've *never* been able to get iTunes to play CDs on your computer, and you're up to date on software upgrades from your drive's manufacturer, it's remotely possible that your drive simply doesn't work with iTunes. If this is the case, submit your drive's make and model number to Apple via the iTunes Feedback page at *www.apple.com/feedback/itunes.html* to make the company aware of the issue.

"iPod Is Linked to Another Library"

If you're trying to plug your iPod into a different computer, an alert box may tell you that this particular iPod is already linked to another music library. iTunes then offers to *replace all of the music* on your iPod with whatever is in *its* library.

Click No here (unless, of course, this second machine's music library is much better than your own).

You can avoid this message by turning on "Manually manage songs and playlists" in the iPod's Preferences box (which appears when you plug the iPod in and click the iPod-shaped icon at the bottom of the iTunes window).

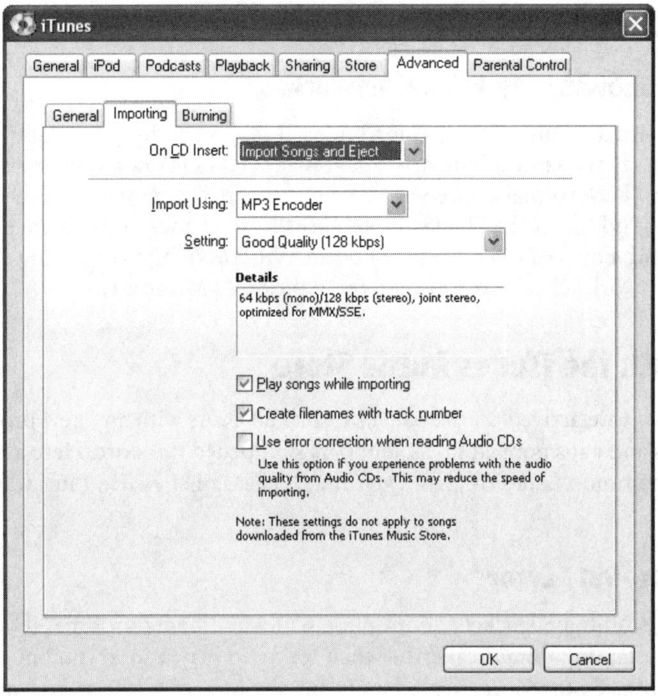

Figure 12-6:
Choose iTunes → Preferences → Advanced → Importing (Mac) or Edit → Preferences → Advanced → Importing (Windows) to open the Preferences dialog box shown here. Once you get there, turn off "Use error correction when reading Audio CDs," and click OK. That option might be interfering with the song-importing process.

When it comes to the iPod Shuffle, alas, you are stuck having to use it with just one computer or face having its library replaced. By design, the Shuffle will either wipe its contents and prepare itself for songs from this new computer's library if you click Yes, or refuse to show itself in the iTunes Source list if you click No in the box.

Tip: If you're not the only person who uses a certain Mac or PC—or if you're not the only person using the iPod—turning on "Manually manage songs and playlists" should make everybody happy (page 47). This way, the iPod won't alert you to other iTunes music libraries each time you plug it in, and the rest of the family can manually drag their own choices of music to the iPod without erasing anything accidentally.

The iPod Always Says, "Do Not Disconnect"

If you've turned on the "Enable disk use" box in iTunes' iPod Preferences panel, the Do Not Disconnect message appears on the iPod at *all times*. You have to unmount the iPod from the computer manually to make the message go away (page 207).

Even if you haven't set up the iPod to work as an external disk, its hard drive may not have spun down properly. If it's stuck in a loop, the Do Not Disconnect message may also appear. Try clicking the Eject iPod button in iTunes, or dragging the iPod icon on the desktop to the Mac's Trash, to see if you get the "OK to Disconnect" message.

Tip: If that doesn't work, try resetting the iPod, as described on page 242, and then try ejecting it.

The iPod Isn't Showing My Album Artwork

One of the nifty visual features of the color-screen iPods (including the Nano) is their ability to display the same album artwork you applied in iTunes. If your art is missing, however, check to make sure you're using at least iTunes 4.7. If you are, then connect the iPod, open the iTunes Preferences box (iTunes → Preference → iPod on the Mac or Edit → Preferences → iPod in Windows), and make sure the "Display album artwork" checkbox is turned on in the box's Music area.

Problems with the iTunes Music Store

The iTunes Music Store arrived on the scene in April 2003. As with any new product, a few glitches and gaps popped up as shoppers stampeded the store. Here are a few of the more common issues or errors you might occasionally encounter when using the service.

-9800, -9815, or -9814 Error

The Music Store is quite persnickety about punctuality and being on time. If you get this negative-sounding numerical error when trying to play a song you bought from the iTunes Music Store—or even when trying to connect to the store—quit iTunes. Set your computer's clock to the correct time (use System Preferences on Mac OS X; the Control Panel in Windows).

-50 Error in the Music Store (Windows Only)

If you're using iTunes, but clicking the Music Store icon produces only a blank window, then one of these problems is probably afoot:

- You're using an ad- or privacy-filter program, a firewall program, or "Web acceleration" software. Updating to the latest version of iTunes should help.

- Configure your privacy or security software to permit access to specific Web sites, if it offers this feature. Put *phobos.apple.com* and *phobos.apple.com.edgesuite.net* on the list. Now you should be able to get into the iTunes Music Store even when your moatware is enabled.

- You're using McAfee Privacy Service, which doesn't work well with the iTunes Music Store.

-5000 or -35 Error When Downloading (Mac Only)

This error refers to scrambled Mac OS X permissions for the iTunes Music folder. (*Permissions* are behind-the-scenes Unix settings that permit only some people and not others to open and inspect certain folders.) This problem occurs (and recurs) if several people are sharing the same copy of iTunes. It can also happen if someone trashes the iTunes Music folder, or if there's a broken alias for the iTunes Music folder.

If you're using an alias for the iTunes Music folder (page 123), make sure that it works and knows where to find the iTunes Music folder. If the folder has disappeared completely, it's time to make a new one.

How to make a new iTunes Music folder

1. **In iTunes, choose iTunes → Preferences.**

   The Preferences dialog box appears.

2. **Click the Advanced icon and then the General tab,**

   Turn on the checkbox next to "Keep iTunes Music Folder organized." Then click the Change button.

3. **Navigate to, and select, the disk or folder where you'd like to store the new iTunes Music folder.**

   Make sure your new place has enough room on the drive to store all of the digital audio files in your collection. (If you don't specify, iTunes puts a folder called iTunes Music in your Home → Music → iTunes folder.)

4. **Click New Folder. Name the folder and click Create. At the bottom of the Change Music Folder Location box, click Choose.**

   You've just blessed this new folder as your music vault.

5. **Click OK to close the Preferences window.**

   A message advises you, "Changing the location of the iTunes Music Folder requires updating the location of each of the songs in your music library. This update will not move or delete any of your song files."

6. **Click OK when you're done reading.**

   In the next step, you'll actually move your songs to the new folder.

7. **Choose Advanced → Consolidate Library.**

   A message pops up with the warning, "Consolidating your library will copy all of your music into the iTunes Music folder. This cannot be undone."

8. **Click Consolidate to copy all of your music files into this new folder and location.**

   Because this action copies all of your music files to the new folder, it might take a few minutes. It also makes *duplicates* of any song files found outside the iTunes Music folder, so mind your hard drive space. To get that drive space back, drag the old iTunes Music folder (but not the iTunes Library files that may also be in the main iTunes folder) to the Trash or Recycle Bin and empty it.

How to correct permissions for the iTunes Music folder

Mac OS X, which is based on Unix, uses *permissions* to allow different people different access to files. If they get messed up for a certain file or folder—especially the iTunes Music folder—you can wind up with a real six-aspirin headache.

Note: To perform the following steps, your account must be an Administrator account (not a Standard or Normal account). If your Mac won't let you perform these steps, ask the technical whiz who set it up for help. (That person almost *certainly* has an Administrator account.)

1. **In the Finder, locate your iTunes Music folder.**

   It's usually in your Home → Music → iTunes folder. If it doesn't seem to be there, open iTunes, choose iTunes → Preferences → Advanced → General, and check the folder map listed in the middle of the box. It tells you where iTunes believes your music to be.

2. **When you've found the iTunes Music folder, click it once and choose File → Get Info.**

   Of course, you can press ⌘-I instead. Either way, the Get Info dialog box appears.

3. **Click to open the flippy triangle to expand the Ownership and Permissions panel.**

   If you're running Mac OS X 10.3 or 10.4, also expand the Details triangle.

4. **Change the "You can" and Owner Access pop-up menus so they look like Figure 12-7.**

   Of course, your account name should appear where it says Owner. (This, by the way, is where you may be asked for your account password, to prove that you're technically competent—an administrator.) The Group Access and Others pop-up menus should say "Read only."

5. **Click "Apply to enclosed items," and close the Get Info box.**

   If you're not having any luck with the permissions-correction approach, making a whole new iTunes Music folder, as described on page 265, may fix the problem.

Tip: If your Mac is behaving somewhat oddly in general—refusing to open files or programs and being generally sluggish—you might have a larger permissions problem than just the iTunes Music folder. Luckily, in both Mac OS X 10.2 and later, there's a truly useful utility program called Disk Utility that you can run to fix all the permissions on the Mac automatically. Choose Applications → Utilities → Disk Utility, and in the First Aid tab, click the name of your hard drive and then click the Repair Permissions button.

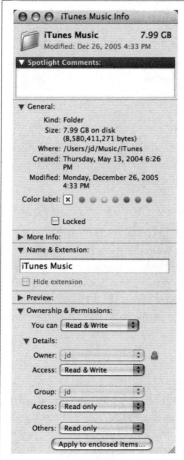

Figure 12-7:
Resetting permissions on the iTunes Music folder can fix some Music Store error messages. The trick is to use Get Info on your iTunes Music folder (shown here in Mac OS X). If you still have trouble after correcting the permissions, you may need to correct the permissions for the folder for the band or singer you were trying to listen to when the trouble started.

Purchased Music Doesn't Play (Mac Only)

If you've purchased some Music Store songs that refuse to play, first make sure that the computer you're using is *authorized* to play the purchased music. Also make sure that you haven't exceeded your five-computer iTunes Music Store limit (page 182).

There's one other remote possibility: the permissions for your Shared folder (a standard Mac OS X folder, designed for sharing documents among account holders) may have become scrambled or even deleted. The Music Store relies on this Shared folder to store the authorization information for your Mac.

Open your hard drive icon, and open the Users folder inside. If you don't see a Shared folder there, create one (File → New Folder). Follow up by setting its permissions as described in the previous steps—except this time, the Owner should be System.

Now try to play your purchased music or buy a song from the iTunes Music Store.

Purchased Video Won't Work in My iMovie Opus

Even though it would be really cool to edit a few clips of Conan O'Brien into your iMovie class project, you can't. This is because the TV shows and other videos purchased from the iTunes Store are copyrighted and contain a special code embedded in the file to keep you from using the files anywhere except on your computer and iPod.

I Can't Buy Music

If you can't complete purchases in the iTunes Music Store, follow the steps described on page 267 for replacing a missing Shared folder. Also, make sure your Internet connection is live and working (not to mention your credit card).

Music Doesn't Download Automatically

You can download your purchases from the iTunes Music Store in one of two ways: either with the 1-Click method, which downloads the songs right away as you buy them, or with the Shopping Cart feature, which collects your songs and then downloads them all when you're done shopping. (See Chapter 7 for details.) If you're expecting instant song downloads, choose iTunes → Preferences on the Mac or Edit → Preferences on the PC, click the Store icon, and make sure the option for 1-Click purchasing is turned on.

I Can't Burn My Purchased Music to CD

If iTunes finds an unauthorized Music Store track on your playlist, it will stop burning the CD in progress and scold you ("One or more of the songs on this playlist are not authorized for use on this machine"). Authorizing the song with your Apple or AOL account name and password will fix it, but remember, you can only burn the same playlist containing purchased music seven times.

I Can't Burn My Purchased Songs to an MP3 Disc

While the iTunes Music Store allows you to burn a playlist containing purchased music up to seven times, you must burn it as an audio CD (page 126) and not an MP3 CD. If you've tried to make an MP3 CD out of purchased music, you've probably seen the foreboding error message, "None of the items in this playlist can be burned to disc."

The songs from the iTunes Music Store are in AAC format and protected from conversion into other file formats like MP3. You can, however, burn them to a regular audio CD or back them up to a data disc. Choose another disc format by choosing iTunes → Preferences, and then clicking the Burning icon.

Note: When you buy a song or album from the iTunes Music Store, it's yours to keep forever—but you can only download it *once* from the store. Additional downloads mean additional payments, so it's a good idea to back up your purchased music files, as described in Chapter 7.

Software Updates for iTunes

Apple updates iTunes at least once a year with new features, (Podcasts! Videos! Pretty Colors!) and enhancements to the program's code. As with any software update, once you download the software, double-click the installer file's icon and follow along as the program takes you through several screens of upgrade adventure.

If you use iTunes for Windows, you can tell the program to alert you to newly available versions by choosing Edit → Preferences → General and turning on "Check for iTunes updates automatically." If you prefer to check yourself, choose Help → Check for iTunes Updates or visit *www.apple.com/itunes*.

If you're in Mac OS X, life is just as easy. The Mac's Software Update program is designed to alert you, via a pop-up dialog box, about new updates for iTunes.

If you've turned Software Update off (in System Preferences), however, you can run it manually by selecting it under the Apple menu and sending it out to look for updates right then. Or you can always hit up the iTunes download page at *www. apple.com/itunes* to see whether your version is the latest and greatest.

If you're having technical troubles, go to Apple's main Support page at *www.apple. com/support/itunes* and choose the version of iTunes (Mac or PC) you're grappling with.

iPod Software Updates

What Apple maketh, Apple shall updateth. Like any other software company, Apple constantly fixes, enhances, and fine-tunes the operating systems it writes— including the iPod's.

In general, Apple updates the iPod's system software a few times a year, but the amount of new stuff varies in each revision. Some updates just fix bugs and improve existing functions (like battery life), while other updates add a whole new world of possibilities (like the ability to play AAC files or use calendars on your iPod).

Apple uses a universal updater program, so no matter what iPod you have, you just download this one file, usually named something bold and inspiring like "iPod Updater 2006-01-10" (Figure 12-8). When you download the latest version, the Updater software will decide if your specific iPod model needs updating or not.

How to Know When It's Time

Notification that a new iPod software version may come to you in any of several ways:

- **Macintosh Software Update.** If you've got the Mac's built-in Software Update feature turned on in your System Preferences or Control Panels, it can regularly check Apple's servers for updates to all your Apple software, including iTunes, iSync, iCal, and the iPod system software. Just pick the software you want from the Software Update list and click Install.

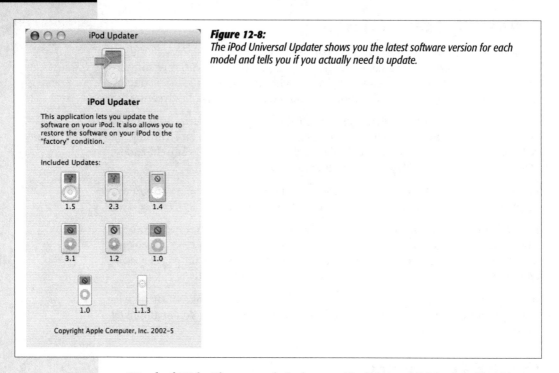

Figure 12-8:
The iPod Universal Updater shows you the latest software version for each model and tells you if you actually need to update.

- **Word of Web.** If you regularly browse iPod-themed Web sites like iLounge (*www.ilounge.com*) or iPoding (*www.ipoding.com*) or tech-oriented forums like Slashdot.org, you'll hear about any new iPod update (software *or* hardware) about five seconds after Apple posts it.

Downloading the Updater

When you get the word, aim your Web browser at *www.apple.com/download/ipod*. Usually, Apple provides updates for both the Macintosh and Windows versions. If you've just purchased a brand-new iPod, load the iPod system software included on the CD that came in the box, and then check to see if there's an updated version. The iPod download page (Figure 12-9) explains what the new software does.

Running the Updater

iPod software updates are relatively painless: You download the installer file from Apple's Web site, connect iPod to computer, and then run the installer program. If you downloaded the updater at some point along with other patches and security fixes, the updater itself may jump in and offer to upgrade your iPod when you plug it into the computer. Depending on what iPod you drive, you may be asked to unplug the USB or FireWire cable once or twice or to plug the iPod into its AC adapter for a toot of electricity during the process to get the new system up and running.

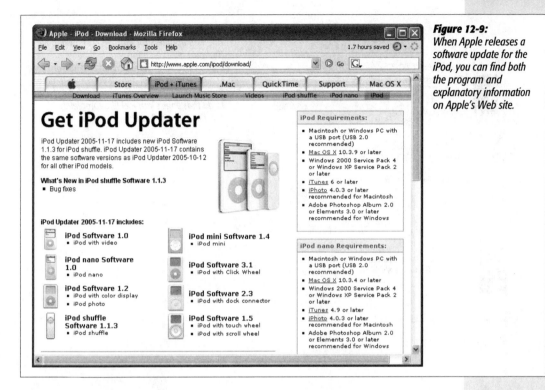

Figure 12-9:
When Apple releases a software update for the iPod, you can find both the program and explanatory information on Apple's Web site.

Updating the Macintosh iPod

1. **Connect the iPod to your Mac using its FireWire or USB cable.**

   Unless you've changed the factory settings, iTunes opens and autosyncs its music with the iPod. Quit iTunes when the iPod's music library is updated.

2. **Open your Home Directory → Applications → Utilities folder. Open the iPod Software Updater application that you downloaded with Software Update.**

   (If you downloaded it to a different folder on your Mac, find the file and double-click the iPod Software Updater icon.)

   As shown in Figure 12-10, at top, the updater software checks your iPod and lets you know if you need to update.

3. **If you're told that your iPod needs updating, click the Update button.**

   You'll probably be asked to type in your Administrator name and password before you can proceed. Let the updater program run.

4. **Follow along as the updater runs its course.**

   Different iPods may behave differently during the update process, so pay attention to both what your Mac's screen and the iPod's screen are telling you to do.

5. **When the Updater tells you so, it's done.**

   Quit the update program and go about your iPod business.

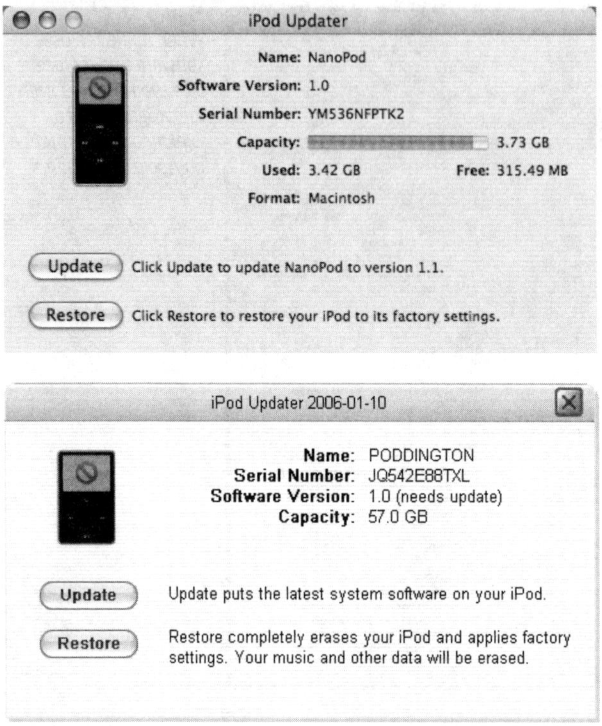

Figure 12-10:
The iPod updaters for Mac (top) and Windows (bottom) give you information about your iPod's current software version and let you know if you're out of date. If you're up to date, Restore is your only option—and you don't want to do that unless you feel like completely erasing your iPod and starting over.

Note: Apple tinkers with the iPod's firmware several times a year and has been known to make changes that affect how the iPod behaves during its own updates. Your iPod experience may not be exactly the same as described here, but the software should guide you as you go.

Updating the Windows iPod

1. **Connect the iPod to your PC with its cable.**

   Unless you changed the factory settings, iTunes opens and updates the iPod with any new songs or playlists you've created since the last time you synced PC with Pod. Quit iTunes when it's done.

2. **Choose Start menu → Programs → iPod → iPod Updater.**

   The update program shown in Figure 12-10 at bottom appears.

3. **Click the Update button.**

   If it's grayed out, you're already up to date.

   A progress bar creeps along the screen as the update runs. If you have an older iPod running iPod Software 2.0 or later, your work is done here unless your FireWire-friendly iPod isn't connected to a powered FireWire port. In most cases with Window machines, it's not, and you'll get a message asking you to unplug the iPod and a graphic of an AC adapter going into an electrical outlet on the iPod's screen.

4. **Find your AC adapter and FireWire cable and plug the iPod into the wall.**

The Apple logo appears and the gray progress bar marches across the screen. This is iPod loading its new software. When it's done, close the Updater box on the computer and unplug the iPod from the AC adapter, unless you need to charge it up anyway.

Compared to Windows service packs or Mac OS system updates, the iPod upgrades go very quickly. (If anything goes wrong, check the iPod support area of Apple's Web site for troubleshooting articles.)

Restoring the Software

Restoring the iPod software isn't the same thing as updating it. Restoring is a much more drastic procedure, like reformatting the hard drive on your Mac or PC. For one thing, *restoring the software erases the iPod's hard drive entirely.*

Of course, you won't lose any of your music, calendars, contacts, or notes because all of that is nothing more than a reflection of what's on your Mac or PC if you've been performing automatic synchronization. If you manually manage your music, though, you'll lose any songs that are not already stored in your iTunes library, so you'll want to harvest them off the player with any of the tools described in Chapter 2 for copying your songs back to the computer. You'll lose all the random computer files you've manually dragged onto the iPod's hard drive as well. If your iPod has been freezing, crashing, or behaving erratically, a good solid software restore may be just the thing it needs to feel better.

Note: If you think there might be a more recent version of the iPod software than what came with your iPod CD, go to *www.apple.com/ipod/download* and snag yourself a piping fresh copy of the iPod updater posted there.

Before you begin, insert your iPod software CD or have an update installer on your desktop. Then restore the iPod software (also called its *firmware*) like this:

1. **Connect the iPod to the computer with its FireWire or USB cable.**

Let iTunes automatically synchronize and update the iPod's library, if it seems to want to.

2. **Double-click the iPod Software Updater icon on your desktop, or the installer on your iPod CD.**

If your iPod software is a version or two behind the current one, you'll see buttons labeled Restore and Update; if the Update button is dimmed and unavailable, then you're already up to date. (If Update is available, run Restore to clean off and reformat the iPod's hard drive, and *then* run Update.)

3. **Click Restore.**

   An alert box pops up asking if you really want to do this. Assure it that you do. (If you're using Mac OS X, Windows 2000, or Windows XP, you may be asked to confirm your technical prowess by typing in your Administrator account password.)

   After you affirm your decision, the installer program gets down to work completely erasing the drive and returning your iPod's factory settings to their original, untouched state.

4. **If the screen requests it, unplug the computer cable from the iPod. Replug it when and where you're asked to do so.**

   As the iPod completes the restoration process, you see the Do Not Disconnect message on its screen. iTunes leaps back into action.

5. **Follow your computer's onscreen instructions through the set-up process, just as you did when you first got an iPod.**

   Here's where you give your iPod a name and choose whether you want to have the player updated automatically when you connect it to the computer. (You don't have to answer these questions the same way you did originally.)

6. **Refill the iPod with your music library from iTunes.**

   Since your iPod is empty now and all of your music is still on your computer, this may take a few minutes.

7. **When you see a message stating that the iPod update is complete, unmount or eject the iPod, and then quit the iPod Software Updater program.**

   See page 207 for details on unmounting the iPod.

8. **Unplug the computer cable from the iPod and let it start itself up again.**

   You'll have to go through the setup process on the iPod as well, doing things like picking the language you wish to use with it.

Once you've gone through all these steps, check the iPod to make sure all your songs and playlists are back where they belong. Then use it as you normally do and see if that nasty freezing problem was fixed.

Updating and Restoring the iPod Shuffle's Software

Just like its big brothers, the iPod Shuffle's software may need to be updated or restored on occasion. As with the hard drive–based iPods, *Update* just puts a newer version of the system software on the Shuffle and leaves your songs and data intact, while Restore wipes everything completely off the drive and forces you to start fresh by reloading your songs and files from the computer.

You can get a copy of the latest Shuffle software online at *www.apple.com/support/ ipod*.

1. Once you've downloaded the file to your computer, double-click the installer file and follow the onscreen instructions.

   Windows users need to restart after running the installer program.

2. **Connect the iPod Shuffle to the computer.**

   Most Macs will jump right up and get going with the update, but if your Windows PC just sits there, give it a shove by going to Start → All Programs → iPod, and then choose the file you just downloaded from Apple's site.

3. **Click Update or Restore and let the software guide you.**

Tip: If the iPod software updater doesn't realize you have your player plugged in already, flip the Shuffle off and then back on again.

Where to Get Help Online

Apple keeps an online library of technical help articles for the iPod on the Web, along with manuals and details about each new iPod hardware and software update.

- The iPod Service & Support page, which includes links to tips, tricks, tutorials, videos, a Frequently Asked Questions section, user forums, and top tech-support issues for the iPod is at *www.apple.com/support/ipod*. Links along the right side of the page let you select articles appropriate for your specific iPod.

- The iTunes Service & Support page covers known issues with the program for both Windows and Macintosh systems. A crash course in using Apple's jukebox program is here, plus animated tutorials and How-To articles; all are at *www.apple.com/support/itunes*.

- For problems with billing, downloading, and computer authorization, the direct link to the iTunes Music Store Customer Service Center is *www.apple. com/support/itunes/musicstore*.

- Information about Apple's own $59 Battery Replacement Service for out-of-warranty iPods with dead or dying batteries is at *www.apple.com/support/ipod/ service/battery*.

Specific Help for Sick or Damaged iPods

The Apple Web page for iPod Service is at *www.apple.com/support/ipod/service*. Repairs are free for the iPod's first year (or two, if you bought the extended iPod AppleCare warranty).

If you're experiencing an iPod problem that's not listed or just won't go away, it may be time to visit the iPod Service Request page and fill out the form at *http:// depot.info.apple.com/ipod*. Click the Continue link and, after you've scrolled down to the bottom of *that* page, fill in the form. You need to type in your iPod serial number and set up an Apple ID if you don't already have one.

If you decide to go ahead with the service, you'll be asked to fill in your credit card number and to make arrangements for getting the iPod into good hands for repairs.

The iPodResQ Service is another option for the frantic. For $29, the company will send you a box to overnight your ailing player to the iPodResQ Repair Center, where they diagnose the problem and give you a price quote. If you accept the charge, they fix your iPod within 24 hours and pop it back to you in the overnight mail. Call them at 1-877-POD-REPAIR, or go to *www.ipodresq.com*, for more information.

The TechRestore computer repair site has opened its own Pod Hospital as well and offers a range of fixes for broken screens, busted audio jacks, battery upgrades, and other ailments. There's more information at *http://ipod.techrestore.com*.

Note: Computers and other electronic gear, including the iPod, contain toxic chemicals and other materials that can be harmful to the environment when just dumped in landfills. If your iPod is dead for good with no hope of ever getting better, you can send it back to Apple and have it recycled in a way that might better please Mother Nature and Father Time. You can read more about Apple's recycling policy and its Take-Back program at *www.apple.com/environment/recycling*.

Part Five:
Appendix

5

Appendix A: iTunes, Menu by Menu

iTunes, Menu by Menu

While you can do almost anything in iTunes by clicking buttons or pressing keys, some functions are available only in the menus at the top of the screen. This appendix covers each menu command—left to right, top to bottom.

This appendix assumes that you're using the latest version of iTunes 6 for Mac OS X and Windows. (Differences between the Mac and Windows versions are noted where necessary.) If you find clicking around in menus too slow to bear, there's a list of keyboard shortcuts at the end.

Application Menu (Mac); Help Menu (Windows)

In Mac OS X, commands that pertain to an overall program—like Hide and Quit—appear in the Application menu, the one bearing the program's name, just to the right of the menu.

In Windows, most of the equivalent commands appear in the Help menu (or at least they do in iTunes).

About iTunes

The information in this menu tells you what version of the program you're using, along with the software's creator and copyright information.

iTunes Hot Tips

This little nudge from Apple takes you to a Web page where you can read up on tips and tricks that make using iTunes a little more fun and a lot more efficient.

Preferences

The iTunes Preferences dialog box has eight panels, accessible by icons along the top of the window, which you can use to get the program looking and sounding just the way you like it. *Keyboard shortcut:* ⌘-comma (Mac); Ctrl+comma (Windows).

Note: In iTunes for Windows, the Preferences box is the last command in the Edit menu.

Here are the names of the specific preference panels, and what they do for iTunes:

General

Click the General icon to change the size of your Source and Song list text and make other adjustments to iTunes' overall appearance and behavior. You can turn on the "Show genre when browsing" checkbox to add the third Genre column alongside Artist and Albums in your iTunes Browser window (page 116), or tell iTunes not to show you the Party Shuffle, Radio, and Music Store Link arrows. You can also turn on a checkbox if you want iTunes to automatically check with Apple on a regular basis for iTunes software updates.

iPod

The iPod has its own tab in the Preferences box, but you need to have the player connected to the computer to fiddle with the settings here. Depending on the iPod, you may see more or less in your iPod's preferences box; owners of the video-enabled iPods get the most options:

- **Music.** Choose to automatically or manually update the music on your iPod here, as well as pick which playlists to update between iTunes and iPod. You can also opt to have iTunes open each time the Pod is connected, to turn your iPod into an external disk (page 204), and to display album artwork on color-screen iPods.

- **Podcasts.** These settings let you regulate which podcasts automatically update when you plug your iPod in.

- **Photos.** In this area, you can tell your color-screen iPod what folder to use for syncing photos from the computer, as well as which specific pictures or rolls to copy.

- **Videos.** Just like in the Music preferences, you can tell the iPod to automatically sync up every video file you add to iTunes or let you do it yourself manually.

- **Contacts.** If you use Outlook or Outlook Express on your PC or the Address Book program with Mac OS X 10.4, you can tell the iPod to snag a copy of your address book here.

- **Calendars.** Likewise, Outlook and iCal users can copy their calendars to the iPod with a click or two in this box.

Podcasts

These settings let you tell iTunes how often to check for new episodes of your favorite podcasts, what to do when it finds them, and how many to keep around. There's also a button that clicks you right into the podcast preferences for the iPod (explained in the preceding list).

Playback

The Playback panel is where you customize the sound of your music. The Cross-fade Playback control lets you blend one song into the next and set the amount of time it takes to blend. The Sound Enhancer slider improves the depth of the audio and lets you adjust it to your personal taste for sonic highs and lows. Turning on the Sound Check feature more or less levels out the different volumes of your songs so you're not straining to hear one soft track only to be deafened by the really loud one right after it. (A caveat: Using Sound Check can tax your computer's resources and slow things down while iTunes is fussing with sound levels and making adjustments.) The Smart Shuffle feature lets you fiddle with the frequency iTunes will play songs by the same artist or from the same album when you're set to shuffle your music. Finally, there's a checkbox you can turn on if you want to play your videos in a separate window.

Sharing

Here you can set up iTunes to allow other people to sample your songs over the network, or have your computer seek out music collections on other connected computers (page 129). You can choose how much of your music library you wish to share, whether that's everything or just a few specific playlists. If you want to put a password on your playlists, you can set that up here, too.

Store

In the Store preferences, you can decide whether you want to invite temptation and display the Music Store icon in your Source list or not. With the Music Store displayed, you have two options for buying music: download each song as you buy, or download in one batch (page 168). You can also instruct iTunes to play the songs as soon as it downloads them or load a complete preview before playing.

Advanced

The Advanced preferences panel (not to be confused with the Advanced *menu;* see page 291) contains three subcategories of settings, each under its own tab:

- **General.** Here, you can redirect iTunes to its iTunes Music folder in case you move your song files onto another drive or partition. Turn on the "Keep iTunes Music folder organized" checkbox to have each artist and album neatly tucked away in a properly labeled subfolder when you add songs to the library. Turning on this box also lets iTunes automatically refile a song in the correct folder if you edit the text in the Song Information box (page 117). If you want to make sure that the iTunes Music folder always has a copy of each song you drag or import into the program, turn on the "Copy files to iTunes Music folder when adding to library" box.

The General tab has the settings for making iTunes your default audio player and for using your Airport Express to connect iTunes to your connected stereo. If you find your Internet radio stations plagued by gaps and rebuffering messages, you can choose to increase the size of the buffer here, too.

If you'd like to make sure that your shrunken iTunes window floats on top of all other windows on your screen for easy or emergency access, there's an option to check to "Keep Mini Player on top of all other windows" here, too. Windows owners can also choose to show the iTunes icon in the Notification area and minimize it there as well when the desktop gets just a little too crowded.

- **Importing.** You can also tell iTunes what to do when you insert a CD, and give the program permission to go on the Internet by itself to get track information by turning on the "Connect to Internet when needed" box. The Importing tab lets you pick the file format (AAC, MP3, AIFF, Apple Lossless, or WAV) to use for encoding the songs copied from CDs, as well as the bit rate (page 84). You can also choose to have the songs play while you're ripping them. Turn on the "Create file names with track number" checkbox if you want your songs to fall in the same order as on the original album, even if you don't rip them all at the same time. (iTunes adds the track numbers to the names of the song files in the iTunes Music folder.)

- **Burning.** The Burning preferences let you pick the model of CD recorder you use with iTunes, as well as the type of CD you want to create—either a standard audio disc or an MP3 CD (page 126). (Remember, even though computer drives can handle them, not all CD players and car stereos can play back MP3 CDs.) With iTunes 4 or later, Mac OS X 10.2.4 or later, and an Apple Super-Drive, you can opt to burn copies of your songs to a blank DVD and archive 4.7 gigabytes of music at a time.

Parental Control

Depending on who's using it, not everything in iTunes may be suitable for children. This set of preferences lets Mom and Dad disable the Source list icons for podcasts, the Music Store, and shared music so the young ones don't roam unrestricted. There's also a checkbox to block Music Store songs labeled with the Explicit tag from underage shoppers.

Shop for iTunes Products

If you're hankering to accessorize your iTunes setup with items like speakers and headphones, let this menu command (and a live Internet connection) whisk you away to Apple's site of iPod-friendly audio products.

Provide iTunes Feedback

If you have something to say about iTunes, why not say it directly to the company that makes the program? Selecting this command opens your Web browser and transports you to the iTunes Feedback page on Apple's Web site.

(Don't expect Steve Jobs to read your note and call you right back. Someone at Apple does, however, read and collate these requests—and the biggest choruses of complaint get attention.)

Services (Mac OS X Only)

These commands are the standard Mac OS X services (see *Mac OS X: The Missing Manual*), like Make New Sticky Note and Reveal Finder. Very few of them work in iTunes, but there are a few surprising exceptions:

- **Mail** opens up a new, outgoing piece of email and attaches the selected MP3 file, ready to address and send to someone.
- **Make New Sticky Note** opens the Stickies program, creates a new empty note, and pastes into it a little chart of the selected songs: Title, artist, album, time, and genre. Kind of a cool way to make a label or a list of your collection.
- **Script Editor** lets you run or make new AppleScripts (page 227) that work with iTunes.
- **Speech → Start Speaking Text** command makes iTunes read *out loud* the artists, album names, timings, and genres of the selected songs. How weird can you get?
- **TextEdit → Open Selection** works just like Make New Sticky Note, except that it creates the table of song information in TextEdit.

Hide iTunes (Macintosh Only)

This command makes the iTunes window disappear. Click the iTunes icon in the Dock (or choose Show All) to bring it back. *Keyboard shortcut:* ⌘-H.

Hide Others (Macintosh Only)

All open program windows onscreen except iTunes disappear when you choose this command. *Keyboard shortcut:* Option-⌘-H.

Show All (Macintosh Only)

Selecting the Show All option brings any program windows hidden by the last two commands into view again.

Quit iTunes (Macintosh Only)

This is the polite way to close down the iTunes program. *Keyboard shortcut:* ⌘-Q.

File Menu

As its name implies, the File menu in iTunes (and any other computer program, for that matter) is where you go to do things with files: open them, export them, create new ones, and so on.

New Playlist

The iTunes program was made for music, and the first item on the menu creates a new, empty playlist file that you can fill with the songs of your choice from your music collection (page 122). Now that iTunes is video-friendly, you can also fill a playlist with music videos and TV shows. *Keyboard shortcut:* ⌘-N (Mac); Ctrl+N (Windows).

New Playlist From Selection

When strolling through your library, you can quickly make instant playlists by selecting an artist or album and selecting New Playlist From Selection on the File menu (page 123). To select only certain songs from the artist or album shown in the song details window, press ⌘ (on the Mac), or Ctrl (Windows), while clicking song titles. (Pressing Shift highlights all the songs between your first and second selection clicks.) *Keyboard shortcut:* With the desired songs highlighted, Shift-⌘-N (Mac), or just Shift-click the Add button; Ctrl+Shift+N (Windows).

New Smart Playlist

As described in Chapter 5, Smart Playlists work like this: You give iTunes a set of rules, like the bands you want to hear or the genre you're in the mood for (*"No Air Supply or other '80s Lite on this one, iTunes!"*) and the program goes shopping through your music library to create a customized playlist. The list even updates itself when you add new music to your collection. *Keyboard shortcut:* Option-⌘-N (or Option-click the Add button in the iTunes window) on the Mac; Ctrl+Alt+N (or Shift-click the Add button) on the PC.

New Folder

If you're one of those playlist-happy music lovers with dozens of playlists spilling out of the iTunes window, you can use this menu command to add folders right into your iTunes Source list. Once you make a new folder, click it to name it, and then drag the playlists you'd like to group together right into the folder. Folders are a great organizational tool to keep all your party or workout playlists gathered together. *Keyboard shortcut:* Shift-Option-⌘-N (Mac); Ctrl+Shift+N (Windows).

Add (File) to Library

If you've just downloaded the new MP3 single that a hot new band posted for free on its Web site, you can get it into rotation on your playlists by choosing File → Add to Library and selecting the song file from your download location. You can also add a whole folder of songs by selecting it in the directory navigation box and then clicking Choose. The "Add to Library" command is just one way to add new songs to your iTunes music library (for others, see page 103). *Keyboard shortcut:* ⌘-O (Mac); Ctrl+O (Windows).

Add Folder to Library (Windows Only)

This command lets you add an entire folder's worth of sound files to iTunes for Windows.

Close Window

If you have a bunch of open playlist windows and need to get some screen real estate back in a hurry, use File → Close Window to close the active iTunes window. *Keyboard shortcut:* ⌘-W (Mac), Ctrl+W (Windows).

Tip: Many people find the keyboard command for Close Window (⌘-W) to be much more efficient than taking the mouse for a joyride through the File menu. See page 295 for a list of other keyboard shortcuts.

Import

If you have a playlist of which you're particularly proud on one computer and want to copy it to another computer, you can export it (see the next item) from iTunes. Then you copy it to a disk or email it to yourself, and use File → Import to pull that playlist into iTunes on the second computer. *Keyboard shortcut:* Shift-⌘-O (Mac); Ctrl+Shift+O (Windows).

Export Song List

You can save copies of your masterful iTunes mixes in three different formats: plain text, Unicode text, and XML (Extensible Markup Language, which is, among other things, the new wave of the Web). Saving a song list in one of the text formats is useful for making a printed list for a CD cover or importing into a database. Saving the song list as XML allows you to import it into iTunes on another computer.

Export Library

If you want to export a list of every item in your library at once, choose the Export Library option to create a large XML file containing all the information.

Get Info

Much like the old standard Macintosh command, selecting a song from the library or a playlist and choosing File → Get Info in iTunes opens the Song Information box (page 117). In the Summary tab, you can see such trivia as the name, size, length, and location of the file, plus the last time you played it. Click the Info tab to edit the labels on the songs in the library, and the Options tab to make adjustments like adding a specific equalizer preset or song rating. Click the Lyrics tab to paste in the words to your songs or click the Artwork tab to add photos and graphics to your iTunes files (page 98). Selecting multiple songs or a whole album in the iTunes browser before choosing Get Info will let you change all their tags at once, which can be helpful, say, if you're sorting batches songs into your own genre categories. *Keyboard shortcut:* ⌘-I (Mac); Ctrl+I (Windows). See page 295 for keyboard shortcuts for navigating the Get Info window.

My Rating

Here's a quick way to slap some stars on your songs: Select the track or tracks you want to rate in iTunes and choose File → My Rating to apply your critical assessment from five stars to none to the selected songs. Features like Party Shuffle or the iPod Shuffle's Autofill can be directed to go after songs with the highest ratings, so labeling them can help weed out the duds the next time you let iTunes do the music programming.

Edit Smart Playlist

Even Smart Playlists can start to sound dumb after awhile. If you want to go back and make some adjustments to your automatic song-selection requirements, click the desired Smart Playlist in the iTunes Source list and then choose Edit Smart Playlist. The Preferences box for that particular playlist pops up so that you can adjust its settings. *Keyboard shortcut:* Option-click the + button below the Source list (Mac); Shift-click the + button (Windows).

Show Song File

The song titles listed in the Library and playlists windows are only pointers that link to the actual digital audio file in the iTunes Music folder on your hard drive. The Show Song File command pops open the folder, revealing the actual song file in the Finder or in Windows Explorer. *Keyboard shortcut:* ⌘-R (Mac); Ctrl+R (Windows).

Tip: If you originally ripped the song from a CD, the folder name is usually the same name as the album, which itself is typically buried inside another folder or two, like Russian nesting dolls.

To cut to the chase and see the file path of the song on the Mac, ⌘-click the *window name* in the title bar of the Finder window. You get a pop-up menu that shows your nested-folder hierarchy, revealing the exact location of the actual audio file.

In Windows XP, just glance up at the address bar to see the file's complete path.

Show Current Song

If you want to name that tune but can't remember what it is, choose Show Current Song to refresh your memory. Whatever you're playing at the moment—whether a radio station, MP3 file, or CD track—is highlighted in the song list. *Keyboard shortcut:* ⌘-L (Mac); Ctrl+L (Windows).

Burn Playlist to Disc

You can make a home-cooked compact disc from the current playlist in your iTunes window by selecting a playlist and then choosing "Burn Playlist to CD." Right away, the circular Burn CD button in the top right corner of the iTunes window spins open to reveal its yellow and black icon, and the status display window asks you to insert a blank CD. (To back out of the deal if you change your mind, click the small gray X in the status display window.) iTunes will even let you burn data files to a DVD if your computer has a DVD burner.

Create an iMix

If you want to share one of your most perfect playlists with everyone else in the iTunes Music Store, selecting this option will guide you through making an iMix (page 175) and posting it for all to see in the Store. You need to be connected to the Internet to send the iMix on its way, though.

Update Songs on iPod

If you have the iPod connected while you're ripping new songs or composing new playlists, this command sends the new data directly to the iPod without your having to disconnect and reconnect the player to jump-start the autosync function.

Page Setup

As with the Page Setup box in word-processing and graphics programs, here is where you select your paper size and orientation in preparation for printing.

Print

Printing is a lot of fun in iTunes, and this command sends your preformatted CD jewel-case insert, album listing, or songs list to your connected printer of choice (page 128). There are options here for both color and black-and-white printers.

Exit (Windows only)

Mac fans *quit* their programs; in Windows, you *exit* them by choosing this command from the File menu.

Edit Menu

Like the Edit menus in almost every Mac program, this menu houses the commands that help you move and manage selected bits of information. In iTunes, it also lets you control how information is displayed.

Undo

The Mac's Undo feature reverses the last menu command or keyboard action you took. *Keyboard shortcut:* ⌘-Z (Mac); Ctrl+Z (Windows).

Cut, Copy, and Paste

These familiar text-editing functions come in quite handy for moving around misplaced album titles and artist names in the Song Information box and elsewhere in iTunes. *Keyboard shortcuts:* ⌘-X, -C, and -V (Mac); Ctrl+X, +C, and +V (Windows).

Clear

Selecting a playlist in the Source list, or selecting certain songs on a playlist, and then choosing Edit → Clear removes the item from the iTunes window—without deleting it from your music library. *Keyboard shortcut:* Delete; or, to bypass the confirmation box, press ⌘-Delete (Mac); Ctrl+Delete (Windows).

Select All

Select All does pretty much what it says it does. For example, if you want to select all the song titles in the window at once, click in the window and choose Edit → Select All. *Keyboard shortcut:* ⌘-A (Mac); Ctrl+A (Windows).

Select None

Choose Edit → Select None to release any song titles from selection. *Keyboard shortcut:* Shift-⌘-A (Mac); Ctrl+Shift+A (Windows).

Show/Hide Search Bar

The inner-window Search bar (it appears at the top of the iTunes browser) lets you sort and screen the contents of your iTunes library. Click any of the Search bar's buttons (Music, Audiobooks, Artist, and so on) to whittle down which tracks appear in the browser. Use this menu command to toggle the Search bar off and on. *Keyboard shortcut:* Shift-⌘-B (Mac); Ctrl+Shift+B (Windows).

Show/Hide Browser

The Browser, a secondary song-finding tool, is described on page 115. This command lets you bring it to your screen or hide it again. *Keyboard shortcut:* ⌘-B (Mac); Ctrl+B (Windows).

Show/Hide Artwork

The Artwork pane shows the CD album cover of whatever song is currently highlighted. When the Artwork pane is showing, the Source list can display only about half as many playlists, which is why iTunes offers you this command to reveal or hide the artwork at will. To see a bigger version of the album cover, click the artwork panel. The Selected Song column header in the artwork panel toggles to Now Playing when you click it. *Keyboard shortcut:* ⌘-G (Mac); Ctrl+G (Windows).

Show/Hide MiniStore

Turning on the MiniStore opens up a new pane along the bottom of your iTunes window that shows you the Music Store's current top-selling songs and new releases, all without your having to actually go into the store itself. Be warned, though, that leaving the MiniStore open sends information back to Apple about what you're listening to (at least it did in its first version), so if you have privacy concerns, you may want to shop through the store's Source list icon. *Keyboard shortcut:* Shift-⌘M (Mac); Shift+Ctrl+M (Windows).

Show Duplicate Songs

If you think you've got copies of certain songs lurking around your hard drive and taking up precious megabytes of space, use this menu command to round 'em up into one place in the iTunes window. Once you flush the duplicates out into the open, you can decide what you want to do about them. Just click the Show All Songs button at the bottom of the screen when you're done with your housecleaning to reveal your full library.

View Options

After you select View Options, a box pops up that lets you customize the columns and categories shown in the iTunes song window. If you decide that you don't want to see, say, the Bit Rate setting listed in the window, choose Edit → View Options and turn off the Bit Rate checkbox. Turn on the boxes for the categories you do want to see in your iTunes Details window. *Keyboard shortcut:* ⌘-J (Mac); Ctrl+J (Windows).

Special Characters (Mac Only)

Use the Mac's own Character Palette dialog box to find obscure typographical characters, just in case you have any songs with glyphs, non-Roman letters, or mathematical symbols in the title (or any other song info field). Insert your cursor into the search box in the upper-right corner of iTunes, choose Edit → Special Characters, and then click the character you're looking for.

Tip: Contextual (shortcut) menus are a wonderful thing, once you remember they're there. They list useful options that are especially relevant to whatever you're clicking. For example, the contextual menu for a song offers choices like Get Info and Convert to MP3; for a playlist, you get choices like Export Song List and Burn Playlist to Disc.

To produce these menus, right-click onscreen items (if you have a two-button mouse) or Ctrl-click them (if not).

Controls Menu

This menu can perform many of the same actions as fiddling with buttons and sliders on the iTunes window—or even on a home stereo system.

Play

With a song or playlist selected in your iTunes window, choose Play to start the music. *Keyboard shortcut:* Space bar.

Next Song, Previous Song

The next two items on the Controls menu let you skip to the next song or back to the last one on the playlist or album you're listening to. *Keyboard shortcut:* ⌘-left or -right arrow (Mac); Ctrl+Left or +Right (Windows).

Shuffle

The Shuffle command tells iTunes to get randomly funky with the order of the songs currently listed in your iTunes window at the time—an album listing, a single playlist, or all the songs in the library. A checkmark next to the Shuffle command means that the setting is already turned on; select Shuffle again to toggle it off. *Shortcut:* Click the Shuffle button in the iTunes window.

Repeat Off, All, One

The next three choices on the Controls menu make iTunes automatically play current playlists or albums over and over (Repeat All) or just once (Repeat One). Repeat Off command disables the repeat function. You can only choose one at a time, and the checkmark shows you which setting is active.

Volume Up, Down

Incrementally increase or decrease the iTunes volume with these two menu items. *Keyboard shortcut:* ⌘-up and -down arrow (Mac); Ctrl+Up or +Down arrow (Windows).

Mute

If you need to take a conference call, or your boss is coming down the hall while you're rocking out at your desk to your Black Crowes playlist, get thee to Controls → Mute as fast as your mouse can take you. *Keyboard shortcut:* Option-⌘-down arrow (Mac); Ctrl+Alt+Down (Windows). The same keyboard shortcuts with the up arrow turns your tunes on again.

Eject Disc/Eject iPod

Choosing the Eject Disc command unmounts whatever disc is in the CD or DVD drive and ejects it. If you've got the iPod attached and selected in the source list, you have the option to gently release it from iTunes instead. *Keyboard shortcut:* ⌘-E (Mac); Ctrl+E (Windows).

Tip: If you have an extended Macintosh keyboard, you may find the four buttons across the top row of the numeric keypad a quicker source of volume control. They feature self-explanatory icons for Volume Down, Volume Up, Mute, and Eject. There are also several PC keyboards geared especially for multimedia functions that may also give you volume and other controls without having to use the mouse.

Visualizer

If you get tired of looking at playlists and just want to zone out, the Visualizations feature (page 109) can provide colorful animations in the main iTunes window. This menu lets you make adjustments to the visualization display. Once you've turned on the visual display, click Options in the top-right corner of the iTunes window to adjust things like frame rate and song title display.

Turn Visualizer On/Off

The first menu item toggles off and on the iTunes Visualizations feature (page 109). Choosing Turn Visualizer On transforms your iTunes window into a psyche-delic animation that can make you feel like you're snowboarding down the DNA helix in living color. *Keyboard shortcut:* ⌘-T (Mac); Ctrl+T (Windows).

Small, Medium, Large

These are the three sizes you can choose for the colorful onscreen animations (see previous command). Choosing Small or Medium leaves a black letterbox frame around the animation, while Large fills the entire iTunes window.

Full Screen

Visualizations can become a full-blown screensaver when you select Full Screen (as well as Turn Visualizations On). To get your monitor back to normal, click anywhere onscreen to toggle off the Full Screen mode. *Keyboard shortcut:* ⌘-F (Mac); Ctrl+F (Windows).

Note: If you've installed any third-party visualizations, you'll see them listed at the bottom of the Visualizer menu. To pick the one you want, select it from the menu. A checkmark next to the name tells you which one is currently in use.

Advanced

The Advanced menu deals with several tasks that might appeal to power users, including adjusting ID3 tag formats (page 293) and downloading track information from the Internet.

Switch to Mini Player (Windows Only)

Instead of minimizing the iTunes program window completely into the taskbar, you may sometimes prefer to shrink its window down to convenient minibar size. That way, the essential controls are still visible. This command does that trick. *Keyboard shortcut:* Ctrl+M.

Open Stream

The Open Stream command opens a dialog box where you can type or paste in a URL to go directly to a streaming audio site. If you've never listened to radio streams over the Internet, iTunes has plenty of preprogrammed links for you to check out (page 121). Just click Radio in the Source list, and then click the kind of music or radio programming you wish to listen to. *Keyboard shortcut:* ⌘-U (Mac); Ctrl+U (Windows).

Subscribe to Podcast

If you've found yourself a podcast out in the wilds of the Internet (and not conveniently clickable in the iTunes Music Store), you can paste the subscription URL from its Web page into this box to add it and download all its future episodes right into iTunes.

Convert Selection to AAC (or MP3 or AIFF or WAV)

Depending on the file type (AAC, MP3, AIFF, Apple Lossless, WAV) you've designated in Preferences for importing songs into iTunes (page 282), you can use the Convert Selection command to convert a selected item into your preferred format. For example, if you have some WAV clips on your computer but have chosen MP3 as your preferred import setting, use the Convert Selection to MP3 command to select and convert the files to MP3 and import them into iTunes all in one shot.

Consolidate Library

If you have songs scattered around the computer in any folders other than the iTunes Music folder, you can use the Consolidate Library command to seek out the scattered songs and put copies of them in the iTunes Music folder. This command puts your entire collection conveniently in one place, but it means you'll have the same song in two places on your computer, possibly even duplicated within the iTunes Music folder.

Get CD Track Names

If you don't have iTunes configured to automatically dash out to the Internet and download track information for the songs on the CD you just inserted (page 95), use the Get CD Track Names command to go fetch those song titles from the Gracenote CDDB database. If you have a dial-up Internet connection instead of an "always on" one, this command lets you connect to the Internet only when you're prepared to dial up.

Submit CD Track Names

The Gracenote CDDB database is a wonderful thing (page 96), but it's far from error-free. This command lets you help make things right.

Make corrections in the Song Information box (page 117), and then choose the Submit CD Track Names command to upload the fixed track information to the Gracenote CDDB database. (Of course, you need to be connected to the Internet to use this command.)

Join CD Tracks

Sometimes you don't want two seconds of silence between songs you import from an album. The Join CD Tracks command imports all selected songs as one big track without those mood-breaking sounds of silence (page 119).

Authorize/Deauthorize Computer

Apple allows you to authorize up to five different computers to play the songs purchased from the iTunes Music Store (or Audible files). As described on page 129, this system lets you hear your music on more than one computer, while still helping curb the illegal copying of copyrighted works.

If you push your luck and try to authorize a sixth machine, this feature will kick in and force you to deauthorize one of the previously authorized computers.

Check for Purchased Music

If you bought some songs in the iTunes Music Store but couldn't download them at the time, "Checked for Purchased Music" lets you back to get them. (You need to enter your Apple ID and password.)

Convert ID3 Tags

ID3 is a labelling format that embeds information about a song's title, artist, track number, and so on into the song file itself. There have been several versions of the ID3 tag format over the years, and earlier versions of the format can store less information than the newer standard. If a song's information doesn't look right, try selecting the song and using Convert ID3 Tags to change the tag format.

Window Menu (Macintosh Only)

The Window menu is where you go to open certain windows as well as expand or collapse the main iTunes window.

Minimize

This command sends the iTunes window swirling down into the Mac OS X Dock. As with any Mac OS X program, its windows return to the screen when you click its Dock icon. *Keyboard shortcut:* ⌘-M.

Tip: When iTunes is minimized, hidden, or in the background, you can still control it. Hold your cursor down on the iTunes program icon (which looks like a CD with musical notes on it) in the Dock to produce a pop-up menu filled with commands like Shuffle, Play, Next Song, and so on. You can even rate the song in progress using the My Rating submenu.

Zoom

The Zoom command is the menu bar equivalent of clicking the green circle at the top of the window—it shrinks the full iTunes window down into a tiny compact silver bar. To expand the window back to its full size, choose Zoom again from the menu.

iTunes

You can hide or reveal the program's window—whether in full-screen view or the silver mini control bar—by selecting iTunes from the Window menu. Reselect iTunes from the menu to toggle the window on or off. *Keyboard shortcut:* ⌘-1.

Equalizer

Equalizer toggles the graphic equalizer window onscreen or off. *Keyboard shortcut:* ⌘-2.

Bring All to Front

If your iTunes window is buried behind your Web browser, email inbox, and spreadsheet project, you can pop it to the front by selecting "Bring All to Front." (This command brings the equalizer and any open playlist windows to the front as well.)

Note: Any open playlist windows also appear in the Window menu. A checkmark indicates which playlist is the currently active and visible window. No checkmark next to the playlist name means it's open but buried under other windows. A diamond in front of the name means the playlist or window is open but minimized.

Help Menu

You can find answers to basic questions about the program's features or functions in the iTunes built-in help files. This menu also gives you access and assistance for the iTunes Music Store.

iTunes and Music Store Help

Selecting this item launches Apple's iTunes Help program. Several topics are readily available, and you can search the program for specific words or phrases for technical support articles about how the program works. *Keyboard shortcut:* ⌘-? (Mac); F1 (Windows).

iTunes and Music Store Service and Support

This command takes you to the iTunes Music Store's online Customer Service department. The team can answer questions about your account, passwords, and so on.

iPod Help

The iPod Help program works just like iTunes Help, except that you can search for iPod-specific words and phrases like "playlists."

Keyboard Shortcuts

One item in the Help menu is the list of iTunes keyboard shortcuts, which also appear below in a handy list. Memorizing the shortcuts for the commands you use most often can give you a faster, smoother iTunes experience.

Check for iTunes Updates (Windows)

Although iTunes can be set to automatically check for its own updates, Windows users can also take a manual approach to seeking out the latest versions of the program with this handy menu item (and an Internet connection).

Run CD Diagnostics (Windows)

Unlike Apple, which makes much of its own hardware and software, PC components can vary widely among manufacturers. If your CD drive is giving you fits when you try to burn a disc in iTunes, pop in a disc and choose the Run CD Diagnostics command. After a few seconds, iTunes pops up a screen full of driver information about your computer, plus helpful tips like "Some Dell computers need an update to the ATA bus driver before iTunes recognizes CDs. If you have a Dell computer, check the Dell support Web site for details." It may not be much, but it's more than you knew before.

Keyboard Shortcuts for iTunes 6

Shortcut	Keystroke
Shortcuts for playing songs	
Play the selected song right now	*Mac:* Return or Space bar. *Windows:* Enter or Space bar.
Move within a playing song	*Mac:* ⌘-Option-Right arrow or -Left arrow *Windows:* Ctrl+Alt+Right arrow or +Left arrow.
Play next or previous album	*Mac:* Option-right arrow or -left arrow (or Option-click the ◄◄ or ►►| buttons in the upper-left corner of the iTunes window). *Windows:* Shift+Ctrl+Alt+right arrow or +left arrow.

Shortcut	Keystroke
Next/previous song	*Mac:* ⌘-left arrow or -right arrow (or ⌘-click the ⏮ or ⏭ buttons). *Windows:* Ctrl+left or +right arrow (or Ctrl-click the ⏮ or ⏭ buttons in the iTunes window).

Shortcuts for library and playlist windows

Shortcut	Keystroke
Create a playlist from selected songs	*Mac:* Shift-click the + button (or drag songs to an empty spot in the Source list). *Windows:* Drag songs to an empty spot in the Source list.
Create a new playlists folder	*Mac:* Option-Shift-⌘-N. *Windows:* Ctrl+Shift-N.
Create a new Smart Playlist	*Mac:* Option-click the + button beneath the Source list. *Windows:* Shift-click the + button.
Reshuffle the current playlist	*Mac:* Option-click the Shuffle button. *Windows:* Shift-click the Shuffle button.
Delete selected playlist without confirmation box	*Mac:* ⌘-Delete. *Windows:* Ctrl+Delete.
Delete selected playlist and all songs in it	*Mac:* Option-Delete. *Windows:* Shift+Delete.
Delete selected song from library and all playlists	*Mac:* Option-Delete. *Windows:* Shift+Delete.

Shortcuts for files and windows

Shortcut	Keystroke
Select or deselect all the songs in a list	*Mac:* ⌘-click any checkbox in the list. *Windows:* Ctrl-click any checkbox.
Change the song information columns	*Mac:* Control-click a column title to summon pop-up list of possible columns. *Windows:* Right-click a column title.
Expand or collapse all the triangles in Radio list	*Mac:* ⌘-click a triangle. *Windows:* Ctrl-click a triangle.
Smoother, outline-only window resizing	*Mac:* ⌘-drag the resize box in the lower-right corner of the iTunes window.
Expand iTunes window to optimal size	*Mac:* Option-click the zoom control in the iTunes window's upper-left corner. *Windows:* Shift-double-click the iTunes window title bar.
Go to the next/previous track in Get Info window	*Mac:* ⌘-N, ⌘-P. *Windows:* Ctrl-Left Arrow, Ctrl-Right Arrow.
Next/Previous pane of Get Info or Prefs window	*Mac:* ⌘-left bracket ([ ) or -right bracket ( ]).
See more options for a visual effect onscreen	Press / or ?, then press the desired key to use its option (not all visual effects can do this).
Jump to the iTunes Search box	*Mac:* ⌘-Option-F. *Windows:* Ctrl+Alt+F.
Refresh Radio/Party Shuffle list	*Windows:* F5.

Shortcut	Keystroke
iPod shortcuts	
Prevent iPod from automatically updating	*Mac:* Press ⌘-Option as you connect the iPod to your Mac until it appears in the Source list. *Windows:* Press Shift+Ctrl+Alt as you connect the iPod to your PC until it appears in the Source list.
Music Store	
Previous/Next Music Store page	*Mac:* ⌘-left bracket ([ ), -right bracket ( ]). *Windows:* Ctrl+right bracket ( ]), +left bracket ([ ).
Audible files	
Previous/Next chapter	*Mac:* ⌘-Shift-left arrow, -right arrow. *Windows:* Ctrl+Shift+left arrow, +right arrow.
Application menu (Macintosh)	
Open iTunes Preferences	⌘-comma.
Hide iTunes	⌘-H.
Hide other programs	⌘-Option-H.
Quit iTunes	⌘-Q.
File menu	
New playlist	*Mac:* ⌘-N. *Windows:* Ctrl+N.
New playlist from selected songs	*Mac:* Shift-⌘-N. *Windows:* Ctrl+Shft+N.
New Smart Playlist	*Mac:* Option-⌘-N. *Windows:* Ctrl+Alt+N.
Add file (from hard drive) to the Library	*Mac:* ⌘-O. *Windows:* Ctrl+O.
Close iTunes window	*Mac:* ⌘-W. *Windows:* Ctrl+W.
Import a song, playlist, or library file	*Mac:* Shift-⌘-O. *Windows:* Ctrl+Shift+O.
Open Info window for selected song or CD	*Mac:* ⌘-I. *Windows:* Ctrl+I.
Show hard drive location of a song file	*Mac:* ⌘-R. *Windows:* Ctrl+R.
Show the currently playing song in the list	*Mac:* ⌘-L. *Windows:* Ctrl+L.
Print (playlist, CD covers, etc.)	*Mac:* ⌘-P. *Windows:* Ctrl+P.
Edit menu	
Show/Hide Search bar	*Mac:* ⌘-Shift-B. *Windows:* Ctrl+Shift+B.
Show/Hide iTunes browser	*Mac:* ⌘-B. *Windows:* Ctrl+B.

Shortcut	Keystroke
Show/Hide album artwork	*Mac:* ⌘-G. *Windows:* Ctrl+G.
View iTunes column options	*Mac:* ⌘-J. *Windows:* Ctrl+J.
Controls menu	
Play/Stop	Space bar.
Play previous/next song in the play-list	*Mac:* ⌘-left arrow, -right arrow. *Windows:* Ctrl+left arrow, +right arrow.
Volume down/up	*Mac:* ⌘-down arrow, -up arrow. *Windows:* Ctrl+down arrow, +up arrow.
Mute	*Mac:* Option-⌘-down arrow. *Windows:* Ctrl+Shift+down arrow.
Eject a CD	*Mac:* ⌘-E. *Windows:* Ctrl+E.
Visualizer menu	
Visual effects on/off	*Mac:* ⌘-T. *Windows:* Ctrl+T.
Expand visual effects to full screen	*Mac:* ⌘-F. *Windows:* Ctrl+F.
Advanced menu	
Stream audio file from a specific URL	*Mac:* ⌘-U. *Windows:* Ctrl+U.
Switch to Mini Player (Windows only)	Ctrl+M.
Window menu (Macintosh only)	
Minimize iTunes window to the Dock	⌘-M.
View the main iTunes window	⌘-1.
View the Equalizer window	⌘-2.
Help menu	
Open iTunes & Music Store Help	*Mac:* ⌘-?. *Windows:* F1.

Index

Colophon

Mary Brady was the production editor, and Mary Brady and Marlowe Shaeffer were the proofreaders for *iPod and iTunes: The Missing Manual*, Fourth Edition. Adam Witwer, Genevieve d'Entremont, and Darren Kelly provided quality control. Mary Anne Mayo provided production assistance. Julie Hawks and J.D. Biersdorfer wrote the index.

The cover of this book is based on a series design by David Freedman. Karen Montgomery produced the cover layout with Adobe InDesign CS using Adobe's Minion and Gill Sans fonts.

David Futato designed the interior layout, based on a series design by Phil Simpson. This book was converted by Keith Fahlgren to FrameMaker 5.5.6. The text font is Adobe Minion; the heading font is Adobe Formata Condensed; and the code font is LucasFont's TheSans Mono Condensed. The illustrations that appear in the book were produced by Robert Romano, Jessamyn Read, and Lesley Borash using Macromedia FreeHand MX and Adobe Photoshop CS.

Better than e-books

Buy *iPod & iTunes: The Missing Manual* and access
the digital edition FREE on Safari for 45 days.

Go to www.oreilly.com/go/safarienabled
and type in coupon code UZCR-42VD-FBTB-MTDF-TZP3

Search thousands of top tech books

Download whole chapters

Cut and Paste code examples

Find answers fast

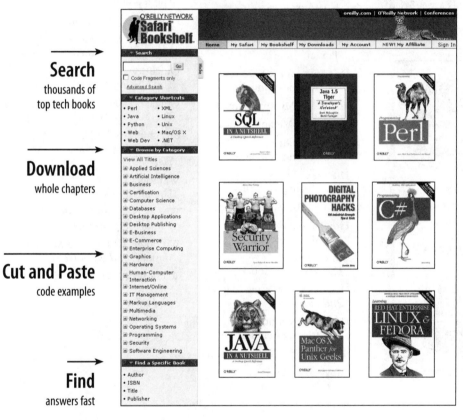

Search Safari! The premier electronic reference
library for programmers and IT professionals.

Related Titles from O'Reilly

Missing Manuals

Access 2003 for Starters:
The Missing Manual

AppleScript:
The Missing Manual

AppleWorks 6: The Missing
Manual

Creating Web Sites:
The Missing Manual

Dreamweaver 8: The Missing
Manual

Dreamweaver MX 2004:
The Missing Manual

eBay: The Missing Manual

Excel: The Missing Manual

Excel for Starters:
The Missing Manual

FileMaker Pro 8:
The Missing Manual

Flash 8: The Missing Manual

FrontPage 2003:
The Missing Manual

GarageBand 2:
The Missing Manual

Google: The Missing Manual,
2nd Edition

Home Networking:
The Missing Manual

iLife '05: The Missing Manual

iMovie 6 & iDVD:
The Missing Manual

iPhoto 6: The Missing Manual

iPod & iTunes: The Missing
Manual, *4th Edition*

iWork '05: The Missing
Manual

Mac OS X: The Missing
Manual, *Tiger Edition*

Office 2004 for Macintosh:
The Missing Manual

PCs: The Missing Manual

Photoshop Elements 4:
The Missing Manual

QuickBooks 2006:
The Missing Manual

Quicken 2006 for Starters:
The Missing Manual

Switching to the Mac:
The Missing Manual,
Tiger Edition

Windows 2000 Pro:
The Missing Manual

Windows XP for Starters:
The Missing Manual

Windows XP Pro: The Missing
Manual, *2nd Edition*

Windows XP Home Edition:
The Missing Manual,
2nd Edition